ALONE IN THE CARIBBEAN

FREDERIC A. FENGER

(1911 Journey)

Table of Contents

ALONE IN THE CARIBBEAN

FREDERIC A. FENGER

Kessinger Publishing reprints thousands of hard–to–find books!

Visit us at http://www.kessinger.net

ALONE IN THE CARIBBEAN

Being the Yarn of a Cruise in the Lesser Antilles
in the Sailing Canoe "Yakaboo"

TO MY MOTHER AND THE MEMORY OF MY FATHER

1

PREFACE

To most of us the West Indies comprise Cuba, Jamaica, Haiti or San Domingo (commonly thought to be two separate islands), Porto Rico and the smaller islands of the Bahamas, the Bermudas and Barbados, somewhere adrift off the Florida coast like a second Sargasso Sea. The lower Caribbees seem as mythical as the lost Atlantis itself. I feel that I shall have accomplished much if by means of a simple explanation and the use of a chart I can set the reader right for all time.

In general the West Indies include the Bahamas (a group of low-lying coral cays just across the Gulf Stream where it sweeps northward past the east coast of Florida) but more particularly they are those islands which stretch to the eastward from Yucatan to just beyond Porto Rico where they take a southward trend forming an almost perfect arc from the Virgins to Trinidad which is in reality the northeast corner of South America. Thus they bound the Caribbean Sea, on the north and east, which in the old days was also called the Northern Ocean in contradistinction to the Southern Ocean or Pacific which Balboa first saw directly to the south from the Isthmus of Panama. The large islands, Jamaica, Cuba, San Domingo and Porto Rico are known as the Greater Antilles while the smaller islands which take up the march to Trinidad are known as the Lesser Antilles. Of the Lesser Antilles, the Virgins, Anguilla, St. Martin, Barbuda, Saba, St. Eustatius, St. Kitts, Nevis, Antigua, Montserrat, Guadeloupe, Dominica and Martinique are known as the Leeward Islands; St. Lucia, St. Vincent, the Grenadines, Grenada, Barbados and Tobago are known as the Windward Islands.

The Bermudas form an entirely separate group quite distinct from the West Indies although their climate is semitropic and lie 750 miles ESE of Hatteras and some eight hundred miles from the nearest Bahamas.

2

ALONE IN THE CARIBBEAN

The Lesser Antilles are apart from the rest of the West Indies in that the Spaniards played very little part in their colonization or development. While it is true that Columbus on his later voyages discovered the Lesser Antilles, a few of which he actually set foot upon and most of which he merely named as he saw them from a distance, the Spaniards made no attempts to settle on these small islands * and they lay unmolested for over a hundred years till early in the seventeenth century they were settled by the English, French and Dutch and a little later by the Danes. Aside from the patois of the Negro which varies more or less in the different islands, there are now but two languages spoken, English in the British, Dutch and Danish possessions and French in the French islands. For a time the Swedes owned St. Bartholomew which was ceded to France in 1878.

* With the exception only of Tobago.

The history of these small islands should be of interest to us on account of their early intimacy with our own colonies and especially because of the part which the Dutch island of St. Eustatius played in aiding us at the time of the Revolutionary War. But our knowledge of their early days is meager, hurricanes and the depredations of the little wood ant (which literally eats away the wooden houses from about their owners) being the two chief destroyers of manuscripts and their containers. What of the life of St. Eustatius scarcely eight miles in area —which had its beginnings before our Plymouth colony and in 1781 when at the height of its prosperity it was destroyed by Rodney it had a population of nearly 40,000 —more than either Boston or New York at that time?

Its printed history does not cover much more than 20,000 words. But with history we have little to do in this account. I have limited myself to those incidents which might have a direct interest for the reader and some of them, in whole or in part, as far as I can ascertain, now appear in print for the first time. Those who are familiar with the literature of the Lesser Antilles will, I hope, be agreeably disappointed in not finding in these pages those hardy perennials of the guide books —the building of schooners at Bottom Town on Saba, eight hundred feet above the sea, and the deadly snakes of the Petit Piton that killed the members of a climbing party one by one till the last man fell only a few feet from his goal.

ALONE IN THE CARIBBEAN

So I have attempted neither a history nor a guide book but have spun out the yarn of a lone cruise in a sailing canoe. I went to study the islands at first hand and in the craft which I believed would be most suitable for the purpose —a deep–sea sailing canoe. The main portion of the cruise has appeared serially in abbreviated form in the "Outing" magazine.

I have made no attempt to discuss the problem of the native —the more one studies it the less one has to say —and my few explosions of choler will, I hope, be forgiven. Throughout the islands from Grenada to St. Thomas, I have made friends whom I count among my best and it is their unexampled courtesy and generosity that go to make up some of the most pleasant memories of the cruise. Those whom I would especially mention are C.V.C. Horne and T.B.C. Musgrave, who at once made me feel at home in St. George's and who, when they could not dissuade me from starting out in the Yakaboo, did everything in their power to facilitate my preparations for the cruise; Dr. William S. Mitchell, who loaned me his cotton ginnery; "Jack" Wildman, who helped me to much interesting material; "Steady" Glean, who rescued me from the mob at Sauteurs (but that is another story) ; Whitfield Smith, now at Grand Turk and whose place at Carriacou has been happily filled by Musgrave; McQueen, of pleasant memory of Top Hill days; Noel Walker —I wonder if he has joined the ranks of the many who have "gone west"; Rupert Otway, whose hospitality I enjoyed at Union; "Old Bill" Wallace; V.J. Monplaisir, "Monty"; Captain Harry Turner, then Harbour Master of Castries and now in Mombasa; Père Remaud, I was going to say Labat; Monsieur Waddy and the whole of the "Union Sportive"; Mr. Frederick Woolworth, who took me in on faith and for whom I acted as cook in times of stress; Dr. John Morgan Griffith, enthusiast, of Statia; Captain "Ben" Hassel, "Freddie" Simmons, and Leslie Jarvis, Commissioner of Tortola.

F.A.F.

Item —I order that my executors purchase a large stone, the best that they can find, and place it upon my grave, and that they write round the edge of it these words : —"Here lies the honorable Chevalier Diego Mendez, who rendered great services to the royal crown of Spain, in the discovery and conquest of the Indies, in company with the discoverer of them, the Admiral Don Christopher Columbus, of glorious memory, and afterwards rendered other great services by himself, with his own ships, and at his own cost. He died. . . . He asks of your charity a Paternoster and an Ave Maria."

Item —In the middle of the said stone let there be the representation of a canoe, which is a hollowed tree, such as the Indians use for navigation ; for in such a vessel did I cross three hundred leagues of sea ; and let them engrave above it this word : "CANOA." From the will of Diego Mendez,
 drawn up June 19th, 1536.

CHAPTER I. THE "YAKABOO" IS BORN AND THE CRUISE BEGINS

"Crab pas mache, il pas gras ; il mache trop, et il tombe dans chodier."

"If a crab don't walk, he don't get fat ;
  If he walk too much, he gets in a pot."

—From the Creole.

IS IT in the nature of all of us, or is it just my own peculiar make–up which brings, when the wind blows, that queer feeling, mingled longing and dread? A thousand invisible fingers seem to be pulling me, trying to draw me away from the four walls where I have every comfort, into the open where I shall have to use my wits and my strength to fool the sea in its treacherous moods, to take advantage of fair winds and to fight when I am fairly caught —for a man is a fool to think he can conquer nature. It had been a long time since I had felt the weatherglow on my face, a feeling akin to the numb forehead in the first touch of inebriety. The lure was coming back to me. It was the lure of islands and my thoughts had gone back to a certain room in school where as a boy I used to muse over a huge relief map of the bottom of the North Atlantic. No doubt my time had been better spent on the recitation that was going on.

5

ALONE IN THE CARIBBEAN

One learns little of the geography of the earth from a school book. I found no mention of the vast Atlantic shelf, that extended for hundreds of miles to seaward of Hatteras, where the sperm whale comes to feed in the spring and summer and where, even while I was sitting there looking at that plaster cast, terrific gales might be screaming through the rigging of New Bedford whalers, hove–to and wallowing —laden with fresh water or grease according to the luck or the skill of the skipper. Nor was there scarcely any mention of the Lesser Antilles, a chain of volcanic peaks strung out like the notched back of a dinosaur, from the corner of South America to the greater islands that were still Spanish. Yet it was on these peaks that my thoughts clung like dead grass on the teeth of a rake and would not become disengaged.

Now, instead of looking at the relief map, I was poring over a chart of those same islands and reading off their names from Grenada to tiny Saba. At my elbow was a New Bedford whaler who had cruised over that Atlantic shelf at the very time I was contemplating it as a boy. And many years before that he had been shipwrecked far below, on the coast of Brazil. The crew had shipped home from the nearest port, but the love of adventure was strong upon the captain, his father,* who decided to build a boat from the wreckage of his vessel and sail in it with his wife and two sons to New York. With mahogany planks sawed by the natives they constructed a large sea canoe. For fastenings they used copper nails drawn from the wreck of their ship's yawl, headed over burrs made from the copper pennies of Brazil. Canvas, gear, clothes, and food they had in plenty and on the thirteenth of May in 1888, it being a fine day, they put to sea. The son traced their course with his finger as they had sailed northward in the strong trade winds and passed under the lee of the Lesser Antilles. Later as a whaler, he had come to know the islands more intimately. "Here !" said he, pointing to the Grenadines, "you will find the niggers chasing humpback whales." On Saint Vincent I should find the Carib living in his own way at Sandy Bay. Another island had known Josephine, the wife of Napoleon, and another had given us our own Alexander Hamilton. And there were many more things which I should come to know when I my self should cruise along the Lesser Antilles. We talked it over. After the manner of the Carib, I would sail from island to island alone in a canoe. Next to the joy of making a cruise is that of the planning and still greater to me was the joy of creating the Yakaboo which should carry me. I should explain that this is an expression use by Ellice Islanders** when they throw something overboard and it means "Good–bye."

ALONE IN THE CARIBBEAN

"Good–bye to civilization for a while," I thought, but later there were times when I feared the name might have a more sinister meaning.

* Captain Joshua Slocum, who sailed around
  the world alone in the sloop Spray.
  ** In the Pacific Ocean just north of the Fiji group.

So my craft was named before I put her down on paper. She must be large enough to hold me and my outfit and yet light enough so that alone I could drag her up any uninhabited beach where I might land. Most important of all, she must be seaworthy in the real sense of the word, for between the islands I should be at sea with no lee for fifteen hundred miles. I got all this in a length of seventeen feet and a width of thirty–nine inches. From a plan of two dimensions on paper she grew to a form of three dimensions in a little shop in Boothbay and later, as you shall hear, exhibited a fourth dimension as she gyrated in the seas off Kick 'em Jinny. The finished hull weighed less than her skipper —one hundred and forty–seven pounds.

From a study of the pilot chart, I found that a prevailing northeast trade wind blows for nine months in the year throughout the Lesser Antilles. According to the "square rigger," this trade blows "fresh," which means half a gale to the harbor–hunting yachtsman. Instead of sailing down the wind from the north, I decided to avoid the anxiety of following seas and to beat into the wind from the lowest island which is Grenada, just north of Trinidad.

My first plan was to ship on a whaler bound on a long voyage. From Barbados, where she would touch to pick up crew, I would sail the ninety miles to leeward to Grenada. A wise Providence saw to it that there was no whaler bound on a long voyage for months. I did find a British trading steamer bound out of New York for Grenada. She had no passenger license, but it was my only chance, and I signed on as A.B.

We left New York on one of those brilliant days of January when the keen northwest wind has swept the haze from the atmosphere leaving the air clear as crystal. It was cold but I stood with a bravado air on the grating over the engine room hatch from which the warm air from the boilers rose through my clothes. Below me on the dock and fast receding beyond yelling distance stood a friend who had come to bid me goodbye. By his side was a large leather bag containing the heavy winter clothing I had sloughed only a few minutes before. The warmth of my body would still be in them, I thought, as the warmth clings to a hearth of a winter's evening for a time after the fire has gone out. In a day we should be in the Gulf Stream and then for half a year I should wear just enough to protect me from the sun. Suddenly the tremble of the steamer told me of an engine turning up more revolutions and of a churning propeller. The dock was no longer receding, we were leaving it behind. The mad scramble of the last days in New York ; the hasty breakfast of that morning ; the antique musty–smelling cab with its pitifully ambling horse, uncurried and furry in the frosty air, driven by a whisky–smelling jehu ; the catching of the ferry by a narrow margin, were of a past left far behind. Far out in the channel, that last tentacle of civilization, the pilot, bade us "good luck" and then he also became of the Past. The Present was the vibrating tramp beneath my feet and the Future lay on our course to the South.

On the top of the cargo in the forehold was the crated hull of the Yakaboo, the pretty little "mahogany coffin," as they named her, that was going to carry me through five hundred miles of the most delightful deep sea sailing one can imagine. I did not know that the Pilot Book makes little mention of the "tricks of the trades" as they strike the Caribbean, and that instead of climbing up and sliding down the backs of Atlantic rollers with an occasional smother of foam on top to match the fleecy summer clouds, I would be pounded and battered in short channel seas and that for only thirty of the five hundred miles would my decks be clear of water. It is the bliss of ignorance that tempts the fool, but it is he who sees the wonders of the earth.

The next day we entered the Gulf Stream where we were chased by a Northeaster which lifted the short trader along with a wondrous corkscrew motion that troubled no one but the real passengers —a load of Missouri mules doomed to end their lives hauling pitch in Trinidad.

On the eighth day, at noon, we spoke the lonely island of Sombrero with its lighthouse and black keepers whose only company is the passing steamer. The man at the wheel ported his helm a spoke and we steamed between Saba and Statia to lose sight of land for another day —my first in the Caribbean. The warm trade wind, the skittering of flying fish chased by tuna or the swift dorade, and the rigging of awnings proclaimed that we were now well within the tropics. The next morning I awoke with the uneasy feeling that all motion had ceased and that we were now lying in smooth water. I stepped on deck in my pajamas to feel for the first time the soft pressure of the tepid morning breeze of the islands.

We lay under the lee of a high island whose green mass rose, surf–fringed, from the deep blue of the Caribbean to the deep blue of the morning sky with its white clouds forever coming up from behind the mountains and sailing away to the westward. Off our port bow the grey buildings of a coast town spread out along the shores and crept up the sides of a hill like lichen on a rock. From the sonorous bell in a church tower came seven deep notes which spread out over the waters like a benediction. There was no sign of a jetty or landing place, not even the usual small shipping or even a steamer buoy, and I was wondering in a sleepy way where we should land when a polite English voice broke in, "We are justly proud of the beautiful harbor which you are to see for the first time I take it. "

I fetched up like a startled rabbit to behold a "West Indie" gentleman standing behind me, "starched from clew to earing" as Captain Slocum put it, and speaking a better English than you or I. It was the harbormaster. I was now sufficiently awake to recall from my chart that the harbor of St. George's is almost landlocked. As we stood and talked, the clanking windlass lifted our stockless anchor with its load of white coral sand and the steamer slowly headed for shore.?

? Carénage of St. George's Grenada ?

The land under a rusty old fort seemed to melt away before our bows and we slipped through into the carénage of St. George's. We crept in till we filled the basin like a toy ship in a miniature harbor. From the bridge I was looking down upon a bit of the old world in strange contrast, as my memory swung back across two thousand miles of Atlantic, to the uncouth towns of our north. The houses, with their jalousied windows, some of them white but more often washed with a subdued orange or yellow, were of the French régime, their weathered red tile roofs in pleasing contrast to the strong green of the surrounding hills.

Here in the old days, ships came to be careened in order to rid their bottoms of the dread teredo. Under our forefoot, in the innermost corner of the harbor, pirate ships were wont to lie, completely hidden from the view of the open sea. At one time this was a hornets nest, unmolested by the bravest, for who would run into such a cul–de–sac protected as it was by the forts and batteries on the hills above?

Moored stern–to along the quays, was a fleet of small trading sloops, shabby in rig and crude of build, waiting for cargoes from our hold. Crawling slowly across the harbor under the swinging impulse of long sweeps, was a drogher piled high with bags of cocoa, a huge–bodied bug with feeble legs.?

? Moored stern–to along the quays was a fleet of small trading sloops, shabby in rig and crude of build. ?

Along the mole on the opposite side of the carénage straggled an assortment of small wooden shacks, one and two–storied, scarcely larger than play houses. Among these my eyes came to rest on something which was at once familiar. There stood a small cotton ginnery with shingled roof and open sides, an exact counterpart of a corncrib. I did not then know that in this shed I should spend most of my days while in St. George's.

The blast of our deep–throated whistle stirred the town into activity as a careless kick swarms an anthill with life, and the busy day of the quay began as we were slowly warped–in to our dock.

A last breakfast with the Captain and Mate and I was ashore with my trunk and gear. The Yakaboo, a mere toy in the clutch of the cargo boom, was yanked swiftly out of the hold and lightly placed on the quay where she was picked up and carried into the customhouse by a horde of yelling blacks. Knowing no man, I stood there for a moment feeling that I had suddenly been dropped into a different world. But it was only a different world because I did not know it and as for knowing no man —I soon found that I had become a member of a community of colonial Englishmen who received me with open arms and put to shame any hospitality I had hitherto experienced. As the nature of my visit became known, I was given all possible aid in preparing for my voyage. A place to tune up the Yakaboo? A young doctor who owned the little ginnery on the far side of the carénage gave me the key and told me to use it as long as I wished.?

? The market place of St. George's Grenada. ?

ALONE IN THE CARIBBEAN

I now found that the cruise I had planned was not altogether an easy one. According to the pilot chart for the North Atlantic, by the little blue wind–rose in the region of the lower Antilles, or Windward Islands as they are called, I should find the trade blowing from east to northeast with a force of four, which according to Beaufort's scale means a moderate breeze of twenty–three miles an hour. Imagine my surprise, therefore, when I found that the wind seldom blew less than twenty miles an hour and very often blew a whole gale of sixty–five miles an hour. Moreover, at this season of the year, I found that the "trade" would be inclined to the northward and that my course through the Grenadines —the first seventy miles of my cruise —would be directly into the wind's eye.

I had been counting on that magical figure (30) in the circle of the wind–rose, which means that for every thirty hours out of a hundred one may here expect "calms, light airs, and variables." Not only this, but, I was informed that I should encounter a westerly tide current which at times ran as high as six knots an hour. To be sure, this tide current would change every six hours to an easterly set which, though it would be in my favor, would kick up a sea that would shake the wind out of my sails and almost bring my canoe to a standstill.

Nor was this all. The sea was full of sharks and I was told that if the seas did not get me the sharks would. Seven inches of freeboard is a small obstacle to a fifteen–foot shark. Had the argument stopped with these three I would at this point gladly have presented my canoe to His Excellency the Governor, so that he might plant it on his front lawn and grow geraniums in the cockpit. Three is an evil number if it is against you but a fourth argument came along and the magic triad was broken. If seas, currents, and sharks did not get me, I would be overcome by the heat and be fever–stricken.

I slept but lightly that first night on shore. Instead of being lulled to sleep by the squalls which blew down from the mountains, I would find myself leaning far out over the edge of the bed trying to keep from being capsized by an impending comber. Finally my imagination having reached the climax of its fiendish trend, I reasoned calmly to myself. If I would sail from island to island after the manner of the Carib, why not seek out the native and learn the truth from him ? The next morning I found my man, with the blood of the Yaribai tribe of Africa in him, who knew the winds, currents, sharks, the heat, and the fever. He brought to me the only Carib on the island, a boy of sixteen who had fled to Grenada after the eruption in Saint Vincent had destroyed his home and family.

11

ALONE IN THE CARIBBEAN

From these two I learned the secret of the winds which depend on the phases of the moon. They told me to set sail on the slack of the lee tide and cover my distance before the next lee tide ran strong. They pointed out the fever beaches I should avoid and told me not to bathe during the day, nor to uncover my head —even to wipe my brow. I must never drink my water cold and always put a little rum in it —and a hundred other things which I did not forget. As for the "shyark" —"You no troble him, he no bodder you." "Troble" was used in the sense of tempt and I should therefore never throw food scraps overboard or troll a line astern. I also learned —this from an Englishman who had served in India —that if I wore a red cloth, under my shirt, covering my spine, the actinic rays of the sun would be stopped and I should not be bothered by the heat.

It was with a lighter heart, then, that I set about to rig my canoe —she was yet to be baptized —and to lick my outfit into shape for the long cruise to the northward. I could not have wished for a better place than the cool ginnery which the doctor had put at my disposal. Here with my Man Friday, I worked through the heat of the day —we might have been out of doors for the soft winds from the hills filtered through the open sides, bringing with them the dank odor of the moist earth under shaded cocoa groves. Crowded about the wide–open doors like a flock of strange sea fowl, a group of black boatmen made innumerable comments in their bubbling patois, while their eyes were on my face in continual scrutiny.

And now, while I stop in the middle of the hot afternoon to eat delicious sponge cakes and drink numerous glasses of sorrel that have mysteriously found their way from a little hut near by, it might not be amiss to contemplate the Yakaboo through the sketchy haze of a pipeful of tobacco. She did not look her length of seventeen feet and with her overhangs would scarcely be taken for a boat meant for serious cruising. Upon close examination, however, she showed a powerful midship section that was deceiving and when the natives lifted her off the horses —"O Lard! she light!" —wherein lay the secret of her ability. Her heaviest construction was in the middle third which embodied fully half of her total weight. With her crew and the heavier part of the outfit stowed in this middle third she was surprisingly quick in a seaway. With a breaking sea coming head on, her bow would ride the foamy crest while her stern would drop into the hollow behind, offering little resistance to the rising bow.

She had no rudder, the steering being done entirely by the handling of the main sheet. By a novel construction of the centerboard and the well in which the board rolled forward and aft on sets of sheaves, I could place the center of lateral resistance of the canoe's underbody exactly below the center of effort of the sails with the result that on a given course she would sail herself. Small deviations such as those caused by waves throwing her bow to leeward or sudden puffs that tended to make her luff were compensated for by easing off or trimming in the mainsheet. In the absence of the rudder–plane aft, which at times is a considerable drag to a swinging stern, this type of canoe eats her way to windward in every squall, executing a "pilot's luff" without loss of headway, and in puffy weather will actually fetch slightly to windward of her course, having more than overcome her drift.

She was no new or untried freak for I had already cruised more than a thousand miles in her predecessor, the only difference being that the newer boat was nine inches greater in beam. On account of the increased beam it was necessary to use oars instead of the customary double paddle. I made her wider in order to have a stiffer boat and thus lessen the bodily fatigue in sailing the long channel runs.

She was divided into three compartments of nearly equal length —the forward hold, the cockpit, and the afterhold. The two end compartments were accessible through watertight hatches within easy reach of the cockpit. The volume of the cockpit was diminished by one half by means of a watertight floor raised above the waterline —like the main deck of a ship. This floor was fitted with circular metal hatches through which I could stow the heavier parts of my outfit in the hold underneath. The cockpit proper extended for a length of a little over six feet between bulkheads so that when occasion demanded I could sleep in the canoe.

Her rig consisted of two fore and aft sails of the canoe type and a small jib.

An increasing impatience to open the Pandora's Box which was waiting for me, hurried the work of preparation and in two weeks I was ready to start. The Colonial Treasurer gave me a Bill of Health for the Yakaboo as for any ship and one night I laid out my sea clothes and packed my trunk to follow me as best it could.

On the morning of February ninth I carried my outfit down to the quay in a drizzle. An inauspicious day for starting on a cruise I thought. My Man Friday, who had evidently read my thoughts, hastened to tell me that this was only a little "cocoa shower." Even as I got the canoe alongside the quay the sun broke through the cloud bank on the hill tops

13

and as the rain ceased the small crowd which had assembled to see me off came out from the protection of doorways as I proceeded to stow the various parts of my nomadic home. Into the forward compartment went the tent like a reluctant green caterpillar, followed by the pegs, sixteen pounds of tropical bacon, my cooking pails and the "butterfly," a powerful little gasoline stove. Into the after compartment disappeared more food, clothes, two cans of fresh water, fuel for the "butterfly," films in sealed tins, developing outfit and chemicals, ammunition, and that most sacred of all things —the ditty bag.

Under the cockpit floor I stowed paint, varnish, and a limited supply of tinned food, all of it heavy and excellent ballast in the right place. My blankets, in a double oiled bag, were used in the cockpit as a seat when rowing. Here I also carried two compasses, an axe, my camera, and a chart case with my portfolio and log. I had also a high–powered rifle and a Colt's thirty–eight–forty.

With all her load, the Yakaboo sat on the water as jaunty as ever. The golden brown of her varnished topsides and deck, her green boot–top and white sails made her as inviting a craft as I had ever stepped into.

I bade good–bye to the men I had come to know as friends and with a shove the canoe and I were clear of the quay. The new clean sails hung from their spars for a moment like the unprinted leaves of a book and then a gentle puff came down from the hills, rippled the glassy waters of the carénage and grew into a breeze which caught the canoe and we were sailing northward on the weather tide. I have come into the habit of saying "we," for next to a dog or a horse there is no companionship like that of a small boat. The smaller a boat the more animation she has and as for a canoe, she is not only a thing of life but is a being of whims and has a sense of humor. Have you ever seen a cranky canoe unburden itself of an awkward novice and then roll from side to side in uncontrollable mirth, having shipped only a bare teacupful of water? Even after one has become the master of his craft there is no dogged servility and she will balk and kick up her heels like a skittish colt. I have often "scended" on the face of a mountainous following sea with an exhilaration that made me whoop for joy, only to have the canoe whisk about in the trough and look me in the face as if to say, "You fool, did you want me to go through the next one ?" Let a canoe feel that you are afraid of her and she will become your master with the same intuition that leads a thoroughbred to take advantage of the tremor he feels through the reins. At every puff she will forget to sail and will heel till her decks are under. Hold her down firmly, speak encouragingly, stroke her smooth sides and she will fly through a squall without giving an inch. We were already acquainted for I had twice had her out on trial spins and we agreed upon friendship as our future status.

It has always been my custom to go slow for the first few days of a cruise, a policy especially advisable in the tropics. After a morning of delightful coasting past the green hills of Grenada, touched here and there with the crimson flamboyant like wanton splashes from the brush of an impressionist, and occasional flights over shoals that shone white, brown, yellow and copper through the clear bluish waters, I hauled the Yakaboo up on the jetty of the picturesque little coast town of Goyave and here I loafed through the heat of the day in the cool barracks of the native constabulary. I spent the night on the hard canvas cot in the Rest Room.

It was on the second day that the lid of Pandora's Box sprang open and the imps came out. My log reads : "After beating for two hours into a stiff wind that came directly down the shore, I found that the canoe was sinking by the head and evidently leaking badly in the forward compartment. Distance from shore one mile. The water was pouring in through the centerboard well and I discovered that the bailing plugs in the cockpit floor were useless so that she retained every drop that she shipped. I decided not to attempt bailing and made for shore with all speed. Made Duquesne Point at 11 A.M., where the canoe sank in the small surf."

She lay there wallowing like a contented pig while I stepped out on the beach. "Well!" she seemed to say, "I brought you ashore —do you want me to walk up the beach?" A loaded canoe, full of water and with her decks awash, is as obstinate as a mother–in–law who has come for the summer —and I swore.

My outfit, for the most part, was well protected in the oiled bags which I had made. It was not shaken down to a working basis, however, and I found a quantity of dried cranberries in a cotton bag —a sodden mass of red. With a yank of disgust, I heaved them over my shoulder and they landed with a grunt. Turning around I saw a six–foot black with a round red pattern on the bosom of his faded cotton shirt, wondering what it was all about. I smiled and he laughed while the loud guffaws of a crowd of natives broke the tension of their long silence. The West Indian native has an uncomfortable habit of appearing suddenly from nowhere and he is especially fond of following a few paces behind one on a lonely road. As for being able to talk to these people, I might as well have been wrecked on the coast of Africa and tried to hold discourse with their ancestors.

ALONE IN THE CARIBBEAN

But the men understood my trouble and carried my canoe ashore where I could rub beeswax into a seam which had opened wickedly along her forefoot.?

? The tall native whom I hit in the chest with the bag of cranberries. On the beach at Duquesne Point. ?

Picturing a speedy luncheon over the buzzing little "butterfly" I lifted it off its cleats in the forward compartment, only to find that its arms were broken. The shifting of the outfit in the seaway off shore had put the stove out of commission. I was now in a land where only woodworking tools were known so that any repairs were out of the question. I was also in a land where the sale of gasoline was prohibited.* My one gallon of gasoline would in time have been exhausted, a philosophical thought which somewhat lessened the sense of my disappointment. And let this be a lesson to all travelers in strange countries —follow the custom of the country in regard to fires and cooking.

* On account of the danger of its use in the hands of careless natives.

??The breaking of the "butterfly" only hastened my acquaintance with the delightful mysteries of the "coal" pot. Wood fires are but little used in these islands for driftwood is scarce and the green wood is so full of moisture that it can with difficulty be made to burn. Up in the hills the carbonari make an excellent charcoal from the hard woods of the tropical forests and this is burned in an iron or earthenware brazier known as the coalpot.

Iron Coal–Pot

By means of the sign language, which consisted chiefly in rubbing my stomach with one hand while with the other I put imaginary food into my mouth, the natives understood my need and I soon had one of my little pails bubbling over a glowing coalpot.

The promise of rain warned me to put up my tent although I could have been no wetter than I was. Food, a change of dry clothes and a pipe of tobacco will work wonders at a

16

time like this and as I sat in my tent watching the drizzle pockmark the sands outside, I began to feel that things might not be so bad after all. This, however, was one of those nasty fever beaches against which my Man Friday had warned me, so that with the smiling of the sun at three o'clock, I was afloat again. The Yakaboo had been bullied into some semblance of tightness. By rowing close along shore we reached Tangalanga Point without taking up much water.

I was now at the extreme northern end of Grenada and could see the Grenadines that I should come to know so well stretching away to windward.** They rose, mountain peaks out of the intense blue of the sea, picturesque but not inviting. As I looked across the channel, whitened by the trade wind which was blowing a gale, I wondered whether after all I had underestimated the Caribbean. Sauteurs lay some two miles around the point and I now set sail for the first time in the open sea.

**In these parts northeast and windward are
 synonymous, also southwest and leeward.

In my anxiety lest the canoe should fill again I ran too close to the weather side of the point and was caught in a combing sea which made the Yakaboo gasp for breath. She must have heard the roar of the wicked surf under her lee for she shouldered the green seas from her deck and staggered along with her cockpit full of water till we were at last safe, bobbing up and down in the heavy swell behind the reef off Sauteurs. The surf was breaking five feet high on the beach and I dared not land even at the jetty for fear of smashing the canoe.

A figure on the jetty motioned to a sloop which I ran alongside. The outfit was quickly transferred to the larger boat and the canoe tailed off with a long scope of line. In the meantime a whaleboat was bobbing alongside and I jumped aboard. As we rose close to the jetty on a big sea, a dozen arms reached out like the tentacles of an octopus and pulled me up into their mass while the whaleboat dropped from under me into the hollow of the sea.

17

Whatever my misfortunes may be, there is always a law of compensation which is as infallible as that of Gravity. One of those arms which pulled me up belonged to Jack Wildman, a Scotch cocoa buyer who owned a whaling station on Île–de–Caille, the first of the Grenadines. By the time we reached the cocoa shop near the end of the jetty the matter was already arranged. Jack would send for his whalers to convoy me to his island and there I could stay as long as I wished. The island, he told me, was healthy and I could live apart from the whalers undisturbed in the second story of his little whaling shack. Here I could overhaul my outfit when I did not care to go chasing humpbacks, and under the thatched roof of the tryworks I could prepare my canoe in dead earnest for the fight I should have through the rest of the islands.

That night I slept on the stiff canvas cot in the Rest Room of the police station —a room which is reserved by the Government for the use of traveling officials, for there are no hotels or lodging houses in these parts. From where I lay, I could look out upon the channel bathed in the strong tropical moonlight. The trade which is supposed to drop at sunset blew fresh throughout the night and by raising my head I could see the gleam of white caps. For the first time I heard that peculiar swish of palm tops which sounds like the pattering of rain. Palmer, a member of the revenue service, who had come into my room in his pajamas, explained to me that the low driving mist which I thought was fog was in reality spindrift carried into the air from the tops of the seas. My thoughts went to the Yakaboo bobbing easily at the end of her long line in the open roadstead. All the philosophy of small boat sailing came back to me and I fell asleep with the feeling that she would carry me safely through the boisterous seas of the Grenadine channel.

CHAPTER II. WHALING AT ÎLE–DE–CAILLE

THERE were thirteen of them when I landed on Île–de–Caille —the twelve black whalemen who manned the boats and the negress who did the cooking —and they looked upon me with not a little suspicion.

What manner of man was this who sailed alone in a canoe he could almost carry on his back, fearing neither sea nor jumbie, the hobgoblin of the native, and who now chose to live with them a while just to chase "humpbacks"? Jack Wildman was talking to them in their unintelligible patois, a hopeless stew of early French and English mixed with Portuguese, when I turned to José Olivier and explained that now with fourteen on the island the spell of bad luck which had been with them from the beginning of the season would end. The tone of my voice rather than what I said reassured him. "Aal roit," he said, "you go stroke in de Aactive tomorrow."

Between Grenada and Saint Vincent, the next large island to the north, lie the Grenadines in that seventy miles of channel where "de lee an' wedder toid" alternately bucks and pulls the northeast trades and the equatorial current, kicking up a sea that is known all over the world for its deviltry. Île–de–Caille is the first of these.

In this channel from January to May, the humpback whale, megaptera versabilis, as he is named from the contour of his back, loafs on his way to the colder waters of the North Atlantic. For years the New Bedford whaler has been lying in among these islands to pick up crews, and it is from him that the negro has learned the art of catching the humpback.?

? In This Channel From January to May, the Humpback Loafs On His Way to the Colder Waters of the North Atlantic. ?

While the humpback is seldom known to attack a boat, shore whaling from these islands under the ticklish conditions of wind and current, with the crude ballasted boats that go down when they fill and the yellow streak of the native which is likely to crop out at just the wrong moment, is extremely dangerous and the thought of it brings the perspiration to the ends of my fingers as I write this story. One often sees a notice like this : "May 1st, 1909. —A whaleboat with a crew of five men left Sauteurs for Union Island ; not since heard of."

The men were not drunk, neither was the weather out of the ordinary. During the short year since I was with them* four of the men I whaled with have been lost at sea. With the negro carelessness is always a great factor, but here the wind and current are a still greater one. Here the trade always seems to blow strongly and at times assumes gale force "w'en de moon chyange."

ALONE IN THE CARIBBEAN

*This was written in 1912.

This wind, together with the equatorial current, augments the tide which twice a day combs through the islands in some places as fast as six knots an hour.

During the intervals of weather tide the current is stopped somewhat, but a sea is piled up which shakes the boat as an angry terrier does a rat. It is always a fight for every inch to windward, and God help the unfortunate boat that is disabled and carried away from the islands into the blazing calm fifteen hundred miles to leeward. For this reason the Lesser Antilles from Trinidad to Martinique are known as the Windward Islands.

And so these fellows have developed a wonderful ability to eat their way to windward and gain the help of wind and tide in towing their huge catches ashore. Even a small steamer could not tow a dead cow against the current, as I found out afterward. While the humpback is a "shore whale," the more valuable deep-water sperm whale is also seen and occasionally caught. True to his deep-water instinct he usually passes along the lee of the islands in the deeper waters entirely out of reach of the shore whaler who may see his spout day after day only a few tantalizing miles away. A sperm whale which by chance got off the track was actually taken by the men at Bequia, who in their ignorance threw away that diseased portion, the ambergris, which might have brought them thousands of dollars and kept them in rum till the crack of doom.

As we stood and talked with José, my eyes wandered over the little whaling cove where we had landed, almost landlocked by the walls of fudge-like lava that bowled up around it. The ruined walls of the cabaret, where in the days of Napoleon rich stores of cotton and sugar were kept as a foil for the far richer deposit of rum and tobacco hidden in the cave on the windward side, had their story which might come out later with the persuasion of a little tobacco.

The tryworks, like vaults above ground with the old iron pots sunk into their tops, gave off the musty rancid smell of whale oil that told of whales that had been caught, while a line drying on the rocks, one end of it frayed out like the tail of a horse, told of a wild ride that had come to a sudden stop. But most interesting of all were the men —African —with here and there a shade of Portuguese and Carib, or the pure Yaribai, superstitious in this lazy atmosphere where the mind has much time to dwell on tales of jumbie and lajoblesse,* moody and sullen from the effects of a disappointing season. So far they had not killed a whale and it was now the twelfth of February.

* The spirits of negro women who have died in illegitimate childbirth.

But even the natives were becoming uneasy in the heat of the noon and at a word from José two of them picked up the canoe and laid her under the tryworks roof while the rest of us formed a caravan with the outfit and picked our way up the sharp, rocky path to the level above where the trade always blows cool.

Here Jack had built a little two–storied shack, the upper floor of which he reserved for his own use when he visited the island. This was to be my home. The lower part was divided into two rooms by a curtain behind which José, as befitting the captain of the station, slept in a high bed of the early French days. In the other room was a rough table where I could eat and write my log after a day in the whaleboats, with the wonderful sunset of the tropics before me framed in the open doorway.?

? Jack's Shack on Ile–de–Caille Where I Made My Home ?

I later discovered that the fractional member of the station, a small male offshoot of the Olivier family, made his bed on a pile of rags under the table. We were really fourteen and a half. In another sense he reminded me of the fraction, for his little stomach distended from much banana and plantain eating protruded like the half of a calabash. A steep stair led through a trap door to my abode above. This I turned into a veritable conjurer's shop. From the spare line which I ran back and forth along the cross beams under the roof, I hung clothes, bacon, food bags, camera, guns and pots, out of the reach of the enormous rats which overrun the island. On each side, under the low roof, were two small square windows through which, by stooping, I could see the Caribbean. By one of these I shoved the canvas cot with its net to keep out the mosquitoes and tarantulas. I scarcely know which I dreaded most. Bars on the inside of the shutters and a lock on the trap door served to keep out those Ethiopian eyes which feel and handle as well as look.

ALONE IN THE CARIBBEAN

Near the shack was a cabin with two rooms, one with a bunk for the cook. The other room was utterly bare except for wide shelves around the sides where the whalemen slept, their bed clothing consisting for the most part of worn out cocoa bags.

Almost on a line between the cabin and the shack stood the ajoupa, a small hut made of woven withes, only partially roofed over, where the cook prepared the food over the native coalpots. As I looked at it, I thought of the similar huts in which Columbus found the gruesome cannibal cookery of the Caribs when he landed on Guadeloupe. A strange place to be in, I thought, with only the Scotch face of Jack and the familiar look of my own duffle to remind me of the civilization whence I had come. And even stranger if I had known that later in one of these very islands I should find a descendant of the famous St.–Hilaire family still ruling under a feudal system the land where her ancestors lived like princes in the days when one of them was a companion of the Empress Josephine.?

 ? Ajoupa—A Reminder of Carib Days ?

Even our meal was strange as we sat by the open doorway and watched the swift currents eddy around the island, cutting their way past the smoother water under the rocks. The jack–fish, not unlike the perch caught in colder waters, was garnished with the hot little "West Indie" peppers that burn the tongue like live coals. Then there was the fat little manicou or 'possum, which tasted like a sweet little suckling pig. I wondered at the skill of the cook, whose magic was performed over a handful of coals from the charred logwood, in an iron kettle or two. Nearly everything is boiled or simmered ; there is little frying and hardly any baking.

With the manicou we drank the coarse native chocolate sweetened with the brown syrupy sugar* of the islands. I did not like it at first, there was a by–taste that was new to me. But I soon grew fond of it and found that it gave me a wonderful strength for rowing in the heavy whaleboats, cutting blubber and the terrific sweating in the tropical heat.

* Muscovado.

As early as 1695 Père Labat in his enthusiasm truly said, "As for me, I stand by the advice of the Spanish doctors who agree that there is more nourishment in one ounce of chocolate than in half a pound of beef."

ALONE IN THE CARIBBEAN

At sunset Jack left for Grenada in one of the whale boats, and I made myself snug in the upper floor of the shack. Late that night I awoke and looking out over the Caribbean, blue in the strong clear moonlight, I saw the white sail of the returning whaleboat glide into the cove and was lulled to sleep again by the plaintive chantey of the whalemen as they sang to dispel the imaginary terrors that lurk in the shadows of the cove.

"Blo–o–ows!" came with the sun the next morning, followed by a fierce pounding on the underside of the trap door. Bynoe, the harpooner, had scarcely reached the lookout on the top of the hill when he saw a spout only two miles to windward near Les Tantes. The men were already by the boats as I ran half naked down the path and dumped my camera in the stern of the Active by "de bum (bomb) box," as José directed. With a string of grunts, curses and "oh–hee's" we got the heavy boats into the water and I finished dressing while the crews put in "de rock–stone" for ballast. As we left the cove we rowed around the north end of the island, our oars almost touching the steep rocky shore in order to avoid the strong current that swept between Caille and Ronde.

When José said, "You go stroke in de Aactive," I little knew what was in store for me. The twenty–foot oak oar, carried high above the thwart and almost on a line with the hip, seemed the very inbeing of unwieldiness. The blade was scarcely in the water before the oar came well up to the chest and the best part of the stroke was made with the body stretched out in a straight line —we nearly left our thwarts at every stroke —the finish being made with the hands close up under our chins. In the recovery we pulled our bodies up against the weight of the oar, feathering at the same time —a needless torture, for the long narrow blade was almost as thick as it was wide. Why the rowlock should be placed so high and so near the thwart I do not know ; the Yankee whaler places the rowlock about a foot farther aft.

While the humpbacker has not departed widely from the ways of his teacher a brief description of his outfit may not be amiss. His boat is the same large double–ended sea–canoe of the Yankee but it has lost the graceful ends and the easy lines of the New Bedford craft. Almost uncouth in its roughness, the well painted topsides, usually a light grey with the black of the tarred bottom and boot–top showing, give it a shipshape appearance ; while the orderly confusion of the worn gear and the tarry smell coming up from under the floors lend an air of adventure in harmony with the men who make up its crew.?

? Grenadine whaleboat showing bow and false–chock. The harpoon is poised in the left hand and heaved with the right arm. ?

The crew of six take their positions beginning with the harpooner in the bow in the following order : bow–oar, mid–oar, tub–oar, stroke and boatsteerer. For the purpose of making fast to the whale the harpooner uses two "irons" thrown by hand. The "iron" is a sharp wrought iron barb, having a shank about two feet long to which the shaft is fastened. The "first" iron is made fast to the end of the whale line, the first few fathoms of which are coiled on the small foredeck or "box." This is the heaving coil and is known as the "box line." The line then passes aft through the bow chocks to the loggerhead, a smooth round oak bitt stepped through the short deck in the stern, around which a turn or two are thrown to give a braking action as the whale takes the line in its first rush.

From the loggerhead, the line goes forward to the tub amidships in which 150 fathoms are coiled down. The "second" iron is fastened to a short warp, the end of which is passed around the main line in a bowline so that it will run freely. In case of accident to the first, the second iron may hold and the bowline will then toggle on the first. Immediately after the whale is struck, the line is checked in such a manner that the heavy boat can gather headway, usually against the short, steep seas of the "trades," without producing too great a strain on the gear. The humpbacker loses many whales through the parting of his line, for his boat is not only heavily constructed but carries a considerable weight of stone ballast "rock–stone" to steady it when sailing. The Yankee, in a boat scarcely heavier than his crew, holds the line immediately after the strike and makes a quick killing. He only gives out line when a whale sounds or shows fight. He makes his kill by cutting into the vitals of the whale with a long pole lance, reserving the less sportsmanlike but more expeditious bomb gun for a last resort, while the humpbacker invariably uses the latter.?

? The humpbacker under sail. ?

A jib and spritsail are carried, the latter having a gaff and boom, becketed for quick hoisting and lowering. Instead of using the convenient "tabernacle" by which the Yankee can drop his rig by the loosening of a pin, the humpbacker awkwardly steps his mast through a thwart into a block on the keel.?

? Unshipping the rig. ?

ALONE IN THE CARIBBEAN

The strike may be made while rowing or under full sail, according to the position of the boat when a whale is "raised." Because of the position of its eyes, the whale cannot see directly fore and aft, his range of vision being limited like that of a person standing in the cabin of a steamer and looking out through the port. The whaler takes advantage of this, making his approach along the path in which the whale is traveling. The early whalemen called the bow of the boat the "head," whence the expression, "taking them head–and–head," when the boat is sailing down on a school of whales.

"Ease–de–oar!" yelled José, for we were now out of the current, bobbing in the open sea to windward of Caille where the "trade" was blowing half a gale. We shipped our oars, banking them over the gunwale with the blades aft. The other boat had pulled up and it was a scramble to see who would get the windward berth.

"You stan' af' an' clar de boom," he said to me, as the men ran the heavy mast up with a rush while the harpooner aimed the foot as it dropped through the hole in the thwart and into its step —a shifty trick with the dripping nose of the boat pointed skyward one instant and the next buried deep in the blue of the Atlantic.

"Becket de gyaf —run ou' de boom —look shyarp!" With a mighty sweep of his steering oar, José pried our stern around and we got the windward berth on the starboard tack. One set of commands had sufficed for both boats ; we were close together, and they seemed to follow up the scent like a couple of joyous Orchas. Now I began to understand the philosophy of "de rock–stone" for we slid along over the steep breaking seas scarcely taking a drop of spray into the boat. As I sat on the weather rail, I had an opportunity to study the men in their element. The excitement of the start had been edged off by the work at the oars. We might have been on a pleasure sail instead of a whale hunt. In fact, there was no whale to be seen for "de balen* soun'," as José said in explanation of the absence of the little cloud of steam for which we were looking. Daniel–Joe, our harpooner, had already bent on his "first" iron and was lazily throwing the end of the short warp of his "second" to the main line while keeping an indefinite lookout over the starboard bow. He might have been coiling a clothesline in the back yard and thinking of the next Policeman's Ball.

* From the French balein, meaning whale.

ALONE IN THE CARIBBEAN

The bow—oar, swaying on the loose stay to weather, took up the range of vision while we of the weather rail completed the broadside. José, who had taken in his long steering oar and dropped the rudder in its pintles, was "feeling" the boat through the long tiller in that absent way of the man born to the sea. With a sort of dual vision he watched the sails and the sea to windward at the same time. "Wet de leach!" and "Cippie," the tub—oar, let himself down carefully to the lee rail where he scooped up water in a large calabash, swinging his arm aft in a quick motion, and then threw it up into the leach to shrink the sail where it was flapping.

Time after time I was on the point of giving the yell only to find that my eye had been fooled by a distant white cap. But finally it did come, that little perpendicular jet dissipated into a cloud of steam as the wind caught it, distinct from the white caps as the sound of a rattlesnake from the rustle of dry leaves. It was a young bull, loafing down the lee tide not far from where Bynoe had first sighted him.

Again he sounded but only for a short time and again we saw his spout half a mile under our lee. We had oversailed him. As we swung off the wind he sounded. In a time too short to have covered the distance, I thought, José gave the word to the crew who unshipped the rig, moving about soft—footed like a lot of big black cats without making the slightest knock against the planking of the boat.

We got our oars out and waited. Captain Caesar held the other boat hove—to a little to windward of us. Then I remembered the lee tide and knew that we must be somewhere over the bull. Suddenly José whispered, "De wale sing!" I thought he was fooling at first, the low humming coming perhaps from one of the men, but there was no mistaking the sound. I placed my ear against the planking from which it came in a distinct note like the low tone of a 'cello. While I was on my hands and knees listening to him the sound suddenly ceased. "Look!" yelled José, as the bull came up tail first, breaking water less than a hundred yards from us, his immense flukes fully twenty feet out of the water.

Time seemed to stop while my excited brain took in the cupid's bow curve of the flukes dotted with large white barnacles like snowballs plastered on a black wall, while in reality it was all over in a flash —a sight too unexpected for the camera. Righting himself, he turned to windward, passing close to the other boat. It was a long chance but Bynoe took it, sending his harpoon high into the air, followed by the snaky line.?

ALONE IN THE CARIBBEAN

? Once more we had the weather berth and bore down on tem under full sail, Bynoe standing high up on the 'box', holding the forestay. ?

A perfect eye was behind the strong arm that had thrown it and the iron fell from its height to sink deep into the flesh aft of the fin. As the line became taut, the boat with its rig still standing gathered headway, following the whale in a smother of foam, the sails cracking in the wind like revolver shots while a thin line of smoke came from the loggerhead. Caesar must have been snubbing his line too much, however, for in another moment it parted, leaving a boatload of cursing, jabbering negroes a hundred yards or more from their starting point. The bull left for more friendly waters. The tension of the excitement having snapped with the line, a volley of excuses came down the wind to us which finally subsided into a philosophical, "It wuz de will ob de Lard."

Whaling was over for that day and we sailed back to the cove to climb the rocks to the ajoupa where we filled our complaining stomachs with manicou and chocolate. While we ate the sun dropped behind the ragged fringe of clouds on the horizon and the day suddenly ended changing into the brilliant starlit night of the tropics. Even if we had lost our whale, the spell was at last broken for we had made a strike. Bynoe' s pipe sizzled and bubbled with my good tobacco as he told of the dangers of Kick 'em Jinny or Diamond Rock on the other side of Ronde.

The men drew close to the log where we were sitting as I told of another Diamond Rock off Martinique of which you shall hear in due time. Bynoe in turn told of how he had helped in the rescue of an unfortunate from a third Diamond Rock off the coast of Cayan (French Guiana) where the criminal punishment used to be that of putting a man on the rock at low tide and leaving him a prey to the sharks when the sea should rise. But there was something else on Bynoe's mind. The same thing seemed to occur to Caesar, who addressed him in patois. Then the harpooner asked me : "An' you not in thees ilan' before?"

I lighted my candle lamp and spread my charts out on the ground before the whalers. As I showed them their own Grenadines their wonder knew no bounds Charts were unknown to them. Now they understood the magic by which I knew what land I might be approaching —even if I had never been there before.

ALONE IN THE CARIBBEAN

Most of the names of the islands are French or Carib ; even the few English names were unknown to the men, who used the names given to the islands before they were finally taken over by the British. One which interested me was Bird Island, which they called Mouchicarri, a corruption of Mouchoir Carré or Square Handkerchief. This must have been a favorite expression in the old days for a whitened shoal or a low lying island where the surf beats high and white, for there is a Mouchoir Carré off Guadeloupe, another in the Bahamas and we have our own Handkerchief Shoals. From the lack of English names it is not at all unreasonable to suppose that it was a Frenchman who first explored the Grenadines. Columbus, on his hunt for the gold of Veragua, saw the larger islands of Grenada and Saint Vincent from a distance and named them without having set foot on them. Martinique was the first well established colony in the Lesser Antilles and from that island a boatload of adventurers may have sailed down the islands, naming one of the Grenadines Petit Martinique, from their own island, because of its striking similarity of contour, rising into a small counterpart of Pelée. Also, it was more feasible to sail down from Martinique than to buck the wind and current in the long channel from Trinidad.

As the fire in the ajoupa died down, the men drew closer and closer to the friendly light of my candle, away from the spooky shadows, and when I bade them good night they were behind the tightly closed door and shutters of their cabin by the time I had reached my roost in the top of the shack.

For several days after our first strike the cry of "blows" would bring us "all standing" and we would put to sea only to find that the whale had made off to windward or had loafed into those tantalizing currents to leeward where we could see it but dared not follow. Finally our chance came again —and almost slipped away under our very noses.

We had been following a bull and a cow and calf since sunrise. At last they sounded an hour before sunset. We had eaten no food since the night before and all day long the brown–black almost hairless calves of the men had been reminding me in an agonizing way of the breast of roasted duck. The constant tacking back and forth, the work of stepping and unshipping the rig, the two or three rain squalls which washed the salt spray out of our clothes and made us cold, had tired us and dulled our senses. Suddenly the keen Bynoe, with the eyes of a pelican, gave the yell. There they were, scarcely a hundred yards from us. The bull had gone his way. I was in Caesar's boat this time and as Bynoe was considered the better of the two harpooners we made for the calf and were soon fast.

If ever a prayer were answered through fervency our line would have parted and spared this baby —although it seems a travesty to call a creature twenty–eight feet long a baby. But it was a baby compared to its mother, who was sixty–eight feet long. As the calf was welling up its life blood, giving the sea a tinge that matched the color of the dying sun, the devoted mother circled around us, so close that we could have put our second iron into her.

It is always this way with a cow and her calf. The first or more skillful boat's crew secures the calf while the mother's devotion makes the rest easy for the other boat. There was no slip this time and the program was carried out without a hitch. José bore down in the Active and Daniel–Joe sent his iron home with a yell. We stopped our work of killing for the moment to watch them as they melted away in the fading light, a white speck that buried itself in the darkness of the horizon. It was an all–night row for us, now in the lee tide, now in the weather tide, towing this baby —a task that seemed almost as hopeless as towing a continent. But we made progress and by morning were back in the cove.

Having eaten three times and cut up the calf, we sailed for Sauteurs late in the afternoon for news of José and the cow. José's flight from Mouchicarri, where we had struck the whales, had been down the windward coast of Grenada. We were met on the jetty by Jack, who told us that the cow had been killed at the other end of Grenada and would not start till the next noon. He had made arrangements for the little coasting steamer, Taw, to tow the carcass up from St. George's.

And so the cow would make the circuit of the island, the first part very much alive, towing a crew of negroes half dead from fright and the last of the way being towed very much dead. While we had been rowing our hearts out, José and his crew had been streaking it behind the whale, not daring to pull up in the darkness for the "kill."

At dawn they dispatched the weakened animal more than thirty miles from their starting point. We learned later that, although the wind and tide had been in their favor and as they neared shore other boats had put out to reach them, they did not reach St. George's till eleven the following night. They had made half a mile an hour.

ALONE IN THE CARIBBEAN

As we turned in on the floor of Jack's cocoa shop, I began to have visions of something "high" in the line of whale on the morrow. I knew the Taw. She could not possibly tow the whale any faster than three miles an hour and would not leave St. George's till one o'clock the next day. The distance was twenty–one miles, so that by the time she could be cut —in the whale would have been dead three nights and two days. I no longer regretted the wild night ride I had missed.

The next afternoon we were again in the whaleboat, Jack with us. Our plan was to wait near London Bridge, a natural arch of rocks half way between Sauteurs and Caille and a little to windward. We did this to entice the captain of the Taw as far to windward as possible for we were not at all certain that he would tow the whale all the way to Île–de–Caille. If he brought the whale as far as London Bridge, the two boats might be able to tow the carcass during the night through the remaining three miles to the island so that we could begin to cut–in in the morning.

So we sailed back and forth till at last, as the sun was sinking, we made out the tiny drift of steamer smoke eight miles away. They were not even making the three miles an hour and Bynoe said that the tongue must have swollen and burst the lines, allowing the mouth to open. We began to wonder why they did not cut off the ventral flukes and tow the whale tail first. But the reason came out later.

The moon would be late, and we continued sailing in the darkness without a light, lest the captain should pick us up too soon and cast off the whale in mid–channel where ten whaleboats could not drag her against the current which was now lee. We lost sight of the steamer for an hour or so but finally decided that what we had taken for a low evening star was her masthead light. In another hour we could make out the red and green of her running lights. She was in the clutches of the tide directly to leeward. She was also two miles off her course and we began to wonder why the captain did not give up in disgust and cast the whale adrift. We sailed down to find out.

First the hull of the steamer began to take shape in the velvety darkness ; then as we swung up into the wind we made out the whaleboat some distance astern. As the bow of the steamer rose on a long sea, her after deck lights threw their rays on a low black object upon which the waves were shoaling as on a reef. At the same instant a stray whiff from the trade wind brought us the message. We were doubly informed of the presence of the cow.

ALONE IN THE CARIBBEAN

But it was not the cow that drew our attention. On the aft deck, leaning far out, stood the captain. His features were distinct in the beams of the range light. Suddenly he started as though he had seen something. Then he bellowed, "Where in hell did you come from?" "We've been waiting to windward for you ; what's the trouble?"

"Trouble?" he shrieked, "trouble? —your damned old whale is fast and I can't get her off."

We guessed the rest. As Bynoe had predicted, the tongue had swollen and burst the lashing that had held the mouth closed. Next the towline had parted. This had happened shortly after the steamer left St. George's and the men who were towing behind in their boat had begged the captain to pass out his steel cable. He didn't know it but it was here that he erred. The whalemen ran the cable through the jaw, bending the end into a couple of hitches. When they started up again, the hitches slipped back and jammed, making it impossible to untie the cable.

Progress had been slow enough under the lee of Grenada but when the steamer got clear of the land she felt the clutches of the current and progress to the northward was impossible. He announced to the pleading whalemen that he was sick of the job and was going to cut loose. But he couldn't. There was not a tool aboard except the engine room wrenches. Not even a file or a cold–chisel. Jack asked him, "What are you going to do?"

"Me? —it's your whale."

"Yes, but you've got it. I don't want it, it's too old now."

And old it was. The smell even seemed to go to windward. But there was only one course left and twelve o'clock found us at Sauteurs, the whale still in possession of the Taw.

The scene of our midnight supper in the cocoa shop that night will long remain in my memory as one of those pictures so strange and far off that one often wonders whether it was a real experience or a fantasy suggested by some illustration or story long since forgotten. We cooked in Jack's little sanctum, railed off at one end of the shop, where the negress brings his tea in the morning and afternoon. At the other end was the small counter with the ledger and scales that brought out the very idea of barter. On the floor space between were bags of cocoa and the tubs in which the beans are "tramped" with red

31

clay for the market. Two coils of new whale line and a bundle

I am firmly convinced that the next morning the odor from that carcass opened the door, walked in and shook me by the shoulders. No one else had done it and I sat up with a start. Shortly after, a courier from the district board brought the following message : (I use the word "courier" for it is the only time I ever saw a native run.)

ST. PATRICK'S DISTRICT BOARD, SECRETARY'S OFFICE,
24th, February, 1911. John S. Wildman, Esq., SIR : —In the interest of sanitation, I am instructed to request that the whale's carcass be removed from the harbor within three hours after the service of this notice.

I have the honor to be, sir,
 Your obedient servant, R.L.B.A., Warden.

We were not unwilling and had what was left of the cow towed out into the current which would carry it far into the Caribbean where for days the gulls could gorge themselves and scream over it in a white cloud. At least that was our intention, but by a pretty piece of miscalculation on the part of Bynoe the carcass fetched up under Point Tangalanga where the last pieces of flesh were removed on the eighth day after the whale's death.

Our work done at Sauteurs, we sailed back to Caille, where we scrubbed out the boats with white coral sand to remove the grease, dried out the lines and coiled them down in the tubs for the next whale.

My real ride behind a humpback came at last in that unexpected way that ushers in the unusual. We were loafing one day near Mouchicarri, lying–to for the moment in a heavy rain squall, when it suddenly cleared, disclosing three whales under our lee. They were a bull, a cow and a yawlin (yearling), with José close on their track. Bynoe hastily backed the jib so that we could "haal aft" and we made a short tack.

Just as we were ready to come about again in order to get a close weather berth of the bull, the upper rudder pintle broke and our chance slipped by. Why Caesar did not keep on, using the steering oar, I do not know. Perhaps it was that yellow streak that is so dangerous when one is depending on the native in a tight place, for we should have had that bull. He was immense.

The rudder was quickly tied up to the stern post, but it was only after two hours of tedious sailing and rowing that we were again upon them. Once more we had the weather berth and bore down on them under full sail, Bynoe standing high up on the "box," holding to the forestay. Except for the occasional hiss of a sea breaking under us, there was not a sound and we swooped down on them with the soft flight of an owl.

As I stood up close to Caesar, I could see the whole of the action. The three whales were swimming abreast, blowing now and then as they rose from a shallow dive. The tense crew, all looking forward like ebony carvings covered with the nondescript rags of a warehouse, seemed frozen to their thwarts. Only one of us moved and he was Caesar, and I noticed that he swung the oar a little to port in order to avoid the bull and take the yawlin. I had guessed right about the yellow streak.

But even the yawlin was no plaything and as he rose right under the bow the sea slid off his mountainous back as from a ledge of black rock, a light green in contrast to the deep blue into which it poured. The cavernous rush of air and water from his snout sprayed Bynoe in the face as he drove the iron down into him. He passed under us, our bow dropping into the swirl left by his tail and I could feel the bump of his back through Caesar's oar.

I wondered for the moment if the boat would trip. There seemed to be no turning, for the next instant the flying spray drove the lashes back into my eyes and I knew we were fast. Blinded for the moment I could feel the boat going over and through the seas, skittering after the whale like a spoon being reeled in from a cast. When I finally succeeded in wiping the lashes out of my eyes there was nothing to be seen ahead but two walls of spray which rose from the very bows of the boat, with Bynoe still clinging to the stay with his head and shoulders clear of the flying water. There was no need to wet the line ; the tub oar was bailing instead.

How the rig came down I do not know and I marvel at the skill or the luck of the men who unshipped the heavy mast in that confusion of motions, for my whole attention was called by the yelling Caesar to the loggerhead, which somehow had one too many turns around it. Caesar was busy with the steering oar, and the men had settled down a little forward of midships to keep the boat from yawing. So I committed the foolhardy trick of jumping over the line as it whizzed past me in a yellow streak and, bracing myself on the port side, I passed my hand aft along the rope with a quick motion and threw off a turn, also a considerable area of skin, of which the salt water gave sharp notice later.

The line was eased and held through this first rush. As the whale settled down to steady flight we threw back that turn and then another, till the tub emptied slower and slower and the line finally came to a stop. We were holding. But we were still going ; it only meant that the yawlin, having gone through his first spurt, had struck his gait ; it was like a continuous ride in the surf. By this time the boat was well trimmed and bailed dry.

"Haal een, now," came from Caesar, and I was again reminded of the missing skin. By the inch first, then by the foot it came, till we had hauled back most of our thousand feet of line. The walls of spray had dropped lower and lower, till we could see the whale ahead of us, his dorsal fin cutting through the tops of the waves. We were now close behind his propelling flukes that came out of the water at times like the screw of a freighter in ballast. Caesar told me to load "de bum lance," and I passed the gun forward to Bynoe. He held it for a moment in pensive indecision —and then placed it carefully under the box.

He now removed the small wooden pin that keeps the line from bobbing out of the bow chocks, and with the blunt end of a paddle he carefully pried the line out of the chock so that it slid back along the rail, coming to rest against the false chock about three feet abaft the stem. We now swerved off to one side and were racing parallel to the whale opposite his flukes. The bow four surged on the line while I took in the slack at the loggerhead, Caesar wrestling frantically with his steering oar that was cutting through the maelstrom astern.

We were now fairly opposite the yawlin, which measured nearly two of our boat's length. It was one of those ticklish moments so dear to the Anglo−Saxon lust for adventure —even the negroes were excited beyond the feeling of fear. But at the sight of the bomb gun, as Bynoe took it out from under the box, a feeling of revulsion swept over me and if it were not for the fatal "rock−stone," or the sharks that might get us, I would have wished the gun overboard and a fighting sperm off Hatteras on our line.

The yawlin continued his flight in dumb fear. Fitting his left leg into the half–round of the box, the harpooner raised his gun and took aim. Following the report came the metallic explosion of the bomb inside the whale. Our ride came to an end almost as suddenly as it had begun ; the yawlin was rolling inert at our side, having scarcely made a move after the shot. The bomb had pierced the arterial reservoir, causing death so quickly that we missed the blood and gore which usually come from the blow–hole in a crimson fountain with the dying gasps of the whale. Bynoe explained that one could always tell if the vital spot had been reached :

"If he go BAM! he no good. W'en he go CLING! de balen mus stop." His way of expressing it was perfect, for the "cling" was not unlike the ringing hammer of trapped air in a steam pipe, but fainter.

Luck was with us this time, for we were well to windward of Caille, with a tide that was lee to help us home.

But it was my last whale at Île–de–Caille, and after we had cut him in and set his oily entrails adrift I turned once more to the Yakaboo. I had had enough of humpbacking and one night I packed my outfit and smoked for the last time with the men.?

? The immense intestines and bladders that looked like a fleet of balloons come to grief. ?

?

CHAPTER III. KICK 'EM JINNY

I FIRMLY believe that it was my lucky bug that did the trick, although under ordinary circumstances I would not carry a tarantula for a mascot. It was on my last night at Île–de–Caille, and as I crawled up through the hatch of my upper story abode, something black stood out in the candle flicker against the wall. Before I knew what it was, instinct told me that it was something to look out for and then I noticed the huge hairy legs that proclaimed the tarantula. Of course, I could not have him running around as he pleased so I took the under half of a sixteen gauge cartridge box and covered him before he had time to think of jumping. The box, which measured four and a half inches square, was not too large for I nipped his toes as I pressed the pasteboard against the wall. Then I slid a sheet of paper between him and the wall. It was no trick at all to superimpose the upper half of the pasteboard box, slip out the paper and push the cover down. He was mine. And a good mascot he proved to be although I gave him a rough time of it in the jumble of sea off Kick 'em Jinny.

Kick 'em Jinny is the sea–mule of the Grenadines. In a prosaic way the cartographer has marked it "Diamond Rock," and then, as if ashamed of himself, has put the real name in small letters underneath. So "steep–to" that a vessel would strike her bowsprit on its sides before her keel touched bottom, Kick 'em Jinny rises from a diameter of a quarter of a mile to a height of nearly seven hundred feet. Cactus–grown, with no natural resources, one would scarcely expect to find on it any animal life other than a few sea fowl. Yet, besides myriads of screaming gulls, boobies, pelicans and wild pigeons, here are goats, the wild descendants of those left by the Spanish pirates, who used to plant them as a reserve food supply that would take care of itself.

The rock lies a third of a mile to the northward of Isle de Ronde, with the jagged Les Tantes a scant two miles to the eastward. With the trades blowing fresh from the northeast the lee tide runs through the passage between Isle de Ronde and Les Tantes at a rate of three knots an hour, whirling past Kick 'em Jinny in a northwesterly direction —at right angles to the wind and sea. The weather tide in returning runs in almost the opposite direction at the rate of a knot and a half. It must be remembered that the constant northeasterly winds move a surface current of water toward the southwest so that this confluence of wind and current makes a tide rip on the weather side of Kick 'em Jinny, from which its name is derived.

Now you may ask, as I did when I discussed the matter with my friends of St. George's over tall, cool glasses of lime squash —Why not sail under the lee of Kick 'em Jinny? If I sailed under the lee of the rock I should lose much valuable ground to windward while if I fought it out along the back or weather side of Ronde and Kick 'em Jinny and then made a port tack to Les Tantes I should be in the best possible position for my jump to Carriacou. That point settled, it was a question of tides. With the lee tide running to the north–north–west I might not be able to clear the rocky windward shore on my starboard tack, and it would be very difficult to claw off on the port tack, the latter being to eastward and away from shore.

ALONE IN THE CARIBBEAN

With the weather tide, however, I could work my way off shore in case of necessity, but I should be fighting the current as I advanced on the starboard tack. With the weather tide I should encounter the rougher sea, and it was here that the Yakaboo would meet her pons asinorum, to carry out the idea of the sea–mule.

Many bets had been offered and some had been taken at St. George's that I would not reach Carriacou, which implied that the cruise would come to an end off Kick 'em Jinny. But I put my faith in one —my Man Friday, who had instructed me in the mysteries of "de lee an' wedder toid," and he had shown me how to watch the weather in regard to the changes of the moon. During my stay on Île–de–Caille, I watched the quarters come and go and kept track of the moon in order to note the changing of the tides. I finally selected a day when the second quarter had promised steady winds, with the weather tide beginning to run at nine o'clock in the morning. If there should be any doubt as to the weather for that day, that doubt would be settled by the time the weather tide had started. With everything as much in my favor as possible I would make the attempt.

I slept that morning till the sun had climbed well up the back of Caille, for when I awoke the warm day breezes were filtering over me through the mosquito bar. I must have eaten breakfast, but later in the day I was puzzled to remember whether I had or not. My mind was not in the present, nor anywhere near my earthly body —it was living in the next few hours and hovering over that stretch of water to the eastward of Kick 'em Jinny. Bynoe and his crew were also going to sail northward to Cannouan in the Baltimore, and I remember standing among the rocks of the whale cove bidding good–bye to the rest of the people. The few shillings I gave them seemed a princely gift and tears of gratitude streamed down the black shiny face of the cook when I presented her with a bottle of rheumatism cure.

The tide would turn at seven minutes after the hour and three minutes later the Yakaboo was in the water. By the feel of her as she bobbed in the heave of the sea I knew that the fight was on. With long rhythmic strokes the whaleboat swung out of the cove, the canoe moving easily alongside like a remora. Cautiously we rowed around the north end of Caille, seeking the currentless waters close to shore. When we reached the windward side of the island we made sail. It did not take many minutes to see that the canoe would be left alone in her fight with Kick 'em Jinny for the whaleboat, with her ballast of "rock–stone" and her twelve hundred pounds of live weight to steady her, caught the wind high above the seas with her tall rig and worried her way through the jumble in a way that made me forget, in a moment of admiration, my own sailing.

But I had other business than that of watching the whaleboat. As I hauled in the sheet to lay the canoe on the starboard tack, a sea seemed to come from nowhere and with scant invitation dropped aboard and filled the cockpit. It was like starting up a sleeping horse with an inconsiderate whip lash. The Yakaboo shook herself and gathered herself for that first essay of windward work. Try as she would, she could find no ease in the nasty, steep sea, and instead of working well along the shore of Ronde in the wake of the whaleboat, she barely crossed the channel from Caille and fetched up at the southern tip of the island.

On the port tack to sea she did better, although the weather tide running abeam carried us back off Caille. We made perhaps a mile to the eastward and then I decided to try the starboard tack again. The canoe did still better this time —for a while —and then we found ourselves in the toils of Kick 'em Jinny. The tide was now running with full force directly against us and at right angles to the wind. There seemed to be no lateral motion to the seas, they rose and fell as though countless imps were pushing up the surface from below in delirious random. One moment the canoe would be poised on the top of a miniature water column to be dropped the next in a hollow, walled about on all sides by masses of translucent green and blue over which I could see nothing but sky. The stiff wind might not have been blowing at all, it seemed, for the sails were constantly ashake, while the centerboard rattled in its casing like the clapper of a bell. It was not sailing —it was riding a bronco at sea.

Bynoe, who was carrying my extra food supply in the whaleboat, was now making frantic motions for me to turn back. I had already decided, however, that the canoe would worry her way through and I motioned to the whalers to come alongside. With the two boats rising and falling beside one another, as though on some foreshortened see–saw, the stuff was transferred from the whaleboat to the canoe. As the whaleboat rose over me the men dropped my bags into the cockpit with an accuracy and ease of aim acquired from years of life in just such jumping water as this. The canoe sailor must at times not only be ambidextrous, but must also use feet and teeth ; in fact, he must be an all around marine acrobat. What wonders we could perform had we but retained the prehensile tail of our animal ancestors! So with the mainsheet in my teeth and my legs braced in the cockpit, I caught the bags with one hand and with the other stowed them in the forward end of the well under the deck. A large tin of sea biscuit, a cubical piece of eight–cornered wickedness, which would neither stow under deck nor pass through the hatches, required two hands for catching and stowing and a spare line to lash it in place just forward of my blanket bag. Then they screamed "Good–bye" at me across the waves, while I yelled "Yakaboo," and we parted company. Of that row of six black faces, two I shall never see again for they have since been lost in the very waters where we said "Good–bye."

Taking quick cross–bearings by eye I could detect from time to time changes in the position of the canoe and I knew that there was some advance to the northward. Finally we were so close to Kick 'em Jinny that I could see the chamois–like goats stuck on its sides like blotched rocks. All progress seemed to cease and for three–quarters of an hour I could detect no change of position. No stage racehorse ever made a gamer fight than did the Yakaboo against her ocean treadmill. The whaleboat was now a vanishing speck to the northward like a fixed whitecap. I began to wonder whether I should stick in this position till the coming of the lee tide. I remember contemplating a small strip of beach on Les Tantes where, in a pinch, I might land through the breast–high surf with enough food to last till the whalers might see some sign that I could put up on the rocks.

Suddenly a blinding flash brought my attention from Les Tantes to my cockpit. It was the tin of sea biscuit. The water sloshing in the cockpit had softened the glue of the paper covering. Finally, an extra large wave, a grandfather, swept the paper entirely off, leaving the shiny tin exposed to the brilliant sun. With a sweep I cut the line, and the next instant I was mourning the loss of a week's supply of sea biscuit.

The forward compartment now proved to be leaking, through the deck as I discovered later, at just the time, when, if the canoe had any soul at all, she would keep tight for my sake. I shifted my outfit as far aft as possible and sponged the water out by the cupful with one hand ready to slam down the hatch in advance of a boarding sea. It was done —somehow —and as a reward I found the canoe was working her way into easier seas. Then she began to sail and I realized that Kick 'em Jinny was a thing of the past. I lay–to off Les Tantes, having traveled three miles in two hours. We had not conquered Kick 'em Jinny, we had merely slipped by her in one of her lighter moods. But the canoe had stood the test and by this I knew that she would carry me through the rest of the channel to Saint Vincent. What her story would be for the larger openings of from twenty–five to nearly forty miles yet remained to be seen.

ALONE IN THE CARIBBEAN

With her heels clear of Kick 'em Jinny the Yakaboo traveled easily in the freer waters and before the tide could draw me out into the Caribbean I was well under the lee of Carriacou. Another half hour and I should have had to fight for six hours till the next weather tide would help me back to land.

Late in the afternoon, I stepped out of the canoe on the uninhabited island of Mabouya, which lies off Carriacou. The beach where I landed was typical of the few low–lying cays of the Grenadines. The sand strip, backed by a cheval de frise of cactus, curved crescentlike, the horns running into sharp, rocky points which confined the beach. The only break in the cactus was a clump of the dreaded manchioneel trees and here I decided to pitch my tent.

Barbot, in relating the second voyage of Columbus, says : "On the shore grow abundance of mansanilla trees, not tall, but the wood of them fine, the leaves like those of the pear tree, the fruit a sort of small apples, whence the Spaniards gave them the name ; of so fine a color and pleasant a scent, as will easily invite such as are unacquainted to eat them ; but containing a mortal poison, against which no antidote has any force. The very leaf of it causes an ulcer, where it touches the flesh, and the dew on it frets off the skin ; nay the very shadow of the tree is pernicious, and will cause a man to swell, if he sleeps under it." I thought I would take a chance —perhaps the manchioneel had become softer and more civilized since the time of Columbus.

If there were any joy in the feeling of relief as I walked up that lonely beach, I knew it not. Tired as I was, I could only think of the hard work that I had to do before I could lie down to rest. The Yakaboo had been leaking steadily all day long and she now lay where I had left her in a foot of water, with my whole outfit except my camera submerged. This did not mean that everything was wet, for my own muslin bags, honestly oiled and dried, would keep their contents dry, but there was the canoe to unload, bail out and drag ashore. There was firewood to collect before dark, and I should have to work sharp before sundown, for there were also the tent to pitch, the supper to cook, and the log to write.

For a moment I stopped to look at the glorious sun racing to cool himself in the Caribbean, and I gave thanks for a strong body and a hopeful heart. In two hours I was sitting under the peak of my tent on my blanket roll, watching my supper boil in a little pail over a lively fire of hard charcoals. The Yakaboo, bailed out, high and dry on the beach, skulked in the darkness as though ashamed to come near the fire.

It is always easy to say "in two hours I was doing so and so," but to the man who lives out of doors and is constantly using his wits to overcome the little obstacles of nature those "two hours" are often very interesting. As a rule, one is tired from the day's work and if accidents are going to happen they are apt to happen at just this time. The early stages of fatigue bring on carelessness, and to the experienced man the advanced stages of fatigue call for extreme caution. Before unloading the canoe, I should have decided just where I would place my tent and then I should have beached the canoe immediately below the tent if possible. As it was, the Yakaboo was sixty yards down the beach and upon returning from one of my trips to her I found that a spark from the fire had ignited my oiled dish bag which was burning with a fierce heat. This had started the bag next to it which contained my ammunition. With one leap I landed on the precious high-power cartridges and began to roll over and over in the sand with the burning bag in my arms. What would have happened had one of my nine-millimeter shells exploded? I had been careless in arranging my outfit upon the sands when I built the fire.

Troubles never come singly —neither do they travel in pairs —they flock. I remember the difficulty I had in starting the fire. The tin in which I carried my matches was absolutely watertight —I have proved that since by submerging it in a bucket of water for two days and nights. And yet when I came to open the tin I found that the tips of the matches were deliquescent. It was my first experience in tropical cruising and I had not learned that the heat of the sun could draw the moisture out of the wood of the matches, condense this moisture on the inside of the tin, and melt the tips. I found some safety matches tucked away in the middle of my clothes bags and they were dry. This became my method of carrying matches in the future. The natives carry matches in a bamboo joint with a cork for a stopper.

And now that I have taken you into my first camp in the islands I shall tell you briefly of the various parts of my outfit as it was finally shaken down for the cruise.

My tent was of the pyramidal form invented by Comstock, seven feet high with a base seven feet square and having the peak directly over the center of the forward edge. In back was a two foot wall. It was made of a waterproof mixture of silk and cotton, tinted green, and weighed eight pounds. My mainmast served as a tent pole, and for holding down I used seventeen pegs made of the native cedar, which is a tough, hard wood and not heavy. For my purposes I have found this the most satisfactory tent for varied cruising, as I could use it equally well ashore or rigged over the cockpit of the Yakaboo when I slept aboard. Let me here offer a little prayer of thanks to Comstock. You will find some "improvement" upon his idea in almost any outfitter's catalogue and given any name but his —one might as well try to improve it as to alter a Crosby cat.?

? My Comstock tent. ?

For sleeping I had two single German blankets, weighing four pounds each. In place of the usual rubber blanket, I used an oiled muslin ground cloth. My blankets were folded in the ground cloth in such a manner that upon drawing them from the blanket bag, I could roll them out on the ground ready for turning in. The blanket bag was made of heavy oiled canvas with the end turned in and strapped so that even when it lay in a cockpit half full of water its contents would still remain dry. One blanket used with pajamas of light duck would have been ample, so far as warmth goes, but for sleeping in the cockpit the second blanket served as a padding for the hard floor.

As for clothes, I started out with a heterogeneous collection of old trousers, shirts and socks, which, according to the law of the survival of favorites, petered out to two pairs of light woolen trousers, two light flannel shirts, and two pairs of thin woolen socks. I indulged myself in half a dozen new sleeveless cotton running shirts, dyed red, B.V.D.'s to correspond, and a dozen red cotton bandana handkerchiefs. For footgear, I carried a pair of heavy oiled tan shoes and pigskin moccasins. A light Swedish dog–skin coat and a brown felt hat with a fairly wide brim, completed my wardrobe.

For cooking I had the "Ouinnetka" kit, of my own design, consisting of three pails, a frypan, two covers, a cup, and two spoons, all of aluminum, which nested and held a dish cloth and soap. There were no handles, a pair of light tongs serving in their stead. This kit, which was designed for two–man use, weighed a trifle under three pounds.

The rest of my working outfit consisted of a two pound axe, a canoe knife, a small aluminum folding candle lantern, two one–gallon water cans, and a ditty bag, containing a sight compass, parallel rule, dividers, hypodermic outfit, beeswax, and the usual odds and ends which one carries. For sailing I used a two–inch liquid compass. This working outfit totaled forty–three pounds. Had the "butterfly" continued in service, its weight would have added a pound and a half.

ALONE IN THE CARIBBEAN

?? My camp at Mabouya. ?

My food at the outset brought this weight up to eighty pounds, but as I later on got down to chocolate, erbswurst and the native foods, there was a reduction of from twenty to thirty pounds.

The heaviest single unit of my whole outfit was a quarter–plate Graflex, which, with its developing tank and six tins of films, added twenty–six pounds. A nine millimeter Mannlicher, .22 B.S.A., 38–40 Colt, a deep sea rod and reel, shells, and tackle brought the total up to 120 pounds. I might as well have left out my armament and tackle for when cruising I find little time for shooting or fishing —I would rather travel.

My charts, twelve in number, had first been trimmed to their smallest working size and then cut into eight–inch by ten–inch panels and mounted on muslin with half an inch separating the edges so that they could be folded to show uppermost whatever panel I happened to be sailing on. The charts with my portfolio I kept in a double bag in the aft end of the cockpit.

The various parts of my outfit were in bags having long necks which could be doubled over and securely tied. These were made of unbleached muslin, oiled with a mixture of raw and boiled linseed oil and turpentine. After a wet bit of sailing, when the canoe had at times literally gone through the seas and there was water in every compartment, it was a great comfort to find the entire outfit quite dry.

The weight of the Yakaboo, with her rig and outfit aboard, varied from 260 to 290 pounds —not much more than that of an ordinary rowboat.?

? Loaded and ready to get off. ?

Nothing is so unalloyed as the joy of pottering over a hot, little fire when the stomach cries out and the body tingles with the healthy fatigue of work in the open. My spirit was at ease, for the canoe had proven herself and even if she did leak, I was getting used to

43

that —as one becomes used to a boil on the neck. To lie on my blankets —no bed was ever so welcome —and to eat and watch the last light fade from the hills of Carriacou made me glad that I had been put on this earth to live. After supper the companionable purr of my faithful pipe made just the conversation to suit my mood. The night was soft and balmy, and as I lay and watched the brilliant constellations of the tropical night the lap–lap of the water on the smooth sand lulled me off to sleep.

CHAPTER IV. CARRIACOU–MAYERO–BEQUIA.

THE next moment I was sitting up, blinking into the fiery face of the sun that had slipped around the earth and was bobbing up again in the east.

It was not the sandy beach, the blue stretch of wind–livened water nor the picturesque hills of Carriacou, rising up before me, that alone brought happiness, for, as my eye wandered down the beach, I saw the buoyant, jaunty Yakaboo, and there came over me the happy satisfaction that the cruise was mine. My eye beheld her with the fondness of a parent for its child —if only she did not leak.

Not until I had cooked and eaten breakfast and was stowing my outfit into the canoe did I think of the mascot I had brought with me from Caille. I found his house in the forward end of the cockpit, unglued by the wash of the day before and empty. I am not sentimental by nature and I did not mourn his black hairy little body, which no doubt, by this time, was being carried far out into the Caribbean. I did thank him, or rather her, for I found out afterwards that it was a female, for the service she had rendered as a mascot in my sail around Kick 'em Jinny. I did not know, in fact, that she was still with the ship and would be my mascot for some time to come.

When I ran alongside the jetty of the pretty little town of Hillsboro, on the shores of Carriacou, a blue–jacketed sailor pointed to where I might beach the canoe, and said, "Mr. Smith is expecting you in his office," a prosaic remark, more fitting to the tenth floor above Broadway than to the beach of a West Indian island. I had scarcely beached the canoe and was walking across the hot stretch, curling my toes under me to ease my soles on the blistering sands, when Mr. Smith met me, a tall, spare figure, accentuated in its leanness by the bulky helmet of the tropics. I liked him instantly. He was a man of about fifty, strong, energetic and young for his age. There was a bit of a brogue in his speech —he was an Irishman —with a university training and cultured as such men usually are, but still with an Irishman's fondness for the world. Perhaps my liking was part of a mutual feeling for he immediately asked me to spend a few days with him at Top Hill. A cozy berth was found for the Yakaboo in a boatshed near by, built, for the sake of coolness, like the cotton ginnery of St. George's, with open sides.?

? On Carriacou looking north. ?

Carriacou might be called the Utopia of the Grenadines. It is here that the work of one man stands out and is not lost. Officially Whitfield Smith is known as the Commissioner,* in reality he is a potentate, while among his people he is known as "Papa."

* Whitfield Smith has been Commissioner at Grand Turk since 1915.

Paternal is the rule of this man, which, after all, is the way all governing should be done. And still with his paternal feeling and his kindness, there is no undermining familiarity. Justice, one feels, holds out her delicately balanced scales and there is no chance for her eye to pierce the blindfold. As in all the West Indies, there is very little crime, petty theft and small squabbles being the principal offenses. Swearing is a punishable offense and one hears but little profanity. The detection of crime is no disgrace and one does not lose caste upon being haled into court. Let the prisoner be convicted and imprisoned and he is forever disgraced.

The curse of the black man is laziness and the curse of the islands is the ease with which life may be sustained. To these may be added a warped idea regarding the tilling of the soil. There is deep rooted from the times of the old planters the West Indian notion that no gentleman dare use his hands in manual labor. The West Indian negro who has received a small smattering of an education spurns hard work and goes to the towns, where he can obtain a position as a clerk in a store. In this way the fields come to be neglected and labor is actually imported for the tilling of the soil. The black man wants to attain his estate by revolution —not physical but mental —while this can only come by a long process of evolution. In his period of transition he should be guided by the highest type of white man, broad minded ; virile, keen and human. Given authority to govern a small community, such as that of Carriacou, and the right man's influence for good among the people is infinite. The ease with which he can accomplish reforms is astonishing. For instance, on my first day at Carriacou I remarked to Smith that there seemed to be scarcely any mosquitoes, indeed, I had not seen any, a remarkable circumstance in view of the fact that the land immediately to the southeast of the town was low and swampy. "You will have a hard time finding any on the island now, although we have a few in the rainy season."

"Kerosene and mosquito bar?" I asked.

"No, million–fish. In Barbados," continued Smith, "it was noticed that on certain freshwater ponds there seemed to be no mosquitoes. Upon investigation it was found that these ponds were the habitat of the 'tap minnow' (Girardinus pocciloides) or 'million–fish,' as it is called, and that these small fellows ate the larvae of the mosquito as they rose to the surface of the water. The fish were introduced to other ponds, water tanks and rain barrels, with the result that there was a considerable reduction of the pest. I sent for some of the fish,* and put them on exhibition in a large glass jar in my office. Then I asked the people to bring in all the larvae they could find floating on the top of the water in rain barrels, tanks and so on. As soon as the larvae were put in the jar, the million–fish swam to the surface and gobbled them up. Then I told the people that if they put million–fish in all the places where mosquitoes breed, the eggs would be eaten up and there would be no more malaria, filaria, and so forth. It was the best kind of an object lesson. The fish were put in all the small ponds, tanks and barrels and they multiplied till there were enough to distribute all over the island."

* The males are an inch long, silver–grey in color and with a
 red spot on each side near the head. The females are
 about an inch and a quarter long but have no red spot.

ALONE IN THE CARIBBEAN

In a similarly easy manner he disposed of a troublesome labor problem. The British government allows six hundred pounds to be spent yearly for the maintenance and building of roads in Carriacou. The work is done by native women who receive nine pence a day or eighteen cents in our money. Smith found that there were more women dependent upon the road work for their livelihood than he could employ at one time and the solution was suggested by the so-called 'paternal system' used in St. Thomas. He secured a list of all the road workers on the island. Of this list he works forty each week, by rote, and in this way the government road money is fairly distributed. He is more like the owner of a large estate than an employee of the British government ruling a small island for a salary. I decided that there might be worse places to live in than Carriacou and that with a man like Smith on the island one's mind would not go altogether fallow. Perhaps my liking for the island was strengthened when I walked into a neat little store, not unlike the kind one finds in a new suburb of a progressive city. Here I could buy small cans of white lead and paint, commodities I could not find in St. George's, and I found sandpaper that had not lain in moldy disuse since the times of the pirates.

As the day cooled into evening, I walked out to the end of the jetty to contemplate the sunset and smoke a quiet pipe. To the west Mabouya, where I had camped the night before, hung a persistent little patch which resisted the efforts of the trade to wash it away towards the horizon of ragged clouds. To the north jagged Union rose, the highest of all the Grenadines, but here my peace came to an end.?

? There had been one house in which the owner had lived at the top of the hill. ?

"What is your reputation?" broke upon my ears. I faced about to find an officious native in a white linen suit, cane and Panama hat standing by me. While I was groping feverishly in my mind for a suitable reply, a native policeman stepped up and hustled off his compatriot before I should forever disgrace myself in this island of soft language. I was no longer in the mood for sunsets and I turned shorewards to find Smith preparing for the drive to his home at Top Hill. The twilight merged into the pale light of the new moon and as we slowly climbed the hills Smith talked about his island.

ALONE IN THE CARIBBEAN

"That is our botanical garden," he said, pointing out an acre or two of planted land that looked like a truck garden, "limes, water lemons, and a flower garden so that we can make up a bouquet when we have a wedding, you know."

On our way we met a Yellow Carib from Demerara. He was the second Carib that I had seen and joy came with the thought that in Saint Vincent I should find more of them, the last remnant of the Yellow Carib in the Lesser Antilles.

We had no sooner alighted in the courtyard at Top Hill than Smith bounded ahead of me and, standing on the top step of his verandah waited for me with outstretched hand, and said, "Welcome to Top Hill." There was a warmth about it that I shall never forget.

With us was MacQueen, an engineer, who might have been taken out of one of Kipling's Indian stories. The two were in a mood for stories that night, stories, for the most part, of the natives, showing their craze for the spectacular, their excitability, and the ease with which they can be fooled. "Did you ever," —there was a slight burr in the "ever," —"did you everr hear the one about New Year's Eve at Goyave, Mac?"

"Not in recent years," said Mac —and we have the story.

"Times had been prosperous and the priest was looking forward to a large contribution at the mass which was to see the Old Year out and the New Year in. He had arranged an impressive ceremony, not the least part of which was the shooting of fireworks on the precise stroke of twelve. Rockets were planted in the churchyard behind the gravestones, and a boy was stationed to touch off the fuses at the given time. The church was packed and in the dim candle light the priest struck awe into the souls of his congregation as he told them what a hell they were surely going to if they did not repent. He spoke with the fervor of a man working for that which was nearest his heart —money.

"The emotional natives became conscience–stricken as they thought, childlike, of their many misdeeds and there was the terror of hell in that blubbering crowd. But there was a chance —a very small one, in truth and the priest pointed to that heaven for which they could make a fresh start with the coming of the New Year. As he raised his hand aloft, the boy thought it was the signal for the fireworks. In the dramatic pause that followed the priest's warning, the awesome silence was intensified by the spasmodic sniveling of the people.

ALONE IN THE CARIBBEAN

"Suddenly there was a blinding flash, and a hissing rocket spurned its way heavenward. Another rocket, and then a bomb exploded. The boy was doing his part well. To the frightened congregation the end of the world must be at hand. With a roar of terror, they rushed from the church taking their pennies with them."

"O Lord," said Smith, the tears rolling down his cheeks, "the poor priest was out the price of the fireworks and lost his contribution."

"No doubt," said Mac, "he more than made up for it in confession fees for he knew that his people were uneasy of conscience."

"And talking about graveyards reminds me of a burial we once had during the rainy season," continued Smith. "A man had died of fever one hot afternoon and I decided to have him buried that night. He was laid out and I ordered a carpenter to make a box for him. By ten o'clock the box was ready and we started down the hill. There was no moon and the clouds shut out the starlight. It was black as pitch and before the days when we had a good road up from town. There were three of us carrying the corpse, myself, the doctor and my man, while the priest walked on ahead chanting the Resurrection. We had no sooner started than it began to rain. Not an ordinary rain or a shower, but the torrential downpour of the tropics. In a short time the roadway was a slippery downward surface over which we were fighting to keep the box with its contents from getting away from us. All this time that lazy beggar was walking ahead of us chanting in a loud voice for us to follow. The doctor, who was a crusty old Scotsman, slipped and fell, pulling the box down with him. Then, before we could take it up again, he gave it a push and it coasted down the hill, catching up the priest on its way. As the black–robed priest disappeared astride the coffin, the doctor yelled, 'Gae 'lang wid ye and yeer Resurrection.'

The next day was the fifth of the moon. In these latitudes where the moon seems to have a decided influence upon the weather, there is a strong tendency towards squalls on or about the fifth day of the new moon. Captain Woolworth, in his book "Nigh onto Sixty Years at Sea," mentions the fact that whenever he ran into trouble it was almost invariably on the fifth day of the new moon. Most of his voyages were made in the tropics. Smith called my attention to the weather on this day and I was careful to note every fifth day during the rest of my six months in the tropics. Almost without fail, from the third to the sixth day and generally on the fifth day of the first quarter there was trouble at sea. Conditions generally were unsettled. Heavy squalls would blow down like the beginnings of small hurricanes. Often I could count four or five squalls at one time whipping up as many spots on the sea to a fury of white caps and drift. There is something uncanny in the way in which the moon seems to affect the weather in these parts and I have often thought that the superstition of the negro is not to be wondered or sneered at.

The next day the weather was settled and continued so for the rest of that quarter.

While overhauling my outfit which I had dumped in a corner of Smith's office I again came upon my little mascot. I was untying a bag containing a few small bits of Carib pottery, which I had dug up near Sauteurs in Grenada, when a black fuzzy object jumped from the heap of duffle before me and scampered across the floor. "Hello! Who's your friend?" asked Smith.

"Oh, that's my mascot," I answered, as I dashed after her on all fours.

"Devil a fine mascot! Why don't you get a nice loving snake? Here! Take this!" said Smith, as he handed me a paper box cover. Having recaptured the tarantula I told the story of the luck she had brought me on my sail around Kick 'em Jinny. I was afraid that she might get into my blanket some time and bite me, so I took her life and carried her hairy carcass in a cotton–padded pasteboard box. I believe that after death her spirit hovered over the masts of the Yakaboo and that she bore me no ill will, for luck stayed with me for the rest of the cruise.

Having remained over the fifth day, I sailed for new islands and landed on picturesque Frigate, which lies off Union. Here I found an abundance of wood and was soon enjoying the crackle of a little blaze. It was good to be a Robinson Crusoe again, if only for a few hours. Before me on the beach lay the Yakaboo, her porpoise–like body suggesting more of the fish than the boat. Across a shallow bay, floored with white coral sand that gave it the appearance of a marble floored pool, Union rose a thousand feet.

I could make out the houses of a village, climbing above the shores of the bay, the most remarkable of its kind in the whole range of the Lesser Antilles, for I found that here one may see a thousand natives, living in small huts clustered close together, in exactly the way their ancestors lived two hundred years ago, when they were first brought over from Africa. One change only from the early days —that of clothing. The men wear trousers and shirts and the women wear skirts. Remove their civilized rags and you have them as they were in Africa. I have heard that in some of the smaller and even more out of the way cays of the Grenadines the natives live among themselves with no clothing but the breech cloth. May the eye of my camera see them thus in their natural state on some future cruise.

While I was cooking my chocolate, a little open boat had been sailing down the wind from the eastward. As she beached close to the Yakaboo, two black men jumped out of her while something in the stern unfolded its attenuated length and I recognized Walker, famous as the tallest man throughout these islands. I knew him before I saw him —that is all of him —for it takes two looks to get in his full height. My eye wandered up and down his length as one views a tall waterfall close by.

The British government had but lately taken over Union Island from private owners and it had been Walker's duty to survey and divide up the land so that it can be sold in small parcels to the natives. With the strength and perseverance of one charmed, Walker has carried his transit in the fierce noon heat and cut his lines through the brush. The soft tissue of his body has long since run off in perspiration so that there is little left for the sun to work upon. He goes about his work unmindful, wearing a flannel shirt with a double thickness over his spine and a large hat, which gives him the appearance of an animated umbrella. He has other dimensions besides height I found, one of them being breadth of heart.

No introduction was necessary for I had long since heard of the tall Walker, and he had expected my coming long before he made out the butterfly rig of the Yakaboo zigzag its way up to the beach on Frigate.

During our conversation I admitted some knowledge of drafting, upon which Walker said, "Come over to Union and help me finish a map of the island and then we can take off a few days for a little loaf." And so it came to pass that my little green tent remained in its bag in the forehold of the canoe and I became for a time an inhabitant of Union.

A span of not much more than three nautical miles separates the islands of Carriacou and Union and yet the natives of Union differ from those of her neighbor by nearly as many hundred years. Up to a short time before I landed on the island, Union had been owned by one man or one family from the time of its discovery. There had been one house in which the owner lived —on the top of a hill. It was now occupied by Rupert Otway, who represented the British government. Another house stood "down de bay," in which the overseer had lived while the rest of the population —slaves —had lived huddled together in the towns of Ashton and Clifton.

In 1838 the slaves were freed and from that time the prosperity of the island began to wane. But the blacks continued to live there, holding no property, a few of them working halfheartedly for the white man and the rest dragging out a mere existence from the fish of the sea. Now the government has bought the island and the ideal thing is being done —that is, the island is being divided into small plots, which are held out with every inducement for the native to buy. The cash price is cheap, from four to eight pounds per acre. There is also a system of payments arranged so that the most impoverished native can take up a small piece of land and from it work out the price to pay for it.?

? Cassava cake drying on a roof at Mayero. Ruins of the old estate house of the St. Hilaires in the background. ?

Not the least charm of these islands are the small private forts which one finds hidden in the bush which has overgrown the top of some hill of vantage, leaving scant evidence to the casual eye of some small pile of heavy masonry, the name and origin of which may have been long since forgotten. At the time of the Napoleonic Wars, when these islands were immensely rich in sugar, the estate owners were forced to defend themselves from the depredations of the privateers who infested these waters like the sharks that swim in them. For this purpose the old estate owners built private forts, one of which I found on Union, undisturbed in its state of dilapidation, four hundred feet above the sea, on the top of an isolated hill so overgrown with cactus that we had to cut our way to it.?

? Drying the cassava, Isle de Ronde. ?

Otway gave me a temporary Man Friday and after an hour's work with our cutlasses we had cleared away enough of the cactus so that we could walk about on the rampart. The top was five–sided, not an exact pentagon, about fifty feet in diameter. Here were four old cannon, lying as they had long ago sunk through their rotting carriages to rest, still pointing in the direction of their old enemies. One aimed at Mayero, two miles away, another covered the channel to the east, a third at one time dropped its death on Prune, while the fourth guarded the little bay where the ruins of the old storehouse or cabaret still stands. The romance of it all seemed intensified in the fierce noonday sun and it required little imagination to picture the days when fighting was an earnest sport. In the center stood the stepping for the flagstaff, the staff itself doubtless long since appropriated for the mast of some native sloop that may even now be resting deep down at the foot of Kick 'em Jinny. As the negro uses his horse till it drops, so he uses his sloop till at last a fierce squall gets him "all standing" and she sinks with her fear–paralyzed crew, leaving no sign, but a hatch or a broken bit of spar which drifts away towards the setting sun.*

Under the steps, which descend from the rampart, was the powder magazine, still intact, resembling an old–fashioned bake oven —and this reminded me that I was due at Government house for luncheon.

The next day as I tried to leave Union, faulty navigation on the part of the skipper caused the centerboard of the Yakaboo to run afoul of a reef. The Yakaboo got the worst of it and I had to put back for repairs. I was on my way to Mayero. Both Walker and Otway were glad to see me back in Union and no sooner had I landed than they ordered their man to carry the canoe up the hill to a shady place, where a native carpenter could relieve me of the work of repairing her. This done, Otway seemed to remember that he owed Mayero a visit in his official capacity, Walker decided to take a day off, and the three of us sailed across in the little government sloop.

* In nearly all cases of loss at sea in these waters, there remains
not the slightest trace of the missing boat or crew and the
relatives blubber for a day or two, murmur,
"It wuz de will ob de Lard" and the tale becomes history.

Our landing on Mayero was a strange performance. The beach was steep–to with a fathom of water less than a boat's length from dry sand. We threw out an anchor astern and then ran the sloop inshore till her bowsprit hung over the surf. Taking off our clothes, we tied them together with our belts and threw them high up on the beach. Three splashes followed and we crawled ashore and dressed. After a climb of about fifteen minutes we gained the top of the island, where "Miss Jane–Rose" rules her little domain.

Mayero is one of those romance islands where in its stagnation one can trace a past once beautiful, now pathetic. At the time of the unrest in France, a cadet branch of the Saint–Hilaire family came to this island, thrived, and finally died with the ebbing fortunes of sugar cane. The last descendant of this famous old family, one of which was a lady–in–waiting to the Empress Josephine at Malmaison, still governs the island under a sort of feudal system. Her name is Jane–Rose de Saint–Hilaire,* and she is a bright, keen woman of about fifty, who rules her subjects with a firm hand and who talks well. The two hundred inhabitants, more or less, representing eighty families, on the island, are, for the most part, descendants of the slaves of the old Saint–Hilaires, and one can still see in their faces the vanishing trace of the French aristocracy like a thin outcropping of gold in the baser rock.

*Miss Jane–Rose died in Feb. 1915.

Each family is allowed to erect a hut free of charge of any kind. This hut is roofed with Guinea grass straw and sided with wattles, cut on the island, and plastered with mud. Most of the huts are floored with American lumber. Each able–bodied inhabitant is allowed as many acres as he or she cares to cultivate, on the metayer or share system. By this arrangement of land tenure, at the time of harvest the produce of the land, cotton and cocoa, is divided equally between the proprietress and the tenants. The people used formerly to give their share of the cotton to Miss Jane–Rose to dispose of for them, but they now sell it direct to the British government at better prices. The fisherman reserve for the proprietress a portion of each day's catch.

The people are essentially French and no religion other than the Roman Catholic is tolerated. Miss Jane–Rose officiates as priestess and occasionally a priest from Carriacou comes to celebrate mass. She also acts the part of mediator or judge in many disputes where no grave issues are involved. The people, generally, are a law–abiding lot and in eight years only two cases of importance have come within the jurisdiction of Whitfield Smith at Carriacou.

ALONE IN THE CARIBBEAN

The little church, close to her house, was opened for our benefit, and it was with great pride that she exhibited the altar and the painted inscriptions on the walls. The building was nothing better than a wooden shed, an ant–eaten sanctuary into which small birds fly to nest through the holes in the roof. As we talked, a pathetic figure stole in to have a glimpse of "de mon in de boat," and to furtively touch his clothes to feel of what strange stuff they might be made. She was a little woman of sixty or more, not shrunken, for that would imply wrinkles, but lessened in size, as though she were slowly evaporating. Her face was still the face of youth, the sepia etching of a French beauty of the old days, the skin dark, somewhat transparent and of fine texture. It was a face beautiful and shapely in every line, the only negro feature that I could detect being the darkness of her skin. She seemed like some incautious mortal, under the spell of a Circe, with an appeal in her eyes to a deliverer who would never come.

With a parting gift of cassava cakes, taken from their drying place on the roof of one of the nearby huts, we scrambled down to the beach where we undressed and swam to the sloop, holding our clothes clear of the water. The wind had dropped with the setting of the sun, and we drifted back to Union in the moonlight before a soft, balmy air that carried no chill.

The next day I was more successful in leaving the island. Walker insisted upon accompanying me in his sloop to pilot me, as he said, through the intricate reefs. It afterwards turned out that he doubted the ability of the Yakaboo to make the passage to Bequia in safety. After three hours of cautious sailing, we ran ashore on Cannouan to cook our luncheon. Here it was that Walker taught me a new trick. The natives of the island had come down to have a close scrutiny of the strange man who was sailing about the islands in "de canoe," and I had come to the conclusion that their presence was far more picturesque than desirable. They handled everything, examined my dishes, and one of them even started to open my food bags. I swore at them, but they did not seem to understand. To my, "What the devil shall I do with these people?" "Oh, I'll fix 'em," said Walker, at which he swept one arm toward them and then pointing at me yelled :

"Get out! or 'de mon' will put a curse on you."

The words were magic. Profanity had made no impression, but the putting on of a curse by one who bordered on the supernatural —that was something different! With one bound they cleared the place of our nooning and with another they were in the brush where for the rest of our stay I could see the tops of their woolly heads and the gleam of white eyeballs, curiosity and fear holding them balanced, as it were, at the nearest point of safety. After that, whenever I was troubled by curious natives I repeated Walker's "magic formula," Get out! Or I'll put a curse on you.

Six o'clock found the canoe and the sloop three and one half miles from West Cape on Bequia with a strong lee tide, that is, off shore, and the wind dropping. The sloop, being heavier with her rock ballast and her crew of three, had outsailed the much lighter canoe in the choppy seas and was leading somewhat to windward. Just as the sun was setting, I saw a number of fins coming down towards the canoe. I now got the greatest fright of my whole cruise. All my past experience as to the cowardice of the shark vanished, leaving a void into which fear rushed as into a vacuum. My imaginative brain could only attach those fins to a school of huge sharks, some of them probably larger than the canoe I was sailing in.

Of what avail would my seven inches of freeboard be to one of those fellows should he choose to slide his ugly head over the gunwale? Of what avail my armament of two rifles, one revolver, and one axe? At a maximum I had a bullet each for nineteen sharks and perhaps my trusty axe would finish up one or two, but here was a horde descending upon me. I remembered how sharks were in the habit of jumping clear of the water and tearing out the blubber on a whale's back ; at any rate, I thought, I would finish one or two of them before they dragged my mangled form into the sea and so forth —oh, happy moment!

There was not the slightest use in altering my course to avoid them, so I held on and the next moment was in the midst of a school of snorting, playing porpoises. I could have jumped overboard and hugged them. I swore that the fun of graining them from the swaying footropes would never again be mine, nor would I even use their oil on my boots. To me the porpoise is henceforth a sacred animal. There were hundreds of them in the school and among them were blackfish of a considerable size. Playful and curious, they would make a dash with torpedo speed and then dive under the canoe or swerve around the ends, fascinating me with their wonderful grace and ease. One of them, making a slight miscalculation, bumped the centerboard and nearly upset the canoe. This made me think it safer to run off the wind and travel with them, presenting the edge of the board rather than the side. And so I kept them company till they had had their fun and resumed their travels.?

ALONE IN THE CARIBBEAN

? Preparing to leave Union. Walker sitting on the rail of his sloop and regarding Yakaboo doubtfully. ?

?

? Coming back for repairs. Six men doing the work of two. ?

Some of them would jump clear of the water and with a half turn in the air would land on their backs with a resounding splash. It was their way of scratching their backs and I could almost see a grin of delight on their mouths. As they left me, twilight gave way, and I was alone in the starry night. Walker in the sloop was somewhere to windward —out of sight. I had taken in sail and was now rowing, using for a guide Orion's Belt, suspended above the swaying top of the stubby little mizzen mast. As the moon rose, I could read the compass.

After an hour or so I must have fallen asleep, still rowing, for I awoke at nine o'clock, the oars still in my hands, to find that I was off my course and about a mile from West Cape, which now loomed up black in the distance. The current had swung the canoe around little by little as I had ceased to take notice of the compass till I was rowing northward instead of nearly due east. In another hour I was headed into Admiralty Bay in the lee of Bequia.

By that same law of compensation which I have already mentioned, I was now rewarded for a hard day of travel at sea. I shall never forget the beauty of that night as I slipped into the easier waters under the long arm of West Cape, which reaches from Bequia three miles out to sea. The moon was high in a brilliant sky across which the trade clouds rolled like a curtain, on their never-ending march to the Spanish Main. The Cape stood lofty and dark and bold and I could see the surf rise from the rocks, high into the air, white and forbidding like a living thing.

As the moon swung over its zenith, I could make out the little huts and trees on the island as in daytime and finally I saw a small fire on the beach, near where I judged the village to be. It was half-past eleven when I rowed up to the jetty, which stood out into the water like an immense centipede. The squeak of my rowlocks betrayed my presence and the natives, who were lying on the beach by the fire, rushed out onto the jetty. They had been waiting for me. Then came the usual babble of voices and torrent of questions.

ALONE IN THE CARIBBEAN

Their curiosity was unappeased for I tied my painter to a sloop at anchor near the jetty and even as I was preparing to turn in, a native policeman drove the crowd inshore.

The Yakaboo was indeed a real "live–aboard–ship" and had my stove been in commission I could have cooked my supper in the cockpit. In fact, I could have lived aboard indefinitely as long as food and water held out, for I could rig up my tent over the cockpit in the event of rain. Cold meat, crackers, and cool fresh water made an excellent repast for a starved and healthy stomach.

One who has never done this sort of thing can scarcely appreciate my sense of complete luxury as I lay in my blankets in the snug cockpit of the Yakaboo. And always at the mention of the Yakaboo I think of her as a thing of life. There was scarcely any motion in the quiet waters of the bay, yet I could feel her buoying me up, as though I were resting on a small cloud suspended in midair, a Mahomet's coffin. Then as I rolled over to lie on my side she would give gracefully–she was always there under me, holding me up out of the sea–my water cradle. A great contentment came over me as I lay contemplating the magical harbor into which I had found my way like a tired gull.

I had hardly fallen asleep when Walker sailed alongside and awoke me. He had lost track of me in the darkness and had been looking for me till the moonlight had shown the Yakaboo crawling into Admiralty harbor. He sent his two men ashore and I passed him some food and one of my blankets. He left again at five in the morning with some food which I insisted upon his taking and a better opinion of the ability of the Yakaboo. There are few men I should care to have with me in the open. Walker is one of them.

With the sun came the incessant babble of an increasing crowd on shore. Sleep was impossible and I landed at nine o'clock. Before I had turned in the night before, I asked the crowd whether "Old Bill" Wallace, the Nestor of whalemen in the Grenadines, was still alive. Yes, they told me, he lived in the hills beyond "Tony Gibbon's."

"Old Bill" came down as I was cooking breakfast over a coalpot in the parsonage. (When I end this life I shall go with an infinite debt to lighthouse keepers, Scotsmen and English parsons.) I gave him a letter I had carried from Boston in my portfolio. It was from a shipmate of his son, who had been lost at sea. In it were two photographs of young Wallace on the next but last of his voyages, showing his active young figure at the "mincing" board and in the cross trees. As the old man opened the letter a look of surprise came over him and he held the photographs in trembling hands. It was like a message from the dead, almost, to see his son at work on the whaler, and a far–off look came into his eyes as he stood there, brought back so suddenly to the vague tragedy that had been the hardest burden of a hard life.?

? "Old Bill" and the skipper of the Yakaboo. ?

"I am old and broken down now, and not much use," he said, "but as long as these old hands can work I'll keep on going till I slip my moorings and get off on my last cruise." Hard work and a rough life had been the lot of this relic of a fast vanishing type of deepwater sailor. In that romance age of fifteen he had spewed the silver spoon from his mouth and left it on the hearth of his Scotland home to taste his first sting of bitterness under the care of a Yankee skipper.

He finally drifted to Bequia with his earnings and bought a large sugar plantation. But the seafaring man rarely prospers on land. The failure of sugar cane in the islands, followed by a disastrous hurricane, brought an end to his few years of ease, and he had to turn to the humpbacking that he had taught the natives, "jumbie crabs," he called them. Now, too old to go whaling, he is rusting away like the ships he used to sail, waiting to "slip his moorings."

In the afternoon, I climbed the hill to his house, rebuilt in a corner of the ruins of his former home, as if backed off in a corner by fate. There I met his blue–eyed little wife and drank with them the bitter tea that had simmered on the coals since morning. It was many years since he had talked to one from the States and as the afternoon grew old his enthusiasm over the adventures of his life rose to the fitting climax of a hurricane off Delos in Africa.

The rickety chair would no longer hold him and he stood in the doorway, dark against the levelled rays of the setting sun, a fiery, Quixotic figure, brandishing his cutlass to illustrate how, as a mate on the almost doomed ship, he had stood years ago in that tense moment with uplifted axe ready to cut the weather shrouds. She was "six points higher than Jordan," he had thought, as she lay with her lee rail under water, not a rag up, held by the force of the wind against her spars. Then —"be th' powers o' Malkenny's cat," she had righted herself and the ship was saved without losing a stick. I can feel his enthusiasm now and I wonder if, in the eternal fitness of things, the good saint will promote him to captaincy on the ghost of that ship on the seas of the world to come.

There was a pathetic touch in his farewell to me, for I had brought back to him the sweet memories of a gallant son. I left him still standing in the doorway, the cutlass hanging forgotten from one arm, the other around the shoulder of his mild little wife.

One hears a great deal of the tropical sunset, but to me there is nothing to compare with the moonlight of these islands, and it was a continual source of pleasure to wander about in the hills in the light of the full moon. There is a color effect that I have found in no other place. The blue sky as in daytime, but softened, with the motion of the large, white, fleecy clouds in contrast. The sea a darker blue with the pattern of the coral reefs showing up yellow and brown. The island itself a subdued blue framed in the thin line of white foam on the rocks. Distance was here and as I stood high above the bay I could see the islands I had left, Cannouan, Mayero, Union, high and dark, and even Carriacou, thirty miles away.

On my way down to the bay, I passed a group of little native huts, where a more or less heated discussion was in progress. "He no sail in de da' —he floy in de noight! You tink dat li'le boat go in de water? Oh, my!" and I realized that I was the topic of conversation. As I neared them, one said, "O Lard, HE come now."

I now understood why I had been so quickly discovered when I rowed into the harbor the night before. One of the natives, with a powerful ship's telescope "obtained" from some Yankee whaler, had picked up my queer rig, late in the afternoon, as I was approaching Bequia and had seen my sails go down shortly after sunset. They knew that the wind was dropping and they believed that I had spread out my sails parallel to the water and flown. In fact, the common belief in Bequia was that the sailing was only a bluff and that I really covered my distances by flying at night.

So they had built a bonfire and were waiting for me on the beach, where they knew I would land. Sure enough, I did land there, but before they had had a chance to see me fly, I had folded the wings of the Yakaboo and was rowing. They could not understand how such a small boat could live in their seas. The cut of the sails suggested wings and the natural deduction was, "He no sail, he floy."?

? The effect of the trade wind on the vegetation, Bequia. ?

I was a man apart and I found out later that the natives regarded me with a great deal of awe and thought that I carried some sort of imp or fetish with me in the canoe. Perhaps I did. Was there not a gru-gru nut the postmaster at Goyave had given me, and how about my little dead mascot? Except for the more intelligent men, they were afraid of me, but curiosity would get the better of their fear and as I talked to them I would now and then feel the furtive fingers of some of the bolder ones touching my clothes as one would a priest's robe.

It was one afternoon, while I was visiting a "tryworks" on the south shore, where they were boiling oil from my friend the porpoise, that I espied a little boat with a peculiar rig coming down from the East. The natives confirmed my guess, it was a Carib canoe. By a lucky chance the canoe beached almost at my feet. There were four Indians in her and I immediately questioned them as to the settlement at Sandy Point, on the north end of Saint Vincent. Yes, they were from the Carib Country and would be glad to have me come up and live with them as long as I wished. What a joy it was to see the lighter color of their skins, their straight black hair, and thin lips. They reminded me of the Japanese and my eye did not miss the ease with which they carried themselves and handled their canoe.

The next morning I said, "Yakaboo," to the Grenadines and laid my course for Saint Vincent and the Carib Country.

CHAPTER V. CLIMBING THE SOUFFRIÈRE OF SAINT VINCENT

MY ENTRY into the port of Kingstown was spectacular, but hardly to my liking. The mail sloop from Bequia had spread the news of my coming and as I neared the shore, I saw that the jetty and the beach were black with black people. A rain squall came down from the hills, but it did not seem to dampen the interest of the people nor dim the eye of my camera. I had scarcely stepped out of the canoe when the crowd rushed into the water, lifted her on their shoulders and she continued on her way through a sea of bobbing heads. Direct was her course for the gate of the building which contains the government offices and she at last came to rest in a shaded corner of the patio, where the police are drilled. As I followed in her wake, I said to myself, "She may be without rudder and without skipper and still find her way to a quiet berth." We were in a land—locked harbor, the crowd as a sea outside, beating against the walls.

My own procedure was as strange a performance as that of the Yakaboo. Among the officials in the patio was one who pushed himself forward and gave me a package of mail. He was His Majesty's Postmaster, Mr. Monplaisir. "Is there anything I can do for you?" asked H.M.P.M., addressing me by my first name.

"Yes, Monty," —he was pleased at this —"you can lead me to a fresh—water shower."

"Come along, then," and the sergeant opened the gate for us. As we walked through the streets, the crowd streaked out behind us like the tail of a comet. We soon gained the house of one Mr. Crichton, where a number of government clerks lived as in a boarding house and where a transient guest might also find lodging. There happened that time to be such a guest, by name, Dr. Theodorini —optometrist. His mission in life, it seemed, was to relieve the eye strain of suffering natives throughout the West Indies. His most popular prescriptions called for gold—rimmed glasses —not always a necessity, but undeniably a distinct social asset. We became good friends.

My comet's tail, like any well behaved appendage, tried to follow me into Mr. Crichton's house but the landlord was too quick for it and, as I stepped over the threshold, he bounded against the flimsy door, thus performing a very adroit piece of astronomic surgery. Divested of my tail, I was led to the bath, which proved to be a small separate building erected over a spacious tank with sides waist high. Over the center of the tank drooped a nozzle with a cord hanging down beside it. What an excellent chance to wash the sea water out of my clothes! I pulled the cord and stood under the shower. Monty handed me a cigarette which I puffed under my hat brim.

In the meantime, Dr. Theodorini, whom I had not yet met, began throwing pennies to the baffled crowd from the second story window. It must have been a queer sight could one have viewed it in section. The swearing of the landlord, accompanied by the orchestration of the voices outside and the staccato "Hurrah's" of Theodorini reminded me in a silly way of Tschaikowsky's 1812 overture.

ALONE IN THE CARIBBEAN

Having washed my clothes, I bathed au naturel and then found to my chagrin that I had brought nothing with me from the canoe. Through the partly opened door I ordered one of the servants to go to my canoe and bring the little yellow bag which contained my spare wardrobe. Dried and unsalted, I emerged from the bath to sit down to a West Indian breakfast at the table of mine host.

My days in Kingstown were mainly occupied in developing the more recent exposures I had made in the Grenadines and in rewashing the films I had developed en route. In the tropics I found that as soon as I had opened a tin of films, it was imperative to expose and develop them as quickly as possible in order to avoid fogging in the excessive heat. Whenever I came to a place like Kingstown where ice was obtainable this was a simple matter, for by the use of the film tank and the changing bag I was independent of a dark room.

On the beaches, however, my chief difficulty was in lowering the temperature of the water, which usually stood at 80° F. —the "frilling" point for films. Having mixed the developing solution in the tank, I would close it and wrap it carefully in a wet flannel shirt. Then with a line tied to it —my mizzen halyard served admirably with its three–inch mast ring to hold in my hand —I would step clear of my tent and whirl the tank around my head at the end of the line. In this way I could bring down the temperature of the liquid to about 75û —a safe temperature for developing. Often I did not have enough fresh water for washing the developed films and would have to use sea water —which meant a thorough rewashing such as at Kingstown. Even under these adverse conditions my failures were only ten per cent of the total.

Ice, in these parts, is used mainly in the making of swizzles, as the West Indian cocktails are called, and when, as at Crichton's, I would send for enough ice to chill gallons of swizzles and withdraw silently to my room after dinner, another topic would be added in the speculation which summed me up as "queer chap that."

On the 22nd of March, I sailed out of the roadstead of Kingstown before a stiff breeze which the trade sent around the southern hills like a helping hand. It was only natural that the wind should become contrary off Old Woman Point where it hauled around to the North. Then it changed its mind, crawled up and down the mast a couple of times, and died out in a hot gasp.

ALONE IN THE CARIBBEAN

The shift from sails to oars in the Yakaboo was quickly made. With a tug and a turn the mizzen was hauled taut and made fast. I worked my lines on "Butler" cleats, a combination of hook and jam cleat that was quick and effective.

A semicircular motion of the hand cleared the line, the same motion reversed made the line fast again. My mizzen boom amidships, I then let go the main halyard and the sail dropped into its lazy jacks like a loose–jointed fan. With three turns of the halyard the furled sail was secured and by making the line fast to its cleat on the port coaming the sail was kept to one side, clear of the cockpit. The lazy jacks held the sail up so that the oar could pass under it without interference. By letting go the mizzen halyard, it likewise fell into its lazy jacks. To furl the mizzen, I pulled taut on a downhaul, the standing parts of which passed around each side of the sail and over the gaff. Thus the gaff was drawn down close to the boom, the line snugly holding the intermediate sail and battens.

These five operations were done in the time it takes a man to remove a case from his pocket and light a cigarette. Then I loosed the light seven–foot oars tied in the cockpit with their blades under the forward decking. With a shove my blanket bag was in the forward end of the cockpit, where it served as my seat when rowing. The rowlock chocks with their sockets and rowlocks were quickly secured in their places on deck, by means of winged nuts that screwed into flush sockets. By the time the man with the cigarette has taken three puffs the Yakaboo is off at a three and a half knot gait.?

? "As I neared the shore I saw that the jetty was black with black people." ?

?

? The usual appearance of the jetty, boat unloading for the market. ?

So far, I had done but little rowing in smooth waters and the sense of stealing quietly along the lee coast to enjoy its intimacy was a new pleasure. All these islands, especially the lower ones, have more or less the same formation —Grenada, Saint Vincent, Saint Lucia, and Dominica. This formation consists of a backbone which rises to a height of from two to three thousand feet and is the main axis of the island with spurs which run down to the Atlantic and the Caribbean, east and west, like the veins of a leaf. The coast is a fascinating succession of points, bays, cliffs, and coves. One may range along shore and find a spot to suit any whim one's fancy may dictate.

ALONE IN THE CARIBBEAN

I chanced to look around —to locate my position on the chart —when I found that I was rowing into a fleet of canoes calmly resting on the heave of the sea like a flock of ducks. They were apparently waiting for me. There was not the usual babble of the native and if I had not turned just then another stroke or two would have shot the Yakaboo into their friendly ambuscade. The canoes were filled with "Black Caribs" —hence the absence of the babble —that sub–race which sprang from Bequia nearly two and a half centuries ago.

In 1675, a slave ship from the West Coast of Africa foundered in a gale on the shores of Bequia which at that time was a Carib stronghold. The negroes were good water people and as the ship went down they swam ashore, men, women, and children, where they were well received by the Caribs. What became of the white skipper and his crew one does not hear —they were presumably murdered.

The Caribs were quick to realize that fortune had sent them a new ally in these negroes whose love for the white man was at a low ebb. The blacks were adopted by the Caribs and a new sub–race was formed. The result was a tribe in which the fighting qualities of both races were distilled to a double strength (an expression which comes naturally enough when one is writing in a rum country). These Black Caribs successfully held the English at bay for a number of years. Nearly a quarter of a century before, the Caribs in Grenada had been completely exterminated by the French and they were now being rapidly driven out of Saint Vincent by the English.

The negro blood very quickly gained ascendancy, as it invariably does, and as far as I could ascertain the traces of the Carib were almost completely obliterated among the Black Caribs whom I saw. The hair is one of the most obvious indices of admixture, varying from the close curly wool of the pure African through diverse shades of dark tow to the straight black of the Indian. Where racial color is well mixed, the hair is often like the frayed end of a hemp rope.

I stopped to talk with them and they begged me to come ashore to see their village of which they were evidently proud. It is called Layou and lies in the bight of a bay by the same name. We landed on a beach furnace of hot black sand. The sand reminded me of iron, and iron reminded me of tetanus. This reminded me that the lockjaw germ is not a rare animal on these inhabited beaches so I put on my moccasins.

ALONE IN THE CARIBBEAN

As I have implied there was heat. Not alone the stifling heat of a beach where the still air, like a spongy mass, seems to accumulate caloric units but also the heat of a vertical tropic sun, pouring down like rain. My felt hat, stuffed with a red handkerchief, made a small circle of shade which protected my neck when I held my head up but left the tips of my shoulders scorching. My forearms hung gorilla–like from my rolled up sleeves, not bare but covered by a deep tan from which sprang a forest of bleached hairs —the result of weather. Heaven preserve me from a nooning on a beach like that!

The village consisted of a single row of one–room huts, thatch–roofed and wattle–sided, each standing on four posts as if to hold its body off the blistering sands. The people conducted me along this row of huts on stilts in exactly the way a provincial will take you for a walk down the main street of his town. Instead of turning into the drug store, we fetched up by a large dugout where a quantity of water–nuts (jelly coconuts) were opened. It was the nectar of the Gods.

I felt like an explorer on the coast of Africa being entertained by the people of a friendly tribe. I was touched by their kindly hospitality and shall tell you later of other friendly acts by these coast natives. I do not believe it was curiosity alone that tempted them to beg me to visit their village. True, they crowded around the Yakaboo, but they had the delicacy not to touch it, a trait which usually obtains among rural or coastal natives whether in these islands or civilization. They seemed deeply interested in me and I felt that they were constantly devouring me with their eyes. When I left them, they filled the cockpit of the Yakaboo with bananas and water–nuts trimmed ready to open at a slice from my knife.

As I rowed out into the bay, I nearly ran down a diminutive craft sailing across my bows. There was something about that double rig —the Yakaboo turned around to look at it as we slid by —and sure enough it was Yakaboo's miniature! Not far off a small grinning boy sat on a small bobbing catamaran. He had seen the Yakaboo in Kingstown and had made a small model of her —and so she was known to a place before she herself got there. I left a shilling on the deck of the Little Yakaboo, but she was not long burdened with her precious cargo.

I was again dreaming along shore. Instead of facing the north, as I had while sailing, and looking at new country, I was now looking toward the south and could still see the outlines of the Grenadines and even distant Grenada, a haunting tongue of misty blue that

66

faded into the uncertain southern horizon. The idea seemed to possess me that I should never get out of sight of that outline. Now I saw it with my own eyes, eaten up by the last point astern that had devoured the Grenadines one by one. I looked around me and could see only shores that were new to me within the hour. There was a strange joy in it. I had made a tangible step northward.

The sun was getting low, and as the reflection came from the broken water, miles to leeward, I felt that I was traveling along the edge of the world. No horizon line to denote finality, the sense was of infinity and I fancied the trade wind, which blew high overhead and met the sea offshore, a siren trying to draw me away from land to the unknown of ragged clouds. It was the effect upon my mind of the ceaseless trade and the westerly current.?

? Along the lee coast of St. Vincent near Layou. ?

With the setting of the sun my row came to an end. I was in the little bay of Château Belaire, at the foot of the Souffrière volcano.

There was a fierce joy of deception in my heart as I sneaked up to the jetty in the dusk and quietly tied my painter to the landing stage. For once I had cheated the native of the small spectacular scene of which he is so fond. As I stepped ashore, dusk gave way to a darkness relieved only by the glow of coalpots through open doors and the smell of frying fish. The stars were not yet in their full glow. I could move about in the murk observing but not observed. I could walk among the fishermen and their garboarded dugouts without the ever–recurrent "Look! de mon!" But I did not walk about for long and for two very good reasons. A lynx–eyed policeman who had discovered the Yakaboo was one, a foot full of sea eggs was the other.

One morning in Kingstown, I went for a sea bath with Monty. It was then I learned that sharks are not the greatest pest of the sea for while incautiously poking among the rocks I managed to fill my foot full of the sharp spines of a sea egg, spines as brittle as glass that break off in the flesh. I had tried to cut them out with my scalpel, but that only tended to increase the damage. Monty had told me the only thing for me to do was to wait till the points worked out of their own accord.

ALONE IN THE CARIBBEAN

So I hobbled back to the jetty to take possession of my canoe. My plan was to leave the Yakaboo at Château Belaire while I made the ascent of the Souffrière and while I visited the Caribs on the windward side where the surf was high and the rocky beaches more friendly to the thick bottom of a log dugout than a quarter inch skin. So the Yakaboo —she was becoming an habitué of the police courts —was unloaded and carried to the station. While I was in the Carib country, the local court was in session and she served as a bench for the witnesses. I hope that her honest spirit permeated upwards through those witnesses so that in the day of judgment they may say, "Once, O Peter, did I speak the truth."

Information regarding the approach and the ascent of the Souffrière was untrustworthy and difficult to obtain. Any number of the natives seemed to have climbed the volcano, but none of them could tell me how to do it —a little subtlety on their part to force me to hire guides. I engaged my men, brewed a cup of tea, chatted with the police sergeant, and turned in, on the stiff canvas cot in the rest–room, with a sheet over me. I now know how a corpse feels when it is laid out.

My guides awoke me at five in the morning, I cooked a hasty breakfast and was with them in their boat half an hour later. There were two of them and as surly as any raw Swede deck hands I have ever had to do with. For an hour we rowed in silence and then we landed at the mouth of the Wallibu Dry River. With some of these natives, although you may have hired them at their own price to serve you, the feeling seems to be not to serve you and do what you wish them to do but to grudge their effort on your behalf and to make you do what they want you to do. It requires continual insistence on the part of the white man to have, at times, the simplest services performed —an insistence that makes one nerve–weary and irritable.?

? My surly guides. ?

As soon as we stepped ashore, I sat down on a convenient rock to grease and bandage my sore foot They seemed to have forgotten my presence entirely and started up the bed of the river without even looking around to see whether I was coming or not. I let them walk till they were almost out of hearing and then I called them back. When they came to me, not without some little show of temper, I told them in unmistakable words of one syllable and most of them connected by hyphens —that we had as yet not started to climb the mountain and that at the end of the day's work I should pay them for being guides and not retrievers to nose out the bush ahead of me.

We proceeded up the bed of the Wallibu River which had been made dry in the last eruption (1902) by a deep deposit of volcanic rocks and dust which had forced the water to seek another channel. As we walked between the cañon–like sides, I was reminded of our own Bad Lands and for the first time I felt a bit homesick. These islands have very little in common with our northern country ; even the nature of the people is different. It seemed queer to me to be walking in this miniature cañon with a couple of West Indian natives instead of riding a patient pony and exchanging a monosyllable or two with a Westerner. I longed for the sight of a few bleached cattle bones and perhaps a gopher hole or a friendly rattlesnake.?

? The Wallibu Dry River where we began the ascent. The Soufrière in the distance, it cone hidden in the mist. ?

A small spur broke the perpendicular face of the northern wall and here we climbed to the upper surface. We were now in bush, most of which was a sort of cane grass, over our heads in height, through which we followed a narrow trail. This upper surface on which we now traveled was in reality the lowest slope of the volcano, a gentle incline where the catenary curve from the crater melts into the horizontal line of the earth's surface. Soon I could see over the top of the grass and found that we were following the ridge of a spur which radiated in a southwesterly direction from the volcano. The ridge itself was not one continuous curve upward but festooned along a series of small peaks between which we dropped down into the bush from time to time. The vegetation between these peaks consisted of the same heavy cane grass we had passed through on the lower slope.

To offset the lack of wind in these valley–like depressions the grass again rose above our heads, keeping the trail well shaded. Thank fortune, the dreaded fer–de–lance does not exist on this island. At about 1,500 feet the vegetation ceased altogether except for a few stray clumps of grass and the greenish fungus that gave the ground a moldy, coppery appearance. There was no sign of the flow of lava on this side of the volcano, merely the rocks and dust which had been thrown up in immense quantities. As we neared the top the wind blew strongly and was cold with the mist torn from the bellies of low–hanging trade clouds. I was fortunate in choosing a day when the crater was at times entirely free of clouds, for only once during the next ten days did I see the top again uncovered, and then for only a few minutes.

ALONE IN THE CARIBBEAN

Contrary to my wishes, my sullen guides had again taken the bit in their teeth and they started the ascent at a brisk pace which killed them before we were half way up the mountain. My sore foot demanded a steady ground eating pace with no rests. Up till this time they had walked a considerable space ahead of me, this lead gradually decreasing as they tired. I could lose no time and dared not rest, and since I could now find my way perfectly well alone, I went on ahead of them. As I neared the top, the force of the wind became more and more violent till I found it impossible to stand up and I finished the last hundred yards on my hands and knees.?

? The rim of the crater. ?

The sight that greeted my eyes as I peered over the rim of the crater literally took my breath away —that is, what breath the wind had not shoved down to my stomach, for it was blowing a hurricane. I could not at once quite grasp the immensity of the crater —for its proportions are so perfect that I would not have believed the distance across to the opposite rim to be more than a few hundred yards, —it is nearly a mile. A thousand feet below me —held in the bowl of the crater —was a lake almost half a mile in diameter. During the last splutters of the eruption of 1902 the ejecta had fallen back and this together with the subsiding of the inner slopes of the crater had effectually sealed up the chimney of the volcano.?

? "A thousand feet below, held in the bowl of the crater, is a lake nearly a half a mile in diameter". ?

The enormous precipitation which is nearly always going on, due to the striking of the clouds against the crater, has collected in the bottom to form this lake. I hardly knew my old friend the trade wind. He rushed up the windward side of the mountain, boarded the crater, and pounced upon the lake like a demon, spreading squalls in all directions. The surface of the water looked like the blushing surface of a yellow molten metal. Then up the leeward side and over the rim where I hung, he came with the scream of a thousand furies. It was as though the spirits of the unfuneraled dead had come back to haunt the place, day and night. As I pulled the slide out of my camera, to make an exposure, the wind bent it nearly to the breaking point. My hat had long since been a tight roll in my pocket and I lay, head on, my toes dug into the slimy surface of the slope, with my face buried in the hood of my camera and the empty case streaming out behind me.

ALONE IN THE CARIBBEAN

I spent an hour in scrambling along the rim and then returned to the guides who were resting some distance below. It was still early for I had reached the rim at 8 :30 after a climb of an hour and thirty–two minutes. My barometer registered a height of three thousand and twenty feet and while the climb had been an easy one, the time was not bad for a foot full of sea eggs.

Higher mountains to the north cut off all possibility of seeing Saint Lucia or Martinique, but as I looked to the south, Grenada showed herself and the Grenadines stretched out like stepping stones. Below lay all the vast area that had been laid waste by the eruption. In place of the forests, now buried deep in the volcanic dust and scoria, was a green blanket of grass, bush and small trees that would belie an eruption that had obliterated every sign of green nine years ago. Scrutiny with the field glasses, however, showed innumerable cañons cut through laminae of volcanic deposit with thin layers of soil between. I could almost throw a stone, I thought, into the little village of Château Belaire four miles away, that by some miracle had escaped destruction by a few hundred yards. But my eyes always came to rest on the Caribbean. The rays of the sun, reflected back from myriad waves, too distant to be seen, gave the sea the appearance of a vast sheet of molten metal with here and there a blush where some trade cloud trailed its shadow. The clouds dissolved away into the horizon, sustaining the feeling that there was nothing beyond but infinity.

The sea eggs were now giving sharp notice of their presence and I decided to rush the descent. I had exchanged but few words with my guides. If there had been discontent during the ascent, there was more cause for it now. The customary grog had not been forthcoming, for I never carry spirits on an expedition like this. In case of accident or exposure there are better things that give no after effects of let down. My guides followed me in my downward rush with hardly breath enough for the proper amount of cursing which the occasion demanded. If they said anything about "de dyam Yonkee" I heard it not, for the trade wind would have carried it high over my head. The enjoyment of the chase kept my mind off the pain in my foot. I reached the boat in forty minutes.

When we arrived at Château Belaire I found the Government doctor on his round of the Leeward coast. What a blessed relief it would be to have him inject Some cocaine into my foot and then cut out the miserable sea egg points. But he was as effective as a Christian Scientist —I should have to wait till I reached Saint Lucia where there was an excellent hospital in Castries and then have the points removed.

ALONE IN THE CARIBBEAN

Batiste promised better. He was a Yellow Carib whom I had found in Kingstown and whom I had engaged to take me into the Carib country the next day. One of the first books I read on the West Indies was by Frederic Ober and what better boatman could I have than the son of his old Batiste with whom he spent months on the slopes of the volcano camping and hunting the Souffrière bird. "W'en we reach up Carib countrie you see de sea egg come out."

That night I was far away from the Caribbean and I dreamed it was Saturday morning in the city. Outside I could hear the familiar sound of the steps being scrubbed with rotten stone. I could feel the glare of the morning sun that had just risen over the roofs of the houses and was shining on the asphalted street —"avenue" it was called. Then came the toot–toot of the toy–balloon man, a persistent sound —too persistent —and I finally awoke with the sun in my eyes and the noise of Batiste's conch in my ears. With a feeling that my youth was forever a thing of the past and that I had assumed some overwhelming burden, I bounded off the high cot and landed on the sea egg foot. There had been no sea eggs and no overwhelming burden in my young life on that city street. For the sake of company I yelled to Batiste to come and have some tea with me.

At last we were off, I comfortably seated in the after end of the canoe with my family of yellow bags around and under me ; Batiste behind me, steering while we were rowed by two Caribs with Christian names. The canoe was as all canoes of the Lesser Antilles —in reality a rowboat. The hull proper is a dugout made of the log of the gommier tree. To this has been added a sheer streak to give the craft more freeboard. In adding the sheer streak a wedge is put into the after end so that above water the boat has the appearance of having a dory stern. Oars have long since taken the place of the primitive paddle and because the boat is deep and narrow, having no real bilge at all, she is ballasted with stones. They are ticklish craft, slow–moving and not particularly seaworthy.

We were passing the point between Richmond River and the Wallibu Dry River where I had begun the ascent of the mountain the day before when Batiste said, "You see w'ere de railin' is?" He pointed to a broad tongue of land about two or three acres in extent which for some reason was fenced in. "De boat walk dere before de eriipshun."

Not far from this place we came upon a curious phenomenon which Batiste called "de spinning tide." In the clay–colored water, that surrounded it, was a circular area of blue, sharply defined, about thirty feet in diameter, set in rotary motion by the coastwise

72

current. The coolness of the water suggested the outflow of some submarine spring, probably from under the bed of the Dry River.

One hears but little of the eruption of the Souffrière of Saint Vincent. It was only because there was no large town near the crater of the Souffrière that only sixteen hundred were killed —a mere handful compared with the twenty–five thousand in the French island. It seems that all these islands, along the arc from Grenada to Saba, lie along a seam where the earth's outer crust is thin. Had the Souffrière of Saint Lucia (which lies between Saint Vincent and Martinique) not been in a semi–active state there would in all probability have been a triple eruption. I found that Pelée and the Souffrière of Saint Vincent have a habit of celebrating together at intervals of approximately ninety years : 1902, 1812, 1718, and there is some mention of disturbances in 1625.

Our chief interest in the eruption of the Souffrière of Saint Vincent is on account of its effect upon the Yellow Carib. This island was the last stronghold of the Caribs in the West Indies and when they were finally subdued and almost exterminated the majority of the few remaining ones were transported by the English to the island of Ruatan near Honduras. The rest were eventually pardoned by the Government and were allowed to settle in various places in the island.

There was for a time a considerable admixture of negro blood, but little by little this was eliminated as the Caribs (Yellow) drew closer and closer together among themselves and began to settle on the windward side of the island at Sandy Bay. Here the Government gave them a considerable grant of land which became known as the "Carib Country." The spread of the Black Carib seems to have stopped shortly after their first union at Bequia. But the Black Carib, more or less a race apart, was more agriculturally inclined than the Yellow Carib, yet possessed the Indian's fondness for the sea.

We find then, before the eruption of 1902, the Yellow Carib to the northeast of the volcano, living more or less in his former state on the windward side of the island ; the Black Carib to the southwest, along the leeward coast, while the negro was more or less evenly distributed throughout the rest of the island. The eruption of the Souffrière differed from that of Pelée in that the volcano of Saint Vincent laid waste a considerable area to windward, devastating most of the Carib Country and killing a goodly number of the Indians. This seems always to have been their favorite spot for as early as 1720 Churchill mentions the fact, and says, "The other side (windward) is peopled by two or

three thousand Indians who trade with those about ,' the river Oronoque, on the continent.
. . .

Immediately after the eruption, the Government gave the Yellow Caribs land among the Black Caribs along the leeward coast and even went so far as to erect small houses for them —houses that were far better than their former huts. But the Yellow Caribs were too much Indian to settle down to the tame life of farming among the Black Caribs and little by little they left their comfortable English—made homes and began to steal back to their former haunts ; one by one at first —then in numbers till there was a well—defined migration. When I visited them —nine years after the eruption —all the Yellow Caribs of Saint Vincent were back at Sandy Bay, there being but two individuals outside the island —one in Carriacou and the other in Grenada.

At one place, where the high cliffs drop sheer into the sea, grudging even a beach, we came upon some Black Caribs fishing from their boats in the deep water. Their method is peculiar and is known as "bulling," probably a corruption of "balling." A single hook on the end of a line is weighted and lowered till it touches bottom. Then the line is hauled in a few feet and a knot is tied so that when the baited hook is lowered it will hang just above the bottom. The line is taken into the boat and the sinker removed from the hook which is now baited with a piece of sardine or smelt. Around this baited hook a ball is formed of meal made of the same small fish. The hook is then gently lowered till the knot indicates that the double bait has reached the haunts of the fish which feeds close to the bottom. With a quick upward jerk the ball is broken away from the hook. The scattered fish—meal draws the attention of the fish which investigates the floating food and presently goes for the large piece hanging in the center. And so like the rest of us who get into trouble when we reach out for the big piece the fish finds that there is a string tied to this food and that the line is too strong for him. The wrist and finger that hold the other end of the line are sensitive to the slightest nibble.

We rounded De Volet Point, which corresponds to Tangalanga on Grenada, and I once more felt the roll of the trades. A sea slopped over the gunwale and wet my leg which I drew into the canoe. We were now all island savages together holding up our ticklish craft by the play of our bodies. I looked across the channel to Saint Lucia with her twin Pitons rising distinct, thirty miles away. Batiste pulled himself together and told me that on very clear days he could see the glint of the sun on the cutlasses in the cane fields on the mountain slopes near Vieux Fort.

ALONE IN THE CARIBBEAN

"You like some sweet water?" he asked, and at the question my throat went too dry for speech. We turned into a little cove —you will find it called "Petit Baleine" on the chart, although if a whale swam into it he could never get out unless he could crawl backwards. While the men held the boat off the rocks, Batiste and I jumped ashore with four empty calabashes. A tiny stream which came from high up on the slope of the Souffrière Mountains, with the chill of the mists still in it, poured out from the dense foliage above us, spread itself into a veil of spray, gathered itself together again on a rocky face, and fell into a deep shaded basin into which we put our faces and drank till our paunches gurgled.?

?How the Caribs Rig a Calabash for Carrying Water

At times it is hard not to be a pig. Then, as if not satisfied with what Nature intended us to carry away, we filled our calabashes. These were as they have always been with the Carib —left whole with merely a small hole about an inch and a half in diameter in the top. They are carried by means of a wisp of grass with a loop for the fingers in one end and with the other end braided around a small piece of wood that is inserted into the hole to act as a toggle. It is easy to carry water in this way without spilling it for when the calabash is full there is but a small surface for the water to vibrate on. Père Labat mentions a curious use of the calabash in his day. In order to make a receptacle in which valuable papers could be hidden without fear of destruction by moisture a calabash was cut across at a point a quarter or a fifth of its length from the stem end. To cover the opening, another calabash was cut with a mouth somewhat larger than the first one and they were bound together with thongs of the mahaut. This calabash safe was then hidden in the branches of trees that had large leaves for the sake of obscurity. They were called coyembouc by the Caribs who invented them.

We put off again, passing the ruined estate of "Fancy," a mute reminder of that smiling day when destruction had come over the top of the mountains to the south —one of Nature's back-hand blows. A little beyond, our row of twelve miles came to an end and we beached through the heavy surf at Owia Bay where I found myself in the midst of a group of Yellow Caribs and negroes. I was a bit disappointed till Batiste told me that this was not Point Espagñol. We should have to go the rest of the way by land for the surf at Sandy Bay, he said, was too high to run with the loaded canoe. I wondered at this till I actually saw the surf two days later.

ALONE IN THE CARIBBEAN

Batiste and his crew packed my family of yellow bags on their heads and marched off on their way to Point Espagñol while I waited for a pony hospitably offered by the manager of an arrowroot estate on the slopes above the bay.

The pony was a heavenly loan but there was a cunning in his eye that did not belong to the realm above. His eye took me in as I mounted him, somewhat stiffly, for the pain of the sea eggs was getting beyond my foot. That eye made careful note that I wore no spurs, neither did I carry a whip nor even a switch. He started off at a brisk pace which he kept up till we were well along the main road. Then he stopped. I clucked and chirruped and whistled and swore. I also beat his leathery sides with my heels. No perceptible inclination to go forward. I talked to him but he did not understand my language. There was something, however, that I knew he would understand and I pulled off my belt. If you must subject by force or punishment, let it be swift, sure and effective. The brute had carelessly neglected to take note of a suspicious lump under my coat which hid a 38–40 Colt. First I circled my legs around his barrel body after the manner of a lead cavalry soldier "Made in Germany." Then with my gun in my left hand and my belt in my right, buckle–end being synonymous with business–end, I gave a warning yell and let him have the buckle in his ribs while the revolver went off close to his left ear. We rapidly caught up with Batiste —in fact, my steed was even reluctant in slowing down when I pulled him up behind the last Indian.

While my little caravan shuffled along ahead of me, I leisurely enjoyed the scenery of this level bit of road which skirts the slope of the Souffrière Mountains at the very edge where it breaks down to the sea. Some two hundred feet below me an intensely blue sea broke against the rocks into a white foam that washed out into a tracery of fine lace at every lull ; the rocks, the blue, and the foam like that of the Mediterranean along a bit of Italian coast. Landwards the slope rose in a powerful curve, heavily wooded, bearing numerous small peaks, to the Souffrière range which hides the volcano from view till one has reached the extremity of Point Espagñol.

The point is a peninsular–like promontory the top of which rises into two hills. Each of these hills is the site of a small Carib village of about forty–five inhabitants, the last of the Yellow Caribs of the Antilles. After a quick survey I decided upon the farther village which is a bit more to seaward and here I dismounted in the cool shade of the grove which gives the huts a pleasant sense of seclusion. After circling around, much as a dog that is preparing to lie down in the tall grass, I selected a spot on the edge of the little group of huts and set up my tent looking out over the Atlantic which lay some three hundred feet below. Since I could not see the setting of the sun, I faced the tent toward his rising. Here the cool trade wind belied the terrific heat of Sandy Bay below with its incessant roar of surf.

CHAPTER VI. DAYS WITH A VANISHING RACE.

I NEEDED no introduction to the Caribs, for they had known that I would come since my first meeting with the men in Bequia. They had also learned of my arrival at Château Belaire and that in another day I should be with them. One poor old woman had been watching all day to see me come flying over the Souffrière Mountains. Batiste told her of the Yakaboo and that if it did not fly it was at least rudderless. She consoled herself with, "He sail widout rudder!"

There was some satisfaction in watching me and as I pitched my tent and put my house in order, I had an interested crowd about me that did not use their fingers as well as their eyes with which to see. About a third of the village was there when I arrived. Besides Batiste and his men, those who gathered around my tent were the younger women who were spending the day in baking cassava cakes for the market, the children, and the old women who could do no other work than tend a coalpot or sweep out the huts. The men were either fishing or were down the coast at Georgetown to sell fish and the produce which the women had raised. The women are the farmers and we could see their patient forms moving goat–like along the furrows high up on the mountain slopes where they cultivate cassava, tanniers, and arrowroot.

One of the old women noticed that I was limping and as soon as I had everything ship–shape in my house, she went to her hut and returned with some soft tallow and a coalpot. Batiste said, "You goin' lose sea egg dis night." First she smeared the sole of my foot with the tallow and then lighting a splinter of dry wood from her coalpot she passed the blaze close to the skin, almost blistering the sole of my foot. Then she told me to bandage the foot and not to walk on it —an unnecessary caution.

ALONE IN THE CARIBBEAN

With Indian tact, they left me to loaf away the waning afternoon on my old companion, the blanket bag. I had begun the day in an idle way —let it end that way. There had been many places where I had loafed away the end of an afternoon on my blanket in just this way, but none of them will hold its place in my memory with this camp of mine on the edge of the Carib village. The huts were behind me and in the vista of my tent door there was no form of the ubiquitous native to distract, for there is no depth of character to romance upon when one sees a silent form shuffle along some bush path. Behind me the Caribs were quiet —I would not have known there were children or dogs in the village. Peace was there with just the rustle of the leaves above me as an accompaniment ; the song of a bird would have been thrilling. Below me the Atlantic rolled under the trade wind through the channel and became the Caribbean. A school of porpoise rounded the point and headed for the Spanish Main, mischief–bent like a fleet of corsairs. Well out in the channel my eye caught a little puff of steam and I knew that it came from a "humpback."

Finally as the sun sent his last long slant across the water whence we had come in the morning, it caught the smoke of the coasting steamer entering the bay of Vieux Fort in Saint Lucia —a hint of industry to speculate upon. With the shutting down of darkness one of the old women brought me a coalpot and I cooked my supper while the stars came out in an inquisitive way to see what I was doing.

By this time the village had assembled and fed itself. When the people found that I was not unwilling, they flocked around the door of my tent and I chatted with those who could talk English, these in turn interpreted our conversation to the others. After a while, my old sea egg woman of the afternoon —I could hardly tell one old woman from another, they were like old hickory nuts with the bark on —said, "Now de sea egg come out." I took off the bandage and she put my foot in her lap. Some one brought a gommier flambeau with its pungent odor that somehow reminded me of a vacant–lot bonfire into which a rubber shoe had found its way.

It would have been one of the best photographs of my whole cruise could I have caught those faces around that burning flambeau. Now for the first time I could really observe them in unconscious pose. Notwithstanding a considerable amount of admixture that must have undergone with the blacks, there was still a satisfying amount of Indian blood left in these people. I said Indian purposely for I do not care to use the expression Carib in this sentence. I believe these people to be more of the peaceful Arawak than the fierce

78

Carib, although time and environment and subjugation may have had this softening effect upon them. How much truth there may be in it I do not know, but the impression seems to be that in these islands the Caribs originally came from the north, advancing from island to island and conquering as they went the peaceful islander, the Arawak, who was the real native of the Lesser Antilles. Upon raiding an Arawak settlement the Caribs would kill most of the men and what women and children they did not eat they took to themselves as wives and slaves. Through their offspring by their Carib masters the Arawak women introduced their language and their softening influence into the tribes so that little by little the nature of the Carib was perceptibly changed. Thus the Arawaks became ultimately the race conquerors. In 1600 Herrera says, "It has been observed that the Caribbees in Dominica and those of Saint Lucia and Saint Vincent scarce understand one another's language," which tends to show that the lingual change was then going on throughout the islands. When I questioned the Caribs of Point Español in regard to the Indians of Dominica they expressed entire ignorance of their fellow savages. These people whom I saw in the light of the flambeau had the softened features of a race dying for the same reason that our pure American is dying —his country is changing and he cannot change with it. I thought of what Père Labat said of them three hundred years ago —"Their faces seemed melancholie, they are said to be good people."

Holding my foot close to the light, the old woman pinched the sole on either side of one of the purple marks which indicated the lair of a sea egg point. At the pressure the point launched forth, with scarcely any pain, eased on its way by a small drop of matter. The blistering with the hot grease had caused each minute wound to fester. In the next minute or two the largest of the points, about fourteen in number, were squeezed out. Some of the smaller points along the edge of the sole had not yet festered, but they came out the next morning.

The fun was over, we had had our preliminary chat, the flambeau had burned down, and the village turned in.

So did I.

On "calm" mornings, that is, when the wind is not blowing more than ten or twelve miles an hour, a stiff squall bustles ahead of the sun as if to say, "Get up! By the time you have cooked breakfast the sun will be having a peep to see how you have begun the day. You must take advantage of the cool morning hours, you know," and in a moment is rushing away toward Honduras. And so it was this morning. Confound Nature and her alarm clock that sprinkled in through my open door ! —but after all she was right.

Fishing was the order of the day and after the sun is up it takes but a short time to warm the black sands of the bay below to a hellish heat. My old woman produced her coalpot —it seemed to be kindled with the everlasting flame of the Roman Vestals —and I soon had my chocolate cooking and my bacon frying while I bade a not reluctant adieu to the last few sea egg points. My foot was free of pain and when I walked I could have sworn that there had been nothing like sea egg points in it the day or even the week before. I stuffed a few biscuits in a clothes bag, dressed my camera in its sea togs, and was off with the fishermen to the beach. There were twelve besides myself, four to a boat, two to row and two to fish —I should be the fifth in Batiste's boat.

The morning was still fresh from the cool night air as we filed down the cliff road to the beach. The surface of the sand was still dew damp. There were three dug–outs waiting for us under the protection of a thatched roof supported by poles, as if some queer four–legged shore bird had just laid them. There was no end of puttering before we could start, a bit of gear to be overhauled, a stitch or two to be taken in a sail so patched that I doubt whether there was a thread of the original cloth in it, and a rudder pintle to be tinkered with. I counted fifty–six patches in our mainsail, although its area was not more than six square yards.?

? Black Carib boy at Owia Bay. his catamaran is taxed at three pence per foot. ?

?

? "There is still a satisfying amount of Indian blood left in these people." ?

When we dragged the three boats down to the edge of the water the sun was just crawling up through the fringe of horizon clouds. The surf was not running so high as on the day before, and yet I could see that we should have to use care in launching the canoes. We dragged the first boat down till its bow was in the foam and with the crew seated at their oars we waited. There was a lull and as a wave broke smaller than the rest we launched the boat on its outgoing tide. The men caught the water and lifted their boat clear of the surf line as a sea curled and broke under their stern. We got off the beach with equal success. Contrary to the lucky rule of three the last boat was swamped and had to try over again.

Once off shore, we stopped rowing and stepped our rig, which consisted of two masts with sprit sails, one smaller than the other, the smaller sail being stepped forward so that we looked like a Mackinaw rig reversed. While these boats have no keel or centerboard, they somehow manage to hang onto the wind fairly well due to their depth of hold. They cannot, of course, beat to any purpose, still they can manage to sail about seven points off the wind which is good enough in the Carib waters where there is always a shore to leeward. With free sheets we ran for a bank to the southeastward where the "black fin" abounds and here we took down our sails and proceeded to fish. The other boats ran to similar banks to the south of us.

?

?

The black fin is a small fish, about the size of a large perch, its scales etched in a delicate red against a white skin. The name comes from a black spot at the hinge of the pectoral fin. Instead of anchoring, the two bow men rowed slowly while the rest of us fished. In this way we could skirt the edge of the reef till we found good fishing and then follow the school as it drifted with the tide while feeding.

We used the ordinary hand line, weighted with a stone about the size of one's fist. Above the stone, a gang of from four to six small hooks is baited with pieces of this same black fin. Like bulling this too is deep–water fishing for we lowered fully two hundred feet of line before the stone reached bottom. The line is then pulled up a few feet and held there to await the nibble of the fish. As soon as a bite is felt (one must develop a delicate touch to feel the nibble of a one pound fish at the end of a weighted line two hundred feet long), the line is given a lightning yank and pulled in as fast as possible. Hand over hand, as quickly as one forearm can pass the other, the line is hauled in over the gunwale while it saws its way into the wood.

ALONE IN THE CARIBBEAN

Sometimes there are two or even three fish on the end of the line when it is hauled into the canoe. I managed, however, to reduce the average considerably at first for I usually found that I had lost both fish and bait. Finally to the joy of Batiste, who considered me his protégé, I began to bring in my share. In the middle of the day we ate our scanty luncheon and then took to hauling in black fins again.

Early in the afternoon a fierce squall came down, dragging half a square mile of breaking seas with it. The Indians began to undress and I did the same, folding my shirt and trousers and stowing them in one of my oiled bags, much to the admiration of the others. We got overboard just as the squall struck and I slipped into the water between Batiste and one Rabat —they were used to fighting sharks in the water. With three of us on one side and two on the other, we held the boat, bow on to the seas, depressing the stern to help the bow take the larger combers and then easing up as the foam swept over our heads. In a jiffy the squall was past, like a small hurricane, and as we crawled into the boat again I watched it race up the mountain slopes and sweep the mists off the Souffrière. In the break that followed, the top of the volcano was exposed for a few minutes, my second and last view of the crater.

We again pulled up black fins till the fish covered the bottom of the canoe and we ran for home toward the end of the afternoon.

I now found out why the puttering of preparation was done in the morning. No sane man would do more than the absolutely necessary work of dragging his boat under the shade of the thatched roof and seeing that his gear was stowed under the roof poles in the heat of that beach. We made all haste for the cliff road and were soon in the breezy shade of our village grove. My share of the black fins went to the old sea egg doctor who selected one of the largest and fried it for me with all sorts of queer herbs and peppers. This with tanniers, tea, and cassava cakes made my supper. It was an easy existence, this with the Caribs, for I did but little cooking. I merely had to indicate what I wanted and some one or other would start a coalpot before my tent and the meal was soon cooking.

I have hinted at the flexibility of the Indian's language and that night I found a similar flexibility in savage custom. No doubt these Caribs had quickly lost most of their ancient rites and customs with the advance of civilization. I found that in like manner they easily adopted new customs, one of them being the "wake." In the day's fishing I had caught fully thirty black fins and had hauled in my line half again as many times, say forty–five.

ALONE IN THE CARIBBEAN

Forty–five times two hundred means nine thousand feet of line hauled in hand over hand as quickly as possible. This kind of fishing was exercise and I was tired. I went to bed early, but I slept not. It was that truly heathen rite, the "wake," which I believe comes from the Emerald Isle. May all Hibernian priests in the West Indies take note —it is the savage side of their religion that takes its hold upon the negro and the Indian. May these same Hibernians know that it was simply the "wake" that the Indians took from their faith for they are in religion Anglicans. Adapted would have been a better word for the wake of the Caribs is a combination of what we know as wake and the similar African custom called saracca. A tremendous feast of rice, peas, chickens, and any other food that may be at hand is cooked for the spirits who come in the night and eat. But the poor spirits are not left to enjoy this repast in peace for the living sit around the food with lighted candles and song. In the morning the food is gone and usually there is evidence that spirits have entered into the stomachs if not the ceremony of the mourners.

There is one pleasing feature in this mourning ceremony ; while it is usually begun with a truly sorrowful mien it often ends with all concerned in a happier mood to take up their worldly burdens again. The Caribs of Point Espagñol were content merely with singing. When one of their number dies they pray on the third night after death and on the ninth they sing during the entire night. This happened to be the ninth. In the evening, then, they all assembled in one of the larger huts, not far from my tent.

At first I thought it was only a sort of prayer meeting and I managed to doze off with a familiar hymn ringing in my ears. They would sing one hymn till their interest in the tune began to flag and their voices lower. Then they would attack another hymn with renewed vigor. At each attack I would awaken and could only doze off again when the process of vocal mastication was nearly completed. They were still singing when the sun rose.

Sunday came, as it always should, a beautiful day and I lay on my blankets till the sun was well above the horizon, watching my breakfast cook on the coalpot as a lazy, well–fed dog lies in his kennel meditating a bone. There seemed to be more than the usual morning bustle in the huts behind me and I found that the whole village was preparing to go to church. I must go with them, so I took off my shirt, washed it, and hung it up to dry. Then I carefully washed my face in warm water and proceeded to shave, using the scalpel from my instrument case for a razor. The polished inside cover of my watch made a very good mirror. A varnish brush, if it be carefully washed out with soap and hot water immediately after it has been used will be just as soft and clean as when new. I had such a brush which I used for painting and varnishing the Yakaboo, —it was not a bad distributor of lather It is remarkable how a shave will bolster one's self respect ; I actually walked straighter afterwards. I donned the trousers that I had washed in the shower bath in Kingstown and with my clean shirt, which had quickly dried in the sun and wind, I made a fairly decent appearance —that is, in comparison with my usual dress. A clean bandana handkerchief completed the toilet.

With church–going came the insufferable torture of shoes —that is, for the aristocrats who owned them. My own I was saving for climbs like the Souffrière and I used moccasins. Shoes, however, are the correct things to wear in these parts at weddings, funerals, and church. Aside from these occasions they are never worn.

The exodus began a little after ten o'clock and in five minutes there was not a soul left in the village. The goodly piece of road to Owia was, I thought, a measure in a certain way of the faith of these people. One is apt to be biased in their favor but still I cannot think that it was merely a desire for a bit of diversion to break the monotony of their lives that they all went to church as they did on this Sunday.

I believed as I walked with them that they were obeying a true call to worship. The call to worship became a tangible one as soon as we had circumvented the ravine and were on the road to Owia. It was the clang of a bell, incessant and regular —irritating to me —not a call but a command —the Sunday morning chore of a negro sexton. The church proper had been destroyed by the earthquakes attendant upon the eruption of the Souffrière —the ruins being another mute piece of evidence of the former splendor of these islands, for it had been built of grey stone and granite brought from overseas, a small copy of an English country church.

The bell was rescued after the earthquake from the pile of debris which had once been its home and mounted where it now hangs, on a cross piece between two uprights. On Sunday mornings the sexton places a ladder against this gallows and climbs up where he pounds the bell as if with every stroke he would drive some lagging Christian to worship. Sheep–like, we obeyed its call till the last of our flock was in the schoolhouse, where the service is held —when the clanging ceased.?

? The Carib boy of St. George's who had been brought to Grenada after the eruption of the Soufrière. ?

ALONE IN THE CARIBBEAN

The congregation was part negro, but we Indians sat on our own side of the building, where we could look out of the windows, across the little patches of cultivation to the blue Atlantic. We were as much out of doors as in, where, in truth, we are apt to find the greater part of our religion —if we look for it.

When I said schoolhouse, I meant a frame shed, about thirty feet by fifty, with unpainted benches for the pupils and a deal table at the far end for the schoolmaster. Letters of the alphabet and numerals wandered about on the unpainted walls and shutters in chalky array like warring tribes on tapestry, doing their utmost to make a lasting impression in the little brown and ebony heads of the school children.

The service was Anglican, read by a negro reader, for the parson is stationed in Georgetown and makes his visit only once a month. We shall let him pass in favor of the woman who led the choir. I knew her as she arose ; I had seen that expression from my earliest days, the adamant Christian whom one finds the world over in any congregation. This woman s voice was as metallic as the bell outside and in her whole manner and bearing was that zeal which expresses the most selfish one of us all, the Christian more by force of will than by meekness of heart. She sang. The choir and the miserable congregation merely kept up a feeble murmur of accompaniment.

I said miserable, for did we not feel that there was no chance for God to hear our weak voices above that clarion clang? Between hymns my mind was free to wander out through the windows, where it found peace and rest.

The offending shoes had come off after the first hymn and now furtive movements here and there proclaimed the resuming of that civilized instrument of torture. The last hymn was about to be sung.

After the heat of the day I wandered back to the village alone. My old sea egg woman was sitting on the grassy slope just below my tent and I took up my notebook and sat down beside her. She was in a reminiscent mood and I soon got her to talk about her natal language. She and two other old women were the only ones who knew the Caribbean tongue in this village —there was an equal number in the other village. When these old people go, with them will go the living tongue of the native of the Antilles —the words that Columbus heard when he discovered these islands. She was intensely pleased at the interest I showed in her language and I had no trouble in getting her to talk.?

85

ALONE IN THE CARIBBEAN

? Yellow Caribs at Point Espagnol. ?

Most of the words were unchanged from the time of Bryan Edwards in 1790, when the conquest of the Arawaks must have been more or less complete. Some words such an Sun —Vehu, now Wey–u ; fire —what–hò, now wah–tuh —were merely softened. Other words showed a slight change such as water —tona, now doonab ; fish —otò, now oodu. There were some words that had been changed completely, such as moon —mòné, now haat or há tí.

Most interesting perhaps to the lay mind are the onomatopoetic words that seem to take their meaning from their sound. A word common to many savage languages all over the world was Wèh–wey for tree, suggesting the waving of the tree's branches, he–wey for snake (pronounced with a soft breath), suggesting the noise of the snake in dry grass, and àh–túgah to chop. I watched her wrinkled old face with its far off look and could see the memory of a word come to the surface and the feeling of satisfaction that came into her mind as she recalled the language of her youth.

I sat there with my notebook open and after I had covered three or four pages I went back to words here and there to test her accuracy —I found that she really knew and was not trying to please. There were some words that would be good for successors to the Yakaboo —Mahouretch —Man o' War Bird ; Hourali —surf ; and Toulouma —pretty girl. At last she turned to me and said, "Ruh bai dahfedi?" —"Give me a penny?" —whereupon I produced a shilling. Her joy knew no bounds ; it would keep her in tobacco for a month.

That night we gathered in one of the huts and swapped yarns to the best of our abilities. I had been with the Caribs for some days and yet there was no hint at that familiarity that would be apt to come with a similar visit to a similar settlement of the natives of these islands. One is very apt to idealize in regard to the Indian, but I can say with absolute certainty that these people lived clean lives and kept themselves and their huts clean.

The huts were all of about the same size, approximately twelve by fifteen feet, of one story, and divided by a partition into two rooms with a door between, each room having a door opening outside. One of the rooms was for sleeping solely, while the other was both a sleeping and living room. While at first the houses seem very small, it must be remembered that the cooking was all done in separate ajoupas, and that most of the time these people live out of doors. They merely use their houses at night for sleeping purposes and as a shelter from rain.

The beds were for the most part rough wooden settees, some with a tick filled with grass and leaves for a mattress. The floors were usually the native soil, tamped hard by the pressure of countless bare feet. A few of the more prosperous families had wooden floors in their huts. The walls were of wattles, woven and plastered with a clay that resembled cement, and the roofs were thatched with Guinea grass. There were usually two small square windows for each room. An attempt was made to conceal the bareness of the walls inside by covering them with old newspapers plastered on like wall paper.

It was in such a newspapered room that we sat and smoked —that is, as many of us as could comfortably squeeze on the settee or squat on haunches on the floor, the overflow crowding about the open door. In this particular room there was one decoration, a pièce de resistance that brought the hut and its owner to even a higher level of grandeur than newspapered wall or floor of American lumber. It hung from the central beam just above headroom and yet low enough so that one might reach up and reverentially touch its smooth surface.

From the darkened look of the inner surface I could see that it was a burned–out sixteen candlepower electric light bulb. When far out to sea in his canoe, the owner had one day picked it up thinking that it was some sort of bottle. When he saw the trembling filament inside and could find no cork or opening he knew that it was for no utilitarian purpose and must be a valuable piece of bric–a–brac. It had probably been thrown overboard from some steamer passing to windward bound for Barbados.

Did I know what it was? Our conversation hung on it for a long time. Yes, I knew, but to make them understand it was a source of light —that was the trouble. Sometimes it is disastrous to know too much. I explained it as simply as I could and the Caribs nodded their heads, but there was a doubt in their eyes that was not to be mistaken. The fact that the tiny black thread inside that globe should be the source of light equal to sixteen candles was utterly beyond their comprehension.

I was turning over the leaves of my portfolio when a photograph of my sister dropped out. The old doctor picked it up and as she passed it to me her eyes fell upon it. She gave a start. Might she look at it closely, she asked? It was one of those ultra modern prints, on a rough mat paper, shadowy and sketchy, showing depth and life. The Caribs all crowded around to look. Such a natural picture they had never seen before. When the old woman at last gave it to me she said of my sister who was looking right at us, "We see she, she no see we," which struck me as a bit uncanny.

I was loafing through my last afternoon in the village. Wandering around the huts in the grove, I stopped at an ajoupa, where one of the women was baking something on the hot surface of a sheet of iron. It somehow reminded me of the thin pancake bread that the people of Cairo bake on the surface of a kettle upturned over a hot dung fire. I sat down to watch her bake and lit my pipe. I was a queer man, she said, to sit down in this humble ajoupa just to watch her bake cassava cakes. "No Englis do dat," she added. I had, of course, eaten the cassava before and on my way up through the Grenadines I had seen the negro women raking the coarse flour back and forth in a shallow dish over a bed of hot coals, but I waited till I was in the Carib country before I should see the mysteries, if there were any, of the making of cassava cakes.

The cassava is a root, Manihot utilissima, which grows very much like our potato and may weigh as much as twenty–five or thirty pounds. Ordinarily, it is dug up when it is about the size of a large beet. In the raw state it is highly poisonous, the juice containing hydrocyanic acid. The root is cleaned by scraping it with a knife, then it is sliced and grated. The grating is done on a board with pieces of tin nailed to it. The tin has previously been perforated so that the upper surface is roughened like the outside of a nutmeg grater. This coarse flour is then heated over a hot charcoal fire. In this way the hydrocyanic acid is dissipated by the heat —a sort of wooden hoe or rake being used to keep the flour from burning.

The woman in the ajoupa had built a hot fire between three stones on which was placed a flat iron plate about two feet in diameter. In the old days a flat stone was used. She prepared the flour by adding just enough water to make it slightly moist. On the hot plate she laid a circular iron band about eighteen inches in diameter —the hoop off some old water cask and inside this she spread the cassava meal to the thickness of a quarter of an inch. She then removed the hoop and levelled the cassava with the straight edge of a flat stick.

The cake baked very quickly and when it was done enough to hang together she turned it with a flat wooden paddle three inches wide in the blade and about eighteen inches long.

As soon as a cake was done she carried it outside and hung it to cool and dry on a light pole supported by two forked uprights. From a distance the cassava cakes looked like a lot of large doilies drying in the sun.

In the evening, when Batiste came from his fishing, I told him that I was ready to go back to Château Belaire. There may have been much more for me to observe among these people —the life was easy and I had never before had a more fascinating view from the door of my tent. But there was the call of the channel, I must have my try at it and it had been many days since I had sailed the Yakaboo. So we had our last palaver that evening around the glow of the coalpot and the gommier flambeau.

The old wrinkled sea egg doctor insisted upon hovering over my coalpot the next morning, while I broke camp and packed my duffle. Her presence had given my parting food a genuine Carib blessing. By sunup I bade them all good–bye and with Batiste and his men before me —my house and its goods balanced on their heads —I left the village. At a sharp bend, where the road curves in by "Bloody Bridge," I turned and had my last peep at the Carib huts.

CHAPTER VII. DELIGHTS OF CHANNEL RUNNING —JOSEPHINE IN SAINT LUCIA

THE NEXT morning, March 30th, found me once more in the Yakaboo rowing out of the bay of Château Belaire half an hour after sunrise. The night had been an anxious one on the morgue–suggesting cot of the rest room in the police station —for the devilish impish gusts had swept down one after the other from the Souffrière and shaken that house till I thought it would blow over like a paper box and go sailing out into the bay. If those fellows caught us in the channel what would the poor Yakaboo do?

I argued that the wind coming down the smooth plane of the mountain slope and shooting out across the water had developed a velocity far greater than anything I should meet in the channel. Perhaps so —but I should learn a bit about it later. I somehow bamboozled my mind into quiescence and at last fell asleep. Almost immediately the big, burly Barbadian awoke me. In an hour and a half I had rowed the six and a half miles to Point DeVolet, where I set sail.

I was now started on my first long channel run and it was with considerable interest if not anxiety that I watched the canoe and the seas. I had a lurking suspicion that I had made a grievous error when I had designed the Yakaboo ; I had perhaps erred on the side of safety and had given her a too powerful midship section in proportion to her ends. That was the feeling I had while sailing in the channels of the Grenadines. I was still traveling eastward as well as northward, and I knew that it would only be by the most careful windward work that I should be able to fetch the Pitons, thirty–one miles away. The wind on this day was the same trade that I had met with lower down, but the seas were longer than those of the Grenadines, and, if not so choppy, were more vicious when they broke ; there would be less current to carry me to leeward.

I had scarcely got her under way and was still under the lee of the land when the first sea came, like the hoary hand of Neptune himself and we turned to meet it. Aft I slid, she lifted her bow —just enough —and the sea broke under us —and we dropped down its steep back, with lighter hearts. In with the mainsheet and we were off again, the canoe tearing along like a scared cotton–tail —a little white bunch under her stern. There was something worth while in this and I kept my eyes to weather for the next sea. Again we met it and came through triumphant. Perhaps I had not erred after all. Another sprint and so on.

After a while the Yakaboo seemed to lag a little and hang her head like a tired pony. It was the forward compartment that was leaking again and I ran her into the wind, dropping the jib and mainsail. The little mizzen aft, flat as a board, held her directly into the wind's eye (which I believe is the best position for a very small craft hove–to), and I could go about sponging out the compartment.

I had, of course, to keep a sharp lookout ahead for breaking seas. If a sea threatened, I would hastily clap on the forehatch and give the screws a couple of turns and then roll back on my haunches into the after end of the cockpit. My precious camera was lashed half way up the mizzen mast. Lightened of the water in her forehold I would hoist the mainsail and jib and give her rein, that is, trim her sheets for another scamper to windward. She was the spirited pony again.

ALONE IN THE CARIBBEAN

That we were traveling well there could be no doubt. The wind was blowing at least twenty miles an hour and the canoe was covering her length with the smooth action of a thoroughbred. Yet when I looked astern after the first hour it seemed as though we were still under the shadow of Saint Vincent. I knew later that we had made five miles. It was discouraging to look backwards, and I did very little of it in my runs afterwards. I would wait till the greyish blue of the island ahead had turned to blue and was shading into green and then I would look back to the island that I had just left and I would estimate that I was perhaps half way across the channel. Having assured myself that I really was half way across, I kept my eyes over the bow, noting the minute changes of the land ahead. But I am not yet half way across this channel.

Soon my eye began to focus on a persistent whitecap that my brain refused to believe was a sail. But the eye insisted and the brain had to give in when the speck refused to move —it was always there, just to leeward of the Pitons —and it grew into a definite shape. Its course must almost cross mine, for as it grew larger and larger, it edged to windward closing in on the Pitons and was at last directly on my course. Nearer it came till I could make out the figure of a man poised erect out over the water. Another second and I could see the line to which he was holding and which ran to the top of the mast. His feet were on the gunwale. Then I distinguished several forms aft of him in the canoe, all leaning far out to windward to see what strange bird the Yakaboo might be, coming up out of the south.?

? Native canoe under sail. ?

The news of my coming had not jumped the channel ahead of me, but these fellows had recognized my rig from afar as a rarity —something to investigate. I shall never forget the picture of them rushing by. They might have been Caribs of old descending, like the Vikings that they were, on some island to be conquered. They came down the wind with terrific speed, the water foaming white under them, a third of the keel showing, the glistening forefoot leaving a train of drops like a porpoise clearing the water.

For an instant my eye held it ; the man poised over the sea ; the figures in the boat, bronze and ebony, tense with excitement ; the white, sun–bleached sails, now outlined against a blue sky and now thrown against an indigo sea, rivaling the brilliant snowy clouds above. As they shot by, close abeam, their arms shot up and they gave me a mighty yell while I waved my hat and shouted back at them. If this sight of a single canoe coming down the wind thrilled the hairs along my spine into an upright position, what would my feeling have been to see a whole fleet of them as in the old days? I would not look back —I wanted the memory of that passing to remain as it was and I sailed on, thinking for some time of each detail as it was indelibly impressed upon my mind.

Like most of us, who are blessed with a lean body, I also have that blessing which usually goes with it —an appetite which is entirely out of all proportion to the size of that lean body. Nervous energy as well as manual labor requires food and when I made my channel runs there was an expenditure of both —and I needed feeding. I always had food handy in my cockpit.

My mainstay was the jelly coconut or water —nut as they call it. This is the coconut that has not yet reached the stage where the meat is the hard, white substance which we meet in the kitchen pantry in the shredded form, but is still in the baby stage when the meat is soft and jelly–like. In this stage the milk is not so rich as later on, but is a sort of sweet coco–tasting water. I never wanted for a supply of coconuts.

The natives along shore invariably saw to it that there were four or five of them in my cockpit, prepared for instant use in the following manner : the native balances the nut on the palm of the left hand, while with a cutlass (not called machete in these islands that have not known the Spaniard, except as a pirate), he cuts through the hard, smooth surface of the husk and trims the pulpy mass, where the stem joins the nut, into a point. At any time, then, with a single slice of my knife, I could lop off this pulpy point and cut through the soft stem end of the inner shell, making a small hole through which I could drink the water.

When first it passes over your tongue, jaded by the civilized drinks which have a tang to them, your judgment will be, "Insipid!" Go out into the open and leave ice water a week behind you and your tongue will recover some of its pre–civilized sensitiveness. You will swear that there is nothing so cool nor delicious as the water of the jelly coconut. After the water has been drunk there is yet the jelly to be eaten. First a slice of the husk is cut oft to be used as a spoon. Then, using my knife as a wedge and my axe as a driver, I split open the nut and scooped out the jelly from the halves.

When my supply of pilot bread ran out I carried soda crackers and sometimes the unleavened bread of the natives. Raw peameal sausage helped out at times and there was, of course, the chocolate of which I have spoken before. I also carried other tropical fruits besides coconuts, mangoes, bananas, pineapples, but I never ate more than one sort on a run. The coconut was my mainstay, however, and that with a little bread and a piece of chocolate would make an excellent stop–gap till I could reach shore and cook a substantial evening meal.

I was now half way across the channel, I judged, for neither island had the advantage of nearness nor distance. After a while Vieux Fort began to work its way to windward of me and the canoe was still hanging bravely on to the Pitons. She was doing excellent work to windward, creeping up the long hollows in pilot's luffs as is the habit of this rudderless craft. The sum total of these small distances eaten to windward a little more than made up for what we lost when we lay–to for a combing sea. Saint Lucia had long since changed from a misty grey to blue grey, and then slowly the green of the vegetation began to assert itself in varying shades as patches of cultivation became defined. Dun–colored spots on the hillsides took the shapes of native huts. It was like the very slow development of a huge photographic plate.

When within a few miles of the island the wind began to draw to the south'ard, and as I eased the sheets of the canoe, she quickened her pace like a horse headed for home. The plate was developing rapidly —I could make out the trees on the mountain ridges and the beaches along shore. Vieux Fort was on our beam, the Pitons towered over us ; then with the hum of tarred rigging in a gale, the centerboard of the Yakaboo crooned its parting song to the channel and we lost our motion in the glassy calm of Souffrière Bay. We had completed our first long jump.

High above me the projectile form of the Petit Piton tore an occasional wraith from the low–flying trade clouds. Inset in its steep side, some twenty feet above where I was now rowing, was a niched shrine to the Virgin Mary, to whom many a hasty prayer had been uttered during the fervor of bare deliverance from the rafales (squalls) of the channel, prayers probably quickly forgotten in these calm waters under the Pitons and the memory of them soon washed away in the little rum shops of the coast town, which gets its name from the Souffrière in the hills above it and gives that name to the bay before it. By this sign of the Virgin Mary, I was leaving for a time the Protestant faith of the outer Antilles and entering the Catholic. In a measure, I was leaving the English for the French, for although Saint Lucia has been in the possession of the English since 1803, there still remains the old creole atmosphere of the French régime.

ALONE IN THE CARIBBEAN

As I swung around the base of the smaller Piton, the leveling rays of the late afternoon sun caught the distant walls of wooden houses weatherworn to a silky sheen. The dull red of a tiled roof here and there, the sharp white of what I soon learned were the police buildings, broke the drab monotone of the town. A little coasting steamer backed out, crab–like, from a cane–laden jetty and as we passed in the bay, three white cotton tufts from her whistle tooted my first welcome to Saint Lucia.

I had planned to show my papers to the police at Souffrière and then to pitch my tent on some sandy beach beyond a point that interested me just north of the town. I should then have a good start for my row along the lee coast on the next day and I should soon be channel running again —to Martinique and the Empress Josephine —I had an especial interest in her.

But one never knows. It happened at Carriacou and it is apt to happen at any time. The perverse imp, whatever his name may be, thrives on the upsetting of plans. I had no sooner crawled up on the jetty of Souffrière and stretched my legs when a black limb of the law confronted me. "Dis no port ob entry," he said ; "you mus' go to Castries."

Castries was sixteen miles farther along the coast and I had already traveled forty–two miles since sunup. I looked at my watch and the hands showed four–thirty. I looked out over the sea and saw the sun, like an impatient boy rushing through his chores, racing for his bath in the horizon, a huge molten drop, trickling down the inverted bowl of the firmament. If I now took to my canoe again and slept on the beach somewhere up the shore, I should get into trouble at Castries for I had already put my foot on shore.

I finally decided that it was two of one and half a dozen of another —two being the trouble I should get into by staying here and six being the trouble I might get into in the proportionately larger town of Castries. Confound a government that spends thirty cents for red tape to wrap up a package worth ten!

Up to this time, my coming had not been detected, but with the increasing agitation of the policeman, it dawned upon the jetty stragglers that something unusual was on foot. Some one noticed the strange canoe tethered like a patient animal to one of the legs of the jetty. Some one else noticed that there was a strange person talking with the policeman. I was rapidly being discovered by a horde of babbling, ragged beach–loafers and fishermen, who followed like swarming bees as we made our way to the police buildings. The swarm was effectually barricaded outside as we entered the building, where I showed my papers to Sergeant Prout.

In these islands when precedent lacks, complexity arises. And here was something complex —a man who traveled alone, voyaging in the daytime and sleeping at night on whatever beach he happened to land. The sergeant must needs have advice, so he sent for the leading merchant of the town and the lawyer. The merchant, being a man of business, said, "Ask your superior," and the lawyer, being a man of caution, said, "Place the responsibility on some one else," at which the sergeant telephoned to His Majesty's Treasurer at Castries. The reply I did not hear. My canoe was carried into the cobbled courtyard of the police buildings and my outfit was locked up in a cell next to that of a thief. "And now," said I, "if you will lend me a coalpot and lock me up with my outfit I shall cook my supper and go to bed." Not a smile on the faces around me.

"But there is an hotel in thee town," came from a voice at my side, and not much higher than my belt, "I will conduc' you there."

He pronounced "hotel" with a lisp that made it more like "hostel," and called the article "thee." I looked down and beheld him who was to be my henchman during my stay in Souffrière. He was a little fellow, black as the record of a trust magnate and with a face that went with the name of Joseph Innocent.

I would take Sergeant Prout's word for anything and his nod in answer to my questioning look was a good voucher for Joseph. And so we walked out, Joseph parting the crowd before me, proudly carrying my camera and portfolio while I followed, a pace or two behind, to observe the quaint old town. Laid out in regular squares, the houses toed the line of the sidewalks in one continuous wall from street to street. For the most part, the walls were bare of paint, or if paint had ever been used, it had long since been crumbled by the sun and washed away by the rain. To relieve the dead geometric regularity, picturesque grilled balconies overhung the sidewalks, giving proof that at some time there had been life in the streets worth observing.

We passed the open square of the market with the bare, sun–heated church at the far end, facing the west, as though its memories lay forever behind it. Joseph stopped at one of the myriad doors in the walls of houses. Would I ever be able to find this door again? —and I stepped from the street into the cool dark salle à manger of this West Indian hotel. The mulatresse, who received me, was of a better looking type, I thought, than the creole negress of the English islands. "Could I have food and room for the night?"

"Mais oui," for in spite of my shifty appearance my camera and portfolio were badges of respectability and vouched for me. I dispatched Joseph for some cigarettes and while awaiting his return I noticed that the mulatresse was setting places for two. I was to have company —a comforting thought when I could not be alone on the beach. I am never so lonesome as when eating alone, where there are people about. On the beach I should have had the company of the setting sun, the tropical starlit night, and the murmur of the little rippling surf on the smooth sands —but here! the shuffling of the silent negress as she placed the food before me would have been loneliness itself.

When Joseph came with the tin of cigarettes, I offered him a "thrupence," for he had served me well. But he was a diplomat from his wide-spreading toes to his apish face. There is a patois saying, "Zo quité yone boudé plein fait zo sote, " —"Don't let a bellyful fool you."

"No! You give me de two copper," indicating the coins in my hand, "for you need de silver for other person." He was an artist, I learned later, and cared little for money —but would I get him some paints and brushes when I reached Castries?

The mulatresse had scarcely announced, "Monsieur est servi," when the other guest entered. He was an Englishman —of the island —spare and well-groomed, as one generally finds them, a government engineer on his monthly tour inspecting the telephone system, which girdles the island. While we ate our thon (tuna) our conversation turned on the tuna fisheries of Martinique and I mentioned Josephine and Trois-Îlets. "Josephine! Martinique! Why man alive! Josephine spent part of her childhood days right here in Souffrière and I don't know but what she was born on this island —in the northern part —at Morne Paix-Bouche."

And so it happened that I was to be denied the beach to stumble upon a page or two of that life of contrasts —pathetic and romantic —of the Empress Josephine. Over our coffee and cigarettes my friend told me of Père Remaud of the parish of Gros-Islet in the north of Saint Lucia —the man who knew more about Josephine's life in this island than any one else. I decided, then, to spend some time in Saint Lucia and I learned many things about her —but who wants to read dry history sandwiched in between salty channel runs? Our conversation turned to other things and then died out even as the glow of our cigarettes. We were both tired and mutually glad to turn in.?

? The camera got them just as they had slipped through the high surf. ?

But the wakening effect of the coffee and the cold funereal sheets of the high antique four–poster onto which I had climbed to rest, kept off slumber for a while. What a cruise of contrasts it was —from the primitive life of the Carib living on fish and cassava, I had sailed in a day from the fifteenth century into the eighteenth. From my roll of blankets on the high ground of Point Espagñol I had come to the more civilized, but not more comfortable, husk mattress of the French régime. I was not long in deciding that the husk mattress was no less aged than the four–poster. Perhaps the friends of Josephine had slept in this bed, on this very mattress —whatever their sins may have been may this have shriven them! Sadness entered my mood and I fell asleep.

Can the lover of small indulgences begin the day better than I began my first morning in Saint Lucia? At six there was a knock at my door, followed by the entrance of the mulatresse bearing a huge basin of cold water with a calabash floating on its surface, the simplest and yet the most delightful bath I have known. Scarcely had I slipped on my clothes —the mulatresse must have known by the sounds the progress of my toilet —when another knock ushered in a small pot of steaming Liberian coffee such as only they of the French islands can grow and brew. There is but one sequence to this —a cigarette. This, then, was my formula, after which I stepped out onto the street where Joseph was waiting for me.

Not far from the town, up in the hills, lies Ventine, the beauty spot of Saint Lucia. This is the safety valve, a sort of Hell's Half Acre, that saved Saint Lucia during the eruptions of Saint Vincent and Martinique. As the well–kept road wound upward, lined with orderly fields and occasional clumps of trees, I could easily imagine myself to be in southern Europe, for the morning was still cool and the road free except for an infrequent figure shuffling along at its ease with its burden balanced on top. It was pleasant to hear the prattle of Joseph with its French construction of the English and that soft inflection, which we lack so much in our own harsh language. "Look! you see that bird there? Eet ees call the cuckoo mayoque by the creole. They say that God, w'en he was building the world (but I don' beleeve it), ask the cuckoo to carry stone to the stream. But the cuckoo would not do it because it would soil his beautiful fethaire. Then God say, 'For that you shall never, drink from the stream an eef you do you will drown. An' now the cuckoo can only get water from the flowers and leaves."

A little farther on, he darted to the side of the road and brought back a leaf of the silver fern. He told me to hold out my hand —"no, wiz zee back upwards." Placing the leaf on the brown skin he gave it a slap and the leaf slipped off leaving the delicate tracery of its form in a silver powder. And so it was on that delightful walk, I came to like the little native, bright and full of spirit. Some day he may, as a regular duty, open my door in the morning and say, "Will you have your, coffee now, sir, or w'en you arize?"

We finally arrived at the Ventine, which is the thin–crusted floor of an ancient crater. The sulphur smell that greeted me brought back memories of Yellowstone Park. From Southern Europe I had been whisked back to the States. And to carry the illusion still further I found there three Americans, Foster, Green and Smith (good plain Yankee names of no pretension), who were working the sulphur of the crater. We fell on each other's necks, so to speak.

One needed a guide and Foster took me about on the hot floor to see the boiling mud pools and the steam jets. On our way up to the cottage where the men lived with their families Foster showed me the natural advantages of living in a place like this. The region of the Ventine would be a wonderful place of retirement for the rheumatic cripple. Here were hot springs of temperatures from tepid to boiling, cold mountain streams that made natural shower baths, as they tumbled down the rocks, and pools of curative mineral water.

As we walked along the path Foster dug his hands into the bank. "When you want to wash your hands just reach into the side of the hill —here —and haul out a lump of this soft clay stuff. Rub your hands together and a little farther on —here —you have the choice of either hot or cold water to wash it off in. You see, my hands are as soft as a baby's skin."

He talked like an advertisement. They are planning to build a hotel at the Ventine some day. If they do it will be a new Souffrière come to life and I can imagine no more delightful resort.

ALONE IN THE CARIBBEAN

We left the Ventine in the cool of the afternoon and passing the town walked out along the broad east road to the ruins of the old French baths, where the aristocracy of France, some of them exiles, and some come to the island to recoup their fortunes, were wont to take the cure. There is but little now remaining, a few walls, a tank into which the sulphur water flows from the mountain stream, and a massive stone arch set in a thick woods that takes two hours from each end of the day and holds a gloom like a shroud for the dead past. A cow was grazing where grace once trod and where perhaps the little Yeyette* came with her elders. That evening I chatted with a man, Monsieur Devaux, whose grandaunt, Mademoiselle Petit L'Étang, had often spoken of having played with the little Josephine, at the estate of Malmaison in the hills to the north of Souffrière.

But there was little else to be learned and the next morning I left for Castries.

Offshore, trying to claw into the wind against the tide, was a little sloop which somehow looked familiar. It was calm alongshore and I rowed for an hour. Then a breeze came directly from the north and I made sail for beating. As I neared the sloop on the out tack she ran up a signal. I dropped my mainsail for an instant to let them know that I understood, and ran in again on the other tack. She was the Glen Nevis from Grenada and had called at Kingstown on her way to Saint Lucia with ice.

When she followed me into port an hour later, I found that my Man Friday of St. George's was in command.

* Childhood name of the Empress Josephine.

They had left Kingstown the day before I had left Château Belaire, and although I had stopped off a day at Souffrière, I beat them into Castries by an hour. In other words, it had taken them seventy–two hours to cover the sixty miles from Kingstown to Castries. My time for traveling the same distance was twenty hours. This showed the advantage of the canoe as a vehicle in these waters, for I could not only sail the rough channels but also slip along under the lee of the islands where the larger boats would be helplessly becalmed. As these fellows sail they must, of necessity, lose valuable ground to windward by dropping away from the island they are leaving to avoid calms and then they must beat their way up to the next island.

Compared with Grenada and Saint Vincent, the lee coast of Saint Lucia is low and uninteresting except for two wonderful harbors, close together, near the northern end ; Cul–de–Sac, the location of the Usine Central for the manufacture of sugar, and Castries, the coaling station of the English islands, with its Vigie, the lately abandoned Gibraltar of the British West Indies.* It was in the hills between these almost landlocked harbors that Sir John Moore fought with the French and the Caribs and learned the real art of warfare that made possible his marvellous retreat at Coruña.

As we approached Castries, a large, white yacht came up from over the horizon and slipped into the harbor. She proved to be the Atinah —belonging to Edouard Rothschild and flying the French flag. She had bumped on a reef south of Cuba and came here to coal before going home to dock. A Norwegian tramp, probably owned by an American company, stole around the south of the island and came up behind me, a huge mass of ocean–going utility, and swung into port after the yacht.

* Shortly after the outbreak of the present war in Europe
 the Vigie was fortified with guns brought over from Martinique
 and garrisoned in 1915 by a company of Canadian soldiers.

An Englishman came out, relieved of coals she had brought from Cardiff, her rusty sides high out of water, the tips of her propeller making a white haystack under her counter. The little coasting steamer, which had saluted me two days before, bustled out of her home on her daily run to Vieux Fort.

There was commerce in this port —I had not been near a steamer for two months. Before sailing into the harbor, we made an inquisitive tack offshore in order to have a peep at Martinique. There she lay —a little to the westward of Saint Lucia ; the arc was swinging back and I should soon be in the Leeward islands. Distinct against the haze of Martinique stood the famous Diamond Rock and here, only six miles off, lay Pigeon Island, lifting its head, a lion couchant with Fort Rodney in its mane.

ALONE IN THE CARIBBEAN

On the other tack we ran into the busy harbor. French, English, and Norwegian flags were there. My little ensign, no larger than a bandana handkerchief, was all that represented the United States in this large company. But the Yakaboo flitted past her overgrown children —for after all the canoe is the mother of them all —to a quiet corner that showed no change since the advent of steam.

I had decided to spend some time in Castries —looking into the past of a certain lady. I ought to make the type appear shamefaced as I write this, but you already know who the lady is, or was, and that she has been dead nearly a century and her past was a romance. There comes an indefinable sense of peace and quiet when one sails into a secure and almost landlocked harbor such as the carénage of Castries, but I did not know that I was only sailing from the vicissitudes of the Caribbean to the uncertainties of a veritable sea of hearsay concerning Josephine.

For instance, there was an old negro who had seen the Empress in Castries when a little child. Whether he was the little child, or she was the little child, I do not know —perhaps it was Castries that was the little child. He was brought to me one day as I stood in the street chatting with one of the merchants of the town.

"Undoubtedly old," I said to my friend, as one would comment upon a piece of furniture. He seemed a youth compared with some of our old Southern darkies, shriveled and cotton–tufted. "Quel âge?' I yelled at him, for he was somewhat deaf.

"Cent onze e' sep' s'mains," came the answer. One hundred and eleven years and seven weeks! If I had not caught him unawares he might have given the days and hours.

But his age was not so remarkable as his memory. He remembered having seen Josephine on the streets and especially at the time when she left Saint Lucia for Martinique on her way to France to marry Beauharnais. There was no doubting that honest old face and there was nothing but admiration for a memory that reached back not only to youth and childhood, but even to prenatal existence. He was born two years after Josephine had paid her last visit to these islands! I took his photograph and paid him a shilling, which shows that a wonderful memory is nothing if not a commercial asset.

My papers from St. George's, which had been viséd from port to port would serve me no longer since I was now leaving for Martinique, which was French. One morning I walked into the office of the French consul, who, it seemed to me, was suspiciously suave and gracious. The idea of traveling about in a boat of less than a quarter of a ton was very amusing. He filled in the blanks of an impressive document, which I stuck in my pocket. When I asked the amount of the fee he said, "Twenty francs." "Whew!" I muttered to myself, "no wonder he was so blasted polite."

Out past the Vigie and I was happy again. One is always glad to run into port, but the voyager is doubly glad to leave it again. There are countless petty annoyances on shore that one never meets on the broad seas. I often worry about the weather, but most of that worry is done when I am ashore. As soon as I stepped into the canoe that morning I felt that I was leaving my small troubles on the stone quay, whimpering like a pack of forlorn dogs. I should lose sight of them and the quay as soon as I rounded the Vigie.

After sailing through two rain squalls and making an investigating tack under Pigeon Island, I headed for the beach of the village of Gros–Islet, for I had business there. I wanted to see Père Remaud and examine some of the parish signatures. As I beached the canoe, Henry Belmar, a fine young colonial Englishman, came through the crowd of natives to meet me. He was riding through Gros–Islet on governmental duties, had seen me in the bay, and had ordered food at one of the houses in the town. The thoughtful hospitality of the colonial Englishman has often made me think upon the manner in which we too often treat the stranger who comes to our shores. If he is outré, we lionize him and the women make a freak of him. If he is of our own kind, we let him shift for himself. We drank our febrifuge with the usual "chin–chin," and after luncheon set out for the house of Père Remaud.

The priest was a young man, full of strength and vigor, much, I thought, as Père Labat would have been had we known him in our age. Père Remaud was interested in the things of the world. He lived for his parish, read, shot ramiers (pigeons), and could talk intimately on the politics of my own country. While I had been eating with Belmar, the priest had been down to the beach to see my canoe and at the moment when we arrived he was hastily turning the leaves of a French sporting catalogue to see whether he might discover to just what species the Yakaboo belonged —much as he would attempt to classify a strange flower which he had found in the hills of his parish.

I spent the afternoon with him, looking over the old parish records. But for the faded paper on which they stood out in bold lines, the letters and signatures might have been written yesterday. There was the signature of Louis Raphael Martin, a planter of Saint Lucia, who had known Josephine here and had been received by her at Malmaison in France. There was that of Auguste Hosten under the date of 1810, who, Frédéric Masson says, loaned a large sum of money to Josephine at the time of the Revolution, when the guillotine had taken her first husband and before she met Napoleon.

We talked, and I made many notes during the long afternoon till at last the yellow sunshine gave warning that I must leave. Père Remaud came down to the beach with me and as we heeled to the evening breeze I heard his last "Bon voyage" above the babble of the natives.

The same puff that carried the last adieux of Père Remaud helped us across the white sandy floor of the bay and left us, close to the shores of Pigeon Island. Three whaleboats were lying on the beach and as I stepped ashore their crews came straggling down to meet me. I found that the man in command of the station was Napoleon Olivier of Bequia, a brother of José at Caille, and I was again in my whaling days of the Grenadines. I was soon as far from Josephine and Père Remaud as the twentieth century is from the eighteenth —but not for long. Accompanied by the two sons of Olivier, I climbed to the famous old fort, now called "Rodney," where that admiral, second only to Nelson, watched for the French fleet to come out of their hiding in the bay of Fort Royal (now Fort de France), thirty miles to the north, in Martinique. His own fleet lay below him in the Saint Croix roads, like impatient hounds tugging at their leashes, eager to be in chase of their quarry.

The French at last slipped out on the night of April 8th, 1782, the news of their departure being signaled to Rodney by means of a chain of English lookout ships. Rodney was immediately on their heels and on the 12th met the French in the Dominica channel, where he fought the battle of "The Saints."

The fort itself is scarcely more than a rampart with a powder magazine on the east side and a flagstaff stepping in the center. There were no guns left and the trees, growing out of the pavement, told of long years of disuse. The sun had dropped below the ridge of the island as we scrambled down again through long rank grass, waist–high, and through a small dark grove of trees, among which there were several tombs of officers, their inscriptions still decipherable, the last narrow earthly homes of men who had died while stationed here, not from the bullets of the French, but from the insidious attack of that enemy which they knew not —the mosquito.

I cooked my supper with the whalemen in the ruins of the old barracks. A rain tank, still intact from the time of the occupation, furnished water and I was soon yarning with Olivier over the bubbling pots. The season had been a bad one, only one small whale had been caught. One of the best harpooners was lying sick with fever in Gros–Islet, and the whole outfit was in a state of black dejection.

Poor Olivier! He was not only doomed to lose his harpooner, for three years later when I sailed my schooner into the quiet haven of Bequia he came aboard and, sitting on the top step of the companionway, he told me with tears in his eyes that one of his sons, who had taken me up to the fort, had died of fever shortly after I had left Pigeon Island. He had no photograph to remember his son by, but he remembered that I had taken a snapshot on the rampart —would I give him a print?

Supper over, we put up impromptu tents in the long, soft grass above the beach where the boats lay, for the ruins, they said, were full of fleas. It may have been fleas or it may have been superstition that inhabited the barracks with jumbies. The tents were impromptu, old sloop sails thrown over the masts of the whaleboats. One end of the masts rested on the ground while the other was supported by crossed oars lashed together about seven feet above ground. Had these shelters not been put up after sunset and taken down before sunrise I might have had an interesting photograph of shipwrecked mariners. I crawled in with Olivier, for it would save me the work of pitching my own tent. I was awakened by the chilly drizzle of a morning squall.

As I got up and shook myself at sunrise —that is 5 :51 on that particular day —(the sun did not rise for us until sometime later, when he edged above the Morne du Cap on Saint Lucia), the weather did not look promising. Had it been the fifth day of the first quarter I would not have started for Martinique, but it was the fifth of the second, which had shown a lamb–like disposition, and there were two days of it left —I was on the safe side. The indications were for rain rather than wind and I decided to take the chance. Olivier was a bit doubtful.

I cooked my breakfast with the men in the barracks, dragged my canoe down to the water's edge and watched the weather. At eight o'clock, the rain having ceased, I bade good–bye to the whalers, who had decided not to try for humpbacks that day, and was off. As we sailed out through the reefs by Burgot Rocks the heavy surf gave warning that there would be plenty of wind outside. Once clear of Saint Lucia I laid my course for Diamond Rock, a good six points off the wind.

What a comfort it was to ease my sheets a bit and to know that if the current began to take me to leeward I could make it up by working closer to windward. Those extra points were like a separate bank account laid up for a rainy day.

The canoe enjoyed this work. She fairly flew, sliding into the deep troughs and climbing the tall seas in long diagonals. In half an hour Saint Lucia behind me was completely hidden by rain clouds and so was Martinique ahead. The two islands seemed to have wrapped themselves in their vaporous blankets in high dudgeon, like a couple of Indian bucks who have failed to wheedle whisky out of a passing tourist. Fearful lest the weather might break and come up from the southwest, I kept a constant watch on the procession of the trade clouds in the northeast, ready to come about with the first weakening of the wind.

Afraid? not exactly —but cautious. The Yakaboo drove on like the sturdy little animal that she was. We flow knew each other so well that we did not even bother to head into the breaking seas, except the very large ones. Some of them we could roll under and slip by. Others came aboard and at times I was waist deep in water and foam, sitting on the deck to windward, my feet braced in the cockpit under the opposite coaming. If there had not been the danger of filling her sails with water, I could have made the mainsheet fast for she practically sailed herself. Between deluges, I bailed out the cockpit with a calabash.

Once in a while she would hang her head and then I hove–to to bail out the forward compartment with a sponge. The exhilaration of the Saint Vincent channel was nothing compared to this. The water was warm and my constant ducking was not unpleasant. I thought I could feel a tingle in the region of my pre–evolute gills.?

? The ruins of the church at Owia. The bell and the ladder can be seen at left. ?

ALONE IN THE CARIBBEAN

It may seem strange that in these channel runs where the trade blew strong, the force of the wind never seemed to bother the canoe. Although it was usually blowing fully twenty miles an hour and often twenty–five, I was obliged to reef my sails but four times on the whole cruise ; on the run to Dominica, when the wind was very strong ; again, under the lee of Dominica ; in the run to Guadeloupe, when the canoe was going too fast in a following sea, and, for the same reason, on my run to Saba. I have often carried full sail when a large sloop has been obliged to reef.

The reason for this is that the wind close to the surface of water, broken up into ridges from three to eight feet in height, is considerably retarded and the stratum through which the low rig of the Yakaboo moved was not traveling at a rate of more than three–fourths the actual velocity of the free wind. Upon approaching land, where the seas began to diminish in size and before I had reached the influence of the down draft from the mountains, I could always feel a slight but definite increase in the force of the wind.

Sailing as I did —seated only a few inches above the water —I had an excellent Opportunity to observe the flying fish which rose almost continually from under the bow of the canoe. Although they were smaller than those I have seen in the channels off the California coast —they were seldom more than about nine inches long —their flight did not seem to be appreciably shorter. Their speed in the water immediately before they emerge must be terrific for they come out as though shot from a submarine catapult ; their gossamer wings, vibrating from the translated motion of the powerful tail, make the deception of flight most real.

The flight is in effect the act of soaring with the body at an angle of from ten to fifteen degrees with the horizontal. The wings are close to the head and the lower part of the body often passes through the crest of a wave from time to time when the tail seems to give an impetus to the decreasing speed of the flight. This, however, may be an illusion, due to the dropping away of the wave, which might thus give the fish the appearance of rising up from the water. I have spent many hours watching these singular fish and, while there can be no doubt that they do not actually fly, it seems almost incredible that a fish can hurl itself from the Water with sufficient force to rise to a height of twenty or more feet and soar for a distance of from three to four hundred feet —perhaps farther.

The land ahead had shaken off its cloud blanket and was now rapidly defining itself, for this channel was shorter than the last one and my old enemy, the lee tide, had been scarcely perceptible. As I held the canoe up for "Diamond Rock," I again noticed the decided veering of the wind to the south'ard, and from time to time I had to ease off my sheets till the canoe was running well off in a beam sea that moderated as I approached land. The sky, which had been well clouded during most of the run, opened at a fortunate moment while I hove–to, stood up in the cockpit, and took a photograph of the famous Rock. There was no hope of landing in that run of sea and I had to be content with a hasty survey of the Rock as the canoe bobbed up and down, her nose into the wind.

Were I writing this narrative true to events, I should have no time to describe the Rock and relate a bit of its history for I had scarcely time to stow my camera when a squall came chasing down on my heels. I hastily raised the mainsail and ran "brad aft," as the harpooner Bynoe would say, to get plenty of sea room. When the squall did catch us, we hove–to with the jib safely stowed and the mainsail securely lashed so that the wind could not get its fingers into it, and with the sturdy little mizzen dutifully holding the canoe into the wind.

You shall have the story now while I am sitting in the cockpit —doing nothing but watch the Rock disappear in the mist to windward, while the Yakaboo is backing off gracefully at a rate of four miles an hour.

Diamond Rock rises in the shape of a dome to a height of five hundred and seventy feet, a mile distant from the Martinique shore. In 1804, when the English and French were making their last fight for the supremacy of the Caribbean, Admiral Hood laid the H. M. S. Centaur close under the lee of the Rock, put kedges out to sea, and ran lines to the shore. Fortunately, calm weather aided the Admiral in his operations and he was able to hoist three long 24s and two 18s to the top of the Rock where hasty fortifications were built. Here Lieutenant Maurice, with one hundred and twenty men, harassed the French fleet.

The Rock was named H. M. S. Diamond Rock and for sixteen months this stationary man–of–war held out against the French, who had two 74s, a corvette, a schooner, and eleven gunboats. Lack of food finally caused these gallant men to surrender and so great was the admiration of the French governor, the Marquise de Bouillé, that he treated them as his guests at Fort Royal (Fort de France), till the proper exchanges could be made. By a strange coincidence, this same Maurice, who had become a captain, in 1811 captured the island of Anholt and successfully held it against the Danes.

ALONE IN THE CARIBBEAN

While I have been yarning to you about Diamond Rock, I have also partaken of my frugal sea-luncheon of coconut, pilot bread, and chocolate. I believe, just to make up for the nastiness of the weather, I raided my larder under the cockpit floor to the extent of a small can of potted meat, and I remember saving the empty tin till I was well in shore, for I did not care to excite the curiosity of a chance shark that might be passing by.

The squall was a mixture of wind and spiteful rain and I thought of the Yakaboo as akin to the chimney sweep's donkey in "Water Babies." For an hour it blew hard and then let up as quickly as it had come, the sea subsiding as if by magic. I found that we were well oft shore nearly due west of Cape Solomon, four miles from the point where the squall had picked me up. Shaping our course past the cape, we soon ran into the calm of the picturesque bay of Fort de France.

Tucked well back from the sea, on the northern shore of the bay, lay the capital of the island. The afternoon was in its decline and the level rays of the sun striking into the low rain clouds that hung over the land threw a golden light on the town and hills, making it a yellow-skied picture by an old Dutch master. The effect of days gone by was heightened by the presence of a large square-rigger that lay in the anchorage with her sails brailed up to dry after the rain. No steamer was there to mar the illusion —the picture was not modern.

As I rowed closer to the town I turned from time to time to see what changes were going on behind my back. On a bluff close aboard were the pretty homes of a villa quarter and over one the tricolor of France proclaimed the governor's house. Beyond was a row of warehouses fronting the sea and beyond these, as though behind a bulwark, rose the cathedral steeple. At the far end of the row of warehouses a long landing jetty ran out at right angles to the water front. Still farther to the eastward Fort St. Louis lay out into the harbor jealously guarding the carénage behind it. At the water's edge and not far from the shore end of the jetty was a building with the revenue flag over it and for this I shaped my course.

As I neared the government landing the harbormaster's boat came out with its dusky crew of douanes (customs officers), wearing blue and white-banded jerseys and the French helmet of the tropics, with its brim drooped in back to protect the nape of the neck. I passed my papers to them and started to follow. The man in the stern, who now held my expensive bill of health, waved me back. "Jettez votre ancre!"

ALONE IN THE CARIBBEAN

I answered that I carried no anchor and they pulled away as from a pest.

"Restez la!" he yelled, pointing indefinitely out into the middle of the bay. The crew landed their officer and then rowed out again, placing themselves between me and the shore. Half an hour passed ; I could see the people of the town trickle down through the streets and gather along the water front. Then I began to notice that there was something wrong with the Yakaboo. She was tired and woman–like she gave way —not to tears, but the reverse. She leaked. She had had a hard day of it and wanted to sit down somewhere ; the bottom of the harbor being the nearest place, she started for that. A seam must have opened on the run across and I had to bail.

But what on earth were those fellows doing with my bill of health and why on earth did they not allow me to come ashore? Between spells of bailing I took up my oars and started to circumnavigate the douanes, but they were inshore of me and had the advantage. The sun sank lower and the crowd along shore became denser. Finally it dawned upon me. My expensive bill of health was dated the day before and the customs officers were trying to guess what I had been doing the day before and where I had been the previous night. Why they did not ask me directly I do not know, and what they actually thought and said to each other I never heard. That they took me for some sort of spy I am certain.

Two weeks in quarantine began to loom up as a vivid possibility. I then remembered that "Monty" at Kingstown had given me a letter to his brother–in–law, a merchant by the name of Richaud, who lived in Fort de France. The next move was to get the letter to Richaud —he might be standing in that crowd on the jetty. So I took the letter out of my portfolio and put it in my pocket where it would be handy. Then I gave the Yakaboo a final sponge–out and started to pull at a smart pace away from the jetty. The crew in the harbormaster's boat swallowed the bait and quickly headed me off.

In a flash I yanked the canoe about and rowed for the jetty, under full steam, at the same time yelling over my shoulder for Monsieur Richaud. Luck was with me. There was a movement in the crowd and a little man was pushed to the outer edge like the stone out of a prune. In a jiffy I was alongside and the letter was in his hands. The baffled douanes, who had turned by this time and were after me full tilt, nosed me away from the jetty, while I lay oft, softly whistling "Yankee Doodle." This seemed to take with the crowd and they applauded. They were not in sympathy with douanes —few West Indians are, for they are all fond of smuggling.

Whether it was Monty's letter backed by the pull of Monsieur Richaud, who seemed to be a man of some importance, or whether the officials decided to call it a day and to go home, I don't know, but I was at last beckoned to come ashore and just in time, for the Yakaboo sank with a gurgle of relief in the soft ooze on the beach. Before I knew what was going on, my whole outfit was bundled into the customs office to undergo the inspection of the officials. Even the canoe was bailed out and carried into the barracks, where she rested on the floor by the side of a gunrack filled with cumbersome St. Étienne rifles. There being no Bible handy I placed my hand on the next most holy thing, the bosom of my shirt, and swore that after this I would cruise in seas more homogeneous as to the nationality of their islands. While this silent ceremony was going on, the douanes looked at me in an awed way and one of them muttered "Fou" (crazy). He was probably right.

But Monsieur Richaud was there and he introduced himself to me. He had been expecting me for some time, he said, and I explained as best I could —it was mental agony to try to recall from a musty memory words that I had not used for ten years or more —that I had spent some time with the Caribs in Saint Vincent and some time in Saint Lucia, since I had left "Monty." Monsieur was a little, jolly round–faced Frenchman with the prosperous air of a business man of some consequence. He was reputed to be one of the rich men of Fort de France. Would I bestow upon him the honor of dining with him at his house? I would bestow that honor. We said "au revoir" to the douanes and stepped out into the street.

CHAPTER VIII. MARTINIQUE —FORT DE FRANCE.

IT WAS DARK and it was raining. My clothes were already wet and I sloshed along the narrow sidewalks behind the little man like a dripping Newfoundland dog. His wife was ill, he said, but he wished to at least give me a dinner, a change of clothes and then find me a lodging place. I had become so used to wet clothing that I forgot to bring my dry duds. I could see little of the town as we walked along the dark streets, but the impression was that of a small city —larger than any I had yet seen in these islands. At our elbows was a monotonous unbroken wall of house fronts with closed doors and jalousied windows, which occasionally gave a faint gleam of light. Presently my friend stopped in front of one of the doors and pushed it in. We stepped into a sort of wide corridor at the farther end of which was another door through which we passed into my friend's house. The house in reality had two fronts, one on the street and this which faced on a sort of patio which separated it from the kitchen and servants' quarters. I made this hasty survey as the master gave some orders in patois to a large negress, whose attention was fixed on my bedraggled figure, which gave the impression of having but lately been fished out of the sea.

First of all there was that enjoyable little liquid ceremony, "a votre santé," in which I rose in the estimation of mine host upon denying allegiance to "wisky soda." This should be further proof that I was no English spy at least. Then I was led upstairs to the guest room which Monsieur was now occupying. Monsieur was short and beamy, while my build was of the reverse order, and the result of the change of dry clothes which I put on was ludicrous —but I was dry and comfortable, which was the main thing. It was pleasant to know that I could now sit down in a comfortable chair without leaving a lasting salt stain behind me, pink-dyed from the color which was continually running from the lining of my coat. What little dignity to which I may lay claim, took wing at the sight of a foot of brown paw and forearm dangling from the sleeve of the coat. In like manner the trousers withdrew to a discreet distance from my feet and hung in desperate puckers around my middle.

Thus arrayed I was ushered into the presence of Madame Richaud, who lay recovering from an attack of fever in an immense four-poster. I paid my respects, assured her of the good health and well-being of her brother, and bowing with as much grace as possible, I followed my host to the drawing room.

The door through which we had passed from the street to the house of Monsieur Richaud was what one might call a general utility door, used by the master of the house on all ordinary occasions and by the servants and tradespeople. This door, as I have said, opened into a sort of corridor or antechamber through which one had to pass before gaining access to the house proper. There was, however, another street door, which opened from the sidewalk directly into the parlor or living room, where I now sat with my friend. This gives an uncomfortable feeling of intimacy with the street —in a step one moves from the living room to the sidewalk. It made me think of one of the smaller canals of Venice, where I had seen an urchin dive from a front window into the street. On either side of this door were two windows, lacking glass, with jalousies between the interstices of which I could now and then see the whites of peeking eyes.

It is in the nature of these people to be fond of street life and during my stay in Fort de France I noticed that the little balconies, with long French windows opening upon them, which projected from the second stories, were occupied most of the time. The aspect of the glaring white and yellow houses, monotonous as the sheer walls of the Wallibu Dry River, could never be so pleasing as the green courtyards in the rear, viewed from large airy galleries. It was just the drift of the street, a casual word now and then and a few exchanges with neighbors similarly occupied.

As we talked, the thought came to me that there was at least one advantage to this parlor street door —it was handy for funerals. Strange to say, I saw such a room put to just this use the very next day. The corpse was laid in state in the parlor and the doors were wide open so that any one, who wished, might enter in and look. There is, of course, some degree of common sense in this, for the rest of the house being practically cut off, the family need not be disturbed by the entrance of numerous friends, some of whom may not alone be satisfied in viewing the corpse, but take a morbid delight in viewing the grief of others.

But mall this had little to do with the dinner which was announced from the door of the adjoining dining room. Monsieur Richaud's two children, a boy and a girl in that nondescript age which precedes the bachfisch, now put in their appearance, the girl proudly taking the place of her mother at the head of the table. The dinner was excellent, but what I ate I did not remember even long enough to write in my note–book the next day, for while I was mechanically eating a soup that was delicious, I could give no specific thought to it, but must concentrate my entire attention to fetching up those few French words which were resting in the misty depths of my mind as in the muddy bottom of a well. Having "dove up" those words, I used them in a conversation which, while it was understood by Monsieur Richaud, afforded considerable amusement to the children. But the little Frenchman fared no better. Wishing to impress me with his familiarity with the English language he described the beauties of the northern coast of Martinique. He came to a fitting climax when he told of a river —"w'ich arrive at zee sea by casharettes."

ALONE IN THE CARIBBEAN

When the substantial part of the meal was over, a wash basin, soap and towel were passed around —satisfactory if not aesthetic —the three articles reminding me of their relations on the back stoop of a western farmhouse. After this, the fruit, which in this case was mango. I will not repeat the ponderous witticism regarding the mango and the bathtub. I have often speculated on this joke, however, and have almost come to the conclusion that it was invented first and the fruit discovered afterward. I can imagine Captain Cook suddenly starting up and slapping his thigh. "What ho!" he shouts, "I have thought up a most excellent joke, but I must find a fruit to fit it." And so he sets forth, discovers the mango and circumnavigates the globe.

However, we ate mangoes and our fingers became messy. As I was looking for some place to rest my hands where they would do the least damage to table linen, the negress, who had been serving us, brought in four plates with large finger bowls on them. There was tepid water in the bowls and by their sides were small beakers about the size of bird-baths. First we took up the beakers, filled them with water from the bowls and set them aside. Then we washed our finger tips in the bowls and finally dipped them in the clean water in the beakers and wiped our lips, an aesthetic proceeding which averaged the use of the wash basin and the soap. This rite concluded, the beaker was upset in the bowl —a signal that the dinner was over.

Thus dried, fed and doubly cleansed, my sum of content lacked only tobacco and a bed. They raise their own tobacco in Martinique —Tabac de Martinique —and that it is pure is where praise halts and turns her back. As for strength —I called it Tabac de Diable. I have shaved the festive plug and smoked the black twist that resembled a smoked herring from the time of the Salem witches, but these are as corn silk to the Tabac de Martinique. I had finished my supply of tobacco from home and now, forced to use the weed of Martinique, I "learned to love it." There was nothing else to do. It reminded me of the tenderfoot who leaned up against a white pine bar in the Far West and asked for a mint julep —"Well frappéd." As the barkeeper produced a tumbler and a bottle he said, "You'll have three fingers of this bug juice and YOU'LL LOVE IT."

But the Tabac de Diable served me a good turn. Half a year later, in the cozy tap room of the Fitzwilliam Tavern, I incautiously left a partly smoked cigar within the reach of a practical joker, who, taking advantage of my preoccupation in a book, watched the cigar go out and then with the aid of a pin inserted a piece of elastic band into the end of the cigar. I did not notice the anticipation of a bit of fun on the faces of the men who had come from an uninteresting game of bridge in another room. I relit the cigar and resumed the smoking of it, still deeply engrossed in my book. I remembered later that one by one the jokers had left the room with silent tread as if in the presence of the dead. For once I was alone in the room and I had the fireplace to myself. I finished the cigar and threw the stump into the fire. It was the Tabac de Diable that had inoculated me and for some time after I left Martinique I found that I could smoke almost anything that was at all porous and would burn if an indraft was applied to it. But I did not enjoy it that first time when Monsieur Richaud handed me a Martinique cigar.

There now remained the last want —a bed —and my friend guessed this for I nearly fell asleep over his cigar.

He led me out into the deserted streets lighted by a faint starlight and still shining from the rain which had let up. We turned into one of the main thoroughfares at the end of which blazed an electric light, yellow, like the moon rising through a mist. Here flourished the "Grand Hôtel de l'Eurôpe," a name, I believe, as legion as Smith. I fully expect, after crossing my last channel, the Styx, to find a sign on the other shore thus —"Grand Hôtel de l'Eurôpe —Coolest Spot in Hades —Asbestos Linen —Sight Seeing Auto Hell/speed leaves at 10 A.M. —Choice New Consignment of Magnates seen at Hard Labor."

My tired senses made scant note of the marble–floored room, the click of the billiard balls, and the questioning glances of the wasp–betrousered French officers, and I bade good night to my host, who had vouched for my harmlessness and left me in charge of the clerk.

The kaleidoscope day came to an end as I crawled under the mosquito bar of an immense four–poster, in a room on the premièr étage, and dove between the sheets with a grunt of satisfaction.

At first I thought it was the love song of a mosquito, but as I began to awaken the sound resolved itself into the thin blare of a trumpet–call and I wondered where I was. My eyes, directed at the ceiling when I opened them, caught the rays of the morning sun, sifted through the jalousies and striking the gauze canopy over me in bands of moted light. The trumpet sounded again —this time almost under my window —and stretching out of bed like a snail from its shell, I peeked through the vanes of the jalousie and saw a company of soldiers returning from their morning drill. There was a delicious novelty about it all that made me feel absolutely carefree, and, as I thought of the Yakaboo and her precious outfit, I hoped that they, as well as I, had rested in the customs station with its antiquated St. Étienne rifles for company. I hoped that there had been no quarrel between my Austrian gun and the Frenchmen and that my little British rifle had not flaunted the Union Jack in their faces. I was in that coma of carelessness when if an earthquake had come to crush out my life with the falling of the ponderous walls about me, I would have reproved it with the dying words, "Oh, pshaw, why didn't you wait till I had finished my cruise?" This feeling is worth traveling to the ends of the earth to experience.

A knock on the door brought forth a hasty "Entrez" as I slid back between the sheets. An aged negress brought in a small pot of coffee and a pitcher of hot milk which I found to my horror would have to stay my hunger until the hour of déjeuner at eleven.

Later, another knock ushered in my clothes from Monsieur Richaud, already washed and dried. My precious shirt looked like a miserable piece of bunting after a rainy Fourth of July, faded and color–run. I dressed and sallied forth to investigate the town.

Fort de France was as new and strange to me as St. George's had been and far more interesting. An impending week of rainy weather decided for me and I made up my mind to spend that week here. Until I was ready to put to sea again and sail for Dominica I could not take my outfit away from the customs office. Camping along shore, then, was out of the question. There was no alternative for me than to become for the time a part of the life of the town. Curiously enough, I find that one passes through various phases during the first few days in a new town or country. At first there is the novelty of the place which appeals to one. This is followed by a period of restlessness —the first blush of novelty has worn off and one comes almost to the point of hating the place. It is like the European tourist who rushes upon a town, gorges himself with what pictures and sights are easily accessible and then in a fit of surfeit hates the thought of the rich optical food before him. But then comes the third stage, which lasts indefinitely, when the spirit of the town makes itself felt and one begins to see through the thin veneer of first impressions and to make friends. Those first impressions —unless they are very striking —vanish little by little till one comes to regard the place more or less with the eyes of the native. After all, this whole process is both natural and human. It is during the last stage (granting always that the town or country has any interest for one at all) that the residence in all out of the way places is brought about of stray Englishmen, Scotchmen, Irishmen and in more recent years Americans. One commonly hears the admission, "I didn't care for the place at all at first but somehow I became fond of it and here I am —let's see, it's blank years now."

My first care was for my outfit which I was allowed to overhaul and put in order in the barracks room. My portfolio and camera I could take with me to the hotel, but the latter was of no use for my films became fogged from the excessive moisture of a rainy week and when I did try to make an exposure it was only of some conventional subject. I could not wander at random from the confines of the town nor edge near the picturesque carénage in back of Fort St. Louis where there is an important coaling station and repair shop without being shadowed by some private apparently detailed for the purpose. While overhauling my outfit I could see that every bag had been carefully searched —nothing, of course, was missing. Through some sort of feigned misunderstanding I was unable to get back my expensive bill of health —perhaps they thought I might alter the date and use it in Guadeloupe (above Dominica), the next French island. I had hoped to bluff the harbor—master at Dominica, but with my French bill of health gone, I could not do otherwise than obtain a new paper for Dominica —the officials saw to that —and it was just as well in the end for I met with the same officiousness that greeted Captain Slocum when I arrived at Roseau.

It had been raining and the deep, old—world gutters were full, miniature canals in which the broken shell of a coconut might be seen sailing down to the sea like the egg shell of Hans Christian Andersen. Apparently most of the refuse of the town is carried off in these gutters. But the canal gutters serve another purpose —they wash the feet of the country people. One sees a woman whose muddy or dusty feet proclaim her to be from the country, walking into town with a monstrous burden on her head. She will suddenly stop on the edge of the sidewalk and balance on one foot while she carefully lowers the other into the running water of the gutter. She may at the same time be passing the time o' day with some approaching acquaintance half a block away. Their conversation seems to have a universal focus for any distance under a quarter of a mile —the intensity is the same for three feet or a block.

Having washed her right foot with the nonchalance of a tightrope walker, she goes on her way till she makes such a turning as will bring her left foot alongside the gutter, and she proceeds as before.

ALONE IN THE CARIBBEAN

It was usually in the afternoon that I saw that most picturesque sang mêle, the creole of Martinique, unaffected by the so-called advance of civilization, wearing the dress of watered silk and the heavy gold ornaments, with just that faint trace of interesting barbarity that goes with the generous features, the wide-spread eyes and the blue-black hair. She is a reminder of creole days of French Louisiana —the coarser progenitor of our so-called "creole." I could see that most of these women were married, by the sign of the madras qualandi which is in reality a silk bandana tied on the head turban-wise, one corner knotted and stuck upright above the forehead like a feather. The unmarried women wear the madras in the usual manner, that is, without the knotted corner upright.

That these women are beautiful there is no denying ; the skin though it may be dark is very clear and the eyes give a frank open expression and by reason of their position seem to diminish what African coarseness may have been left in the nose. The nose may be flattish and a bit heavy but the broad, even high forehead, wide-spread eyes and perfect teeth counteract this effect so that it is hardly noticeable. One finds these people a delightful contrast to the rawboned creole of the English colonies with her male-like figure and eccentricities of hair, nose, lips, hands and feet.

There was a refreshing spirit of enterprise —we get the word from the French —and of varied interests that were a relief after having seen the "live and bear it" spirit of the English islands. The people of Martinique are industrious and they are happy —the one naturally follows the other. In the market I found nearly all the vegetables of the temperate climate besides those of the tropics. They are now extensively growing the vanilla bean and the Liberian coffee is excellent. The wines which they import from France are inexpensive. In drinking the claret they dilute it with water which is the French custom and is as it should be. One might live very comfortably in Fort de France. There were electric lights and book stores where one could buy the current French magazines —illustrated, humorous and naughty. I bought several. There was just one step in their enterprise which I did not appreciate and that was the cultivating of home-grown tobacco —Tabac de Diable.

My walks about town were for the most part sallies from the hotel during intermissions between showers, for it rained almost continually for the entire week. These sallies I alternated with periods of writing in the quiet little cabaret where an occasional acquaintance would sit down for a chat, my French taking courage from day to day like an incipient moustache. I usually occupied a marble-topped table under an open window by which bobbed the heads of passersby.

What front the Hôtel de l'Eurôpe boasts, faces toward the savanna in the middle of which stands the statue of the Empress Josephine. Here she stands, guarded by a high iron fence and surrounded by seven tall palms, their tops, towering to a lofty coronet, above her head, seemed to claim her after all as a child of the West Indies. She is looking pensively across the bay towards Trois Îlets where she may or may not have been born and where so many sentimental steamer–deck authorities on the West Indies may or may not have made pilgrimages to the parish church and perhaps to the ruins of the La Pagerie estate. That she spent a considerable part of her West Indian days in Saint Lucia there can be no doubt and I will say for the benefit of the steamer–deck authorities that there is a very strong likelihood that she was born in that island. Was it some ironical whim that tempted the sculptor to impart a wistfulness in her face which seemed to carry her thoughts far beyond Trois Îlets and across the channel to the little plantation on the Morne Paix–Bouche and perhaps still farther, along that half mythical chemin de la Longue Chasse, which I discovered some time later on an old map of Saint Lucia, leading from the Dauphin quarter down to Souffrière? I have often wondered whether it was mere chance that impelled the sculptor to express that sign of parturient womanhood for which Napoleon longed and the lack of which caused one of the most pathetic partings in history.

One morning I was honored by a call from the clerk of the hotel. A delegation from the Union Sportive Martiniquaise et Touring Club Antillais wished to wait upon me at four o'clock in the afternoon —would I receive them? At four, then, while I was sitting at my table in the cabaret, the delegation of four came, headed by a fiery little man of dark hue —but a thorough Frenchman. His name was Waddy and I came to like him very much. The committee was very much embarrassed as a whole and individually like timid schoolgirls, but if they blushed it was like the desert violet —unseen.

Would I do them the honor to be entertained for the rest of the afternoon? I said that I should be delighted —and felt like a cheap edition of Dr. Cook. Waddy explained to me that the club was very much interested in my cruise and that it was their intention to become familiar with the other islands of the Antilles. The members of the club were for the most part eager to visit the neighboring islands but they were too timid to trust themselves to anything smaller than a steamer and while there was more or less frequent communication by steamer with Europe there was no inter–island service except by

118

sloop. My coming in a canoe had set them a wonderful example, he told me.

We then walked to the jetty and were rowed out into the harbor to visit a West Indian schooner of the type that sailed from Martinique to Cayenne and upon which Waddy hoped the Club as a whole could some day be induced to cruise. She was an old Gloucester fisherman of about eighty tons and perfectly safe (I assured Waddy) for the use of the Touring Club Antillais. Having surveyed the schooner we were rowed ashore where a carriage awaited us. We then drove by a circuitous route, carefully planned out beforehand to include the various sights of note in the town, to the rented house in the Rue Amiral de Gueydon where the Union Sportive Martiniquaise et Touring Club Antillais thrived.

I was escorted to a room on the upper floor where the Union Sportive Martiniquaise et Touring Club was already gathered. To my intense embarrassment, the President of the Union Sportive Martiniquaise et Touring proceeded to read off a long speech from a paper in his hand. What he said I managed to understand for the most part but it concerns us little here. I replied to the members of the Union Sportive Martiniquaise to the best of my ability —in French —and what I said I know but they did not understand —neither does that concern us in this writing. After a pleasant stramash of verbal bouquets we were served with refreshments which consisted of champagne and lady fingers. Champagne is not a rare beverage in the French islands, but I did not imagine that I should see it used with the familiarity with which the German treats his morning coffee ; I mean the habit of dipping his toast in it. But dipping seemed the custom and into the champagne went the lady fingers of the Union Sportive, and mine. To me these people were warmhearted and impulsive and as I got to know them, thoroughly likable.

According to my almanac, it was Easter Sunday and I almost felt ashamed of my morning cigarette as I left the hotel for a little stroll before I should sit down to my notes at the marble—topped table. But somehow or other I thought I must be mistaken in the day. While there were few people on the streets, to be sure, all the small shops were open. I walked over to the covered market and to my surprise I found that open also but most of the business had already been transacted. But the large stores, emporiums and magasins as they were called, were closed. Then I passed a church and saw that it was packed. Another church was packed. The priests were doing a thriving business and I realized that perhaps after all it was Easter Sunday. I did not know that with the ending of Lent the people were having a last injection of the antitoxin of religion to inoculate themselves from the influence of Satan which was sure to follow on Monday. And it was on account of Monday that the small shops and the market were open, for everybody went to the country for the Easter holidays, that is everybody who was anybody, and they left the town to the proletariat. Those who were fortunate enough to be able to spend the week in the country must need get their last fresh supplies at the market and the little necessities such as sweets, tobacco and so on which were apt to be forgotten in the press of Saturday could yet be bought on the way home from church.

The next morning I found that the market was not open and that all the shops were closed. So were the houses for that matter —everybody had made an early departure, the devil was having his due and the town was left to the rest. Various members of the Union Sportive played soccer football beneath the unheeding eyes of the Empress, in costumes that would have brought a smile to those marble lips, I believe, could she have looked down at them. With utter disregard for the likes or dislikes of one color for another these members of the Union Sportive wore jerseys of banded red, green and purple and with an equal disregard for the fierce tropical heat, they raced over the savanna, most of them with knickerbockers but some with trousers, brailed up, if one might use the seagoing term. But all the trousers did not calmly submit to this seagoing treatment and generally slipped down as to the left leg. (After some consideration I have come to the conclusion that this phenomenon was on account of the left leg usually being smaller than the right ; hence the left trouser leg would be more prone to come down.) One would see an energetic member of the Union being carried rapidly after the ball by a pair of legs, one decorously covered and the other exposed in all its masculine shamelessness of pink underwear, livid "Y" of garter, violent hose of Ethiopian choice and shoe of generous dimension with long French toe, cutting arcs in advance and bootstrap waving bravely behind. Even to stand perfectly still in the shade of a tree to watch this performance was heating and I moved on.

The unearthly squeal of a flute brought me across the savanna to a shady grove where something was holding the attention of a large crowd. The flute, I found, was only one of four instruments held captive in a ring of prancing wooden horses that circled on an iron track like fish in a well. Each horse was mounted on an iron wheel with pedals and those who could afford the necessary five sous were allowed to circle for a time on this merry–go–round, in mad delight, the power coming from their own mahogany limbs which showed a like absence of stockings in both sexes. The riders wore shoes and the impression when they were in motion was that they also wore stockings but when the ride came to an end the illusion vanished. There was no central pivot, merely this bracelet of horses fastened to each other and kept from cavorting away over the savanna by the U–shaped track wherein ran the wheels under their bellies. It was a piece of engineering skill —the evident pride of the owner —and being machinery it must needs be oiled. For this purpose a boy wandered about in the confines of this equine circle with a long–spouted oilcan in his hand. The shrieking axles, while in motion, were guarded by the pumping legs of the riders and therefore could not be oiled ; there remained only one other part for lubrication and that was the track. So the boy very adroitly followed the wheel of some favorite steed with the nose of the oilcan. But, you ask, why not oil the axles at the end of the ride? Ah, but everybody is resting then, the horses and the orchestra ; besides the axles are no longer squeaking.

But let's have that delicious tidbit —the orchestra. After the flute–player, I name them in the order of their effective strength ; there was the man who played on the fiddle, which ages ago in these parts had slipped from its customary place under the chin to the hollow of the left shoulder. Then came the man who shook a gourd filled with small pebbles and the drummer who beat on a huge section of bamboo with two pieces of wood like chop sticks. These last two instruments were extremely effective, mainly because they were of African origin and played upon by African experts. They were artists of rhythm —a metronome could have done no better. In the hands of the drummer the bamboo echoed the jungle from the light patter of rain drops on palm fronds to the oncoming thunder–roll of an impending storm. From the complacent beating of time this master lashed himself into a fury as the orchestra periodically rose to a climax under the spur of the flute–player. But it was the gourd which held my eye longest. The hard surface of the gourd, a calabash about eighteen inches long, was banded with deep grooves across which the performer rubbed his thumbnail, producing a noise that reminded me of the dry grass of the prairies where the rattlesnake sounds his note of warning. For an instant the gourd would be poised above the head of the player to suddenly swoop, twirling and whistling, through a fathom of orbit to fetch up for a moment hugged in the curving form of its master where it gurgled and hissed under the tickle of a thumbnail of hideous power.

In the evening, after dinner, I would walk out across the savanna to the still waters of the carénage —I was living in such a civilized state that canoe cruise, whalers, and Caribs seemed to have slipped back into the remote haze of memory —where an aged steamer, clipper–stemmed and with a ship's counter, lay rusting at her mooring, her square ports and rail with gingerbread white—painted life—net, a delight to one who revels in a past that is just near enough to be intimate. From the carénage my walk would continue along the quay, past the barracks of the naval station across the street from which a tribe of cozy little cabarets blinked cheerfully into the night through open doors and windows.

Before long a quartet of French sailors, wearing Peter Thompson caps with red or blue fuzzy tassels set atop like butter—balls, would come singing up the street and swing into one or another of the cabarets as though drawn by some invisible current, the song being continued to its end.

If the singing were good —and it usually was —the little room would gradually fill, to the joy of the beaming landlord. The song finished, there would be refreshments and then one of the audience would get up and sing some catchy little Parisian tune and if there were sufficient talent among those present, the entertainment might last long after the goodwife had withdrawn with her knitting and her children and until the landlord himself had closed the shutters outside and was making furtive attempts to put his place in order. With the stroke of ten, the guests would pour out and the door would close behind them to cut off its rectangular beam of light and leave the street in darkness.

But this life in Fort de France was becoming too demoralizing and I should soon be too lazy to cook another meal. The rainy week was over and I bade adieu to the statue of Josephine, extracted my outfit from the jealous care of the douanes, and sailed for the ruined city of St. Pierre.

CHAPTER IX. ST. PIERRE —PELÉE.

DURING MY week of idleness I had found time to coax the Yakaboo into an amiable mood of tightness —not by the aid of cabarets, however, but with white lead and varnish and paint for which she seemed to have an insatiable thirst. I was always glad to be sailing again and, to show the fickleheartedness of the sailor, I had no sooner rounded

ALONE IN THE CARIBBEAN

Negro Point in a stiff breeze than Fort de France —now out of sight —took her place among other memories I had left behind.

The thread of my cruise was once more taken up and I was back into the canoe, enjoying the lee coast panorama with my folded chart in my lap for a guide book. It was early in the afternoon when I made out the little beacon on Sainte Marthe Point beyond which lay the roadstead of St. Pierre. A heavy, misty rain squall —a whisk of dirty lint —was rolling down the side of Pelée and I was wondering whether or no I should have to reef when something else drew my attention. Pulling out from a little fishing village beyond Carbet was a boatload of my old friends the douanes, a different lot, to be sure, but of the same species as those of Fort de France. They were evidently making desperate efforts to head me off and as long as they were inshore and to windward of me they had the advantage. Little by little I trimmed my sheets till I was sailing close–hauled.

There were eight or ten of the dusky fellows and they fetched their boat directly on my course and a hundred feet away. This was some more of their confounded nonsense and I decided to give them the slip. I motioned to them to head into the wind so that I might run alongside, and while they were swinging the bow of their heavy boat, I slipped by their stern, so close that I could have touched their rudder, eased off my sheets, and the Yakaboo, spinning on her belly, showed them as elusive a stern as they had ever tried to follow. It took them a few seconds to realize that they had been fooled and they then proceeded to straighten out their boat in my wake and follow in hot pursuit. They hoisted their sail but it only hindered their rowing, for the heeling of the boat put the port bank out of work altogether while the men to windward could scarcely reach the water with the blades of their oars. It would only be truthful to say that I laughed immoderately and applied my fingers to my nose in the same manner that midshipman Green saluted his superior officer.

I was soon lost to their sight in the squall which had now spread over the roadstead. Rain and mist were ushered along by a stiff breeze. Under this friendly cover I held on for a bit and then came about on the inshore tack, thinking that the douanes would little suspect that I would come ashore under their very noses. It was not a bad guess for I afterwards learned that they had sent word to the next station to the north to watch for me.

Although I could not see more than a hundred feet ahead of me, I knew by the floating pumice that I must be well into the roadstead of St. Pierre. I snatched up a piece out of the sea and put it in my pocket as a souvenir. Then we passed out of the mist as from a wall and I saw the ruins of St. Pierre before me, not a quarter of a mile away. A heavy mist on the morne above hung like a pall over the ruined city cutting it off from the country behind.

It was truly a city of the dead, the oily lifeless waters of the bay lapping at its broken edges and the mist holding it as in a frame, no land, no sky —just the broken walls of houses. The mist above me began to thin out and the vapors about the ruins rolled away till only those on the morne remained and the sun shining through arched a rainbow over St. Pierre, one end planted by the tumbled statue of Our Lady and the other in the bed of the Roxelane. It was like a promise of a better life to come, to those who had perished. At first glance, the extent of the ruins did not seem great, but as I ran closer to shore I saw that for a mile and a half to the northward broken walls were covered by an inundation of green foliage which had been steadily advancing for nearly ten years.

You may but vaguely recall the startling news that St. Pierre, a town hitherto but little known, on a West Indian island equally little known, was destroyed in one fiery gasp by a volcano which sprang to fame for having killed some twenty–five thousand people in the space of a minute or two.

For nearly a month the volcano had been grumbling, but who could suspect that from a crater nearly five miles away a destruction should come so swift that no one could escape to tell the tale? When I was in Fort de France, I found a copy of Les Colonaries, of Wednesday, May the 7th, 1902, the day before the explosion of Pelée. Under the heading, "Une Interview de M. Landes," it says : —"M. Landes, the distinguished professor of the Lyceum, very willingly allowed us to interview him yesterday in regard to the volcanic eruption of Mount Pelée . . . Vesuvius, adds M. Landes, only had rare victims (this is a literal translation). Pompeii was evacuated in time and they have found but few bodies in the buried cities. Mount Pelée does not offer more danger to the inhabitants of St. Pierre than Vesuvius to those of Naples."

The next morning, a few minutes before eight o'clock, that awful holocaust occurred, a bare description of which we get from the survivors of the Roddam, the only vessel to escape of sixteen that were lying in the roadstead. Even the Roddam which had steam up and backed out, leaving her ground tackle behind, paid her toll and when she limped into Fort de France two hours later, a phantom ship, her decks were covered with ashes still hot and her woodwork was still smoking from the fire.

The story of the survivors was quickly told. The volcano had been rumbling, according to its custom of late, when about a quarter before eight there was an explosion in which the whole top of the mountain seemed blown away. A thick black cloud rose up and from under it a sheet of flame rolled down the mountainside, across the city, and out over the roadstead. There had been barely time to give the signal to go astern and the few passengers of ready wit had hardly covered their heads with blankets when the ship was momentarily engulfed in flame. It was all over in a few seconds and those who had not been caught on deck or in their cabins with their ports open, came up to the blistering deck to behold the city which they had looked at carelessly enough a few minutes before, now a burning mass of ruins.

Fortunately some one had been near the capstan and had tripped the pawls so that the chain had run out freely. Otherwise the Roddam would have met the fate of the cable ship Grappler and the Roraima and the sailing vessels that were unable to leave their moorings. After she had backed out, the Roddam steamed into the roadstead again and followed the shore to discover, if possible, some sign of life. But the heat from the smoldering city was so great that there could be no hope of finding a living being there. The steamer then turned southward to seek aid for her own dying victims.

It was the suddenness of the catastrophe that made it the more awful. One man whom I met in Fort de France told me that he was talking at the telephone to a friend in St. Pierre when the conversation was interrupted by a shriek followed by a silence which brought no answer to his question. Rushing from his office, he found others who had had the same experience. There was no word to be had from St. Pierre and the noise of the explosion which came from over the hills confirmed the fear that some terrible disaster had befallen the sister city. It was not until the Roddam steamed into port that the people of Fort de France learned just what had happened.?

? Native canoe—St. Lucia. ?

I have said that there was no survivor of St. Pierre to tell the tale thereof, but I may be in error. They tell a fanciful tale of a lone prisoner who was rescued from a cell, deep down in the ground, some days after the first explosion and before subsequent explosions destroyed even this retreat. His name is variously given as Auguste Ciparis and Joseph

125

ALONE IN THE CARIBBEAN

Surtout, and in a magazine story "full of human interest and passion," which could not have been written by the man himself, as Ludger Sylbaris. I was told in confidence, however, by a reputable citizen of Fort de France, that the story was in all probability gotten up for the benefit of our yellow journals.

Reviewing these things in my mind, I ran alongside the new jetty built since the eruption and hauled up the Yakaboo under the roofing that covers the shore end. There were about ten people there, nearly the entire population of what was once a city of forty thousand.

These people, I found, lived in a few rooms reconstructed among the ruins, not with any hope of rebuilding but because at this point there is a natural outlet for the produce of the rich valleys behind St. Pierre which is sent in droghers to Fort de France. Among them I found a guide, a huge Martinique saccatra, who knew Pelée well, he said, and we arranged to make the ascent in the morning.

I have always been fond of moonlight walks in strange places and as I cooked my supper I said to myself, "That is how I shall first see the dead city —by moonlight." As I struck in from the jetty I knew that no negro dared venture forth in such a place at night and that I was alone in a stillness made all the more desolate by the regular boom of the surf followed by the rumble as it rolled back over the massive pavement of the water front. There was no human sound and yet I felt the ghost of it as I heard the noise of the sea and knew that same sound had mingled for over a century with the sounds of the cafés of the Rue Victor Hugo where I was now walking, and had been a roar of second nature to the ears of the thousands who had lived in the cubes of space before my eyes, now unconfined by the walls and roofs which had made them rooms.

The moon rode high, giving a ghostly daylight by which I could distinguish the smallest objects with startling ease. The streets were nearly all of them cleared, the rubbish having been thrown back over the walls that stood only breast high. Here and there a doorway would be partly cleared so that I could step into the first floor of a house and then mounting the debris, travel like a nocturnal chamois from pile to pile, and from house to house. There was not the slightest sign of even a splinter of wood. A marble floor, a bit of colored wall, the sign of a café painted over a doorway and the narrow sidewalks reminded me of Pompeii and had there been the familiar chariot ruts in the roadways the illusion would have been complete. There was a kinship between the two ; they had alike been wicked cities and it seemed that the wrath of God had descended upon them through

126

the agency of a natural phenomenon which had hung over them and to which they had paid no heed.

I wondered how many of the dead were under these piles of debris. At one place I came to a spot where some native had been digging tiles from a fallen roof. There was a neat pile of whole tiles ready to be taken away while scattered about were the broken pieces which would be of no use. Where the spade had last struck protruded the cranium of one of the victims of that fateful May morning.

I picked my way to the cimitière where I loafed in the high noon of the moon which cast short shadows that hugged the bases of the tombs and gravestones. There was a feeling of comfort in that moonlight loaf in the cimitière of St. Pierre and had I thought of it in time I might have brought my blankets and slept there. In comparison with the ruined town about it, there was the very opposite feeling to the spookiness which one is supposed to have in a graveyard.

I sat on the steps of an imposing mausoleum and loaded my pipe with the Tabac de Martinique which I smoked in blissful reverie. Here would I be disturbed by no mortal soul and as for the dead about and beneath me were they not the legitimate inhabitants of this place? Those poor fellows over whom I had unwittingly scrambled might have some reason to haunt the places of their demise, but these of the cimitière had no call to play pranks on a visitor who chanced in of a moonlight night. I was not in a joking mood —neither did I feel serious.

A sort of moon dreaminess came over me —I felt detached. I saw my form hunched against the face of the mausoleum with my long legs stretched out before it, but it did not seem to be I. I was a sort of spirit floating in the air about and wondering what the real life of the dead city before me had been. I should have liked to have the company of the one whose bones rested (comfortably, I hoped) in the tomb behind me and to have questioned him about the St. Pierre that he had known. But I could only romance to myself.

The mere bringing down of my pipe from my mouth so that my glance happened to fall on its faithful outline with its modest silver band with my mark on it brought me to myself. The pipe seemed more a part of my person than my hands and knees and I knew that I was merely living through an incident of a canoe cruise. I sat there and smoked and

127

idled till the moon began to shimmer the sea before me and with her light in my face I found my way back to the jetty and the Yakaboo.

I was awakened at five by my guide who had with him a young boy. It was always a case of Greek against Greek with these fellows and I reiterated our contract of the night before. His first price was exorbitant and I had beaten him down as far as I dared —to fifteen francs. I find that it is a mistake to pull the native down too far for he is apt to feel that you have taken advantage of him and will become sullen and grudging in his efforts.

While I ate my scanty breakfast I impressed upon him the fact that I was paying for his services only and that if the boy wished to follow that was his affair. He prided himself on a very sparse knowledge of English which he insisted upon using. When I had finished he turned to his boy and said, "E —eh? il est bon garçon!" To which I replied, "Mais oui!" which means a lot in Martinique. The boy came with us and proved to be a blessing later on.

The moon had long since gone and we started along the canal–like Rue Victor Hugo with the pale dawn dimming the stars over us one by one. We crossed the Roxelane on the bridge, which is still intact, and then descended a flight of steps between broken walls to the beach and left the town behind us. Another mile brought us to the Sêche (dry) Rivière just as the rose of dawn shot through the notches of the mountains to windward. When we came to the Blanche Rivière, along the bed of which we began the ascent of the volcano as in Saint Vincent, the sun stood up boldly from the mountain tops and gave promise of a terrific heat which I hoped would burn up the mist that had been hanging over the crater of Pelée ever since I had come to Martinique. I did not then know of the prophetic line which I discovered later under an old outline of Martinique from John Barbot's account of the voyage of Columbus —"the Mount Pelée in a mist and always so."

Were I to go into the detail of our ascent of Pelée you would find it a monotonous repetition for the most part of the Souffrière climb. Pelée was a higher mountain and the climb was harder. There was scarcely any vegetation even on the lower slopes, much to my relief, for Martinique is the home of the fer–de–lance. I had with me a little tube of white crystals which I could inject into my abdomen in case I were bitten by one of these fellows but I cannot say that even for the novelty of using it did I relish having my body a battle ground for the myriad agents of Pasteur against the poison of one of these vipers.

ALONE IN THE CARIBBEAN

The sun did not burn up the mist and at a height of 3600 feet we entered the chilly fog, leaving our food and camera behind us. The remaining eight hundred feet made up the most arduous climbing I have ever experienced. We were now going up the steep sides of the crater cone made of volcanic dust, slippery from a constant contact with mist and covered with a hairlike moss, like the slime that grows on rocks in the sea near human habitations. I took to falling down so many times that it finally dawned upon me that I would do much better if I crawled and in this way I finished the last four hundred feet. At times I dug my toes well into the side of the crater and rested half–lying, half–standing, my body at an angle of forty–five degrees.

Although I could scarcely see three yards ahead of me there was no need of the guides to show the way there was only one way and that was up. The negroes were a little ahead of me and I remember admiring the work of their great toes which they stuck into the side of the mountain as a wireman jabs his spikes into a telegraph pole. When I had entered the cloud cap I had come out of the hot sun dripping with perspiration and I put on my leather jacket to prevent the direct contact of the chilly mist upon my body. I was chilled to the bone and could not have been wetter. I could feel the sweat of my exertions streaming down under my shirt and could see the moisture of the condensed mist trickling down the outside of my coat. No film would have lived through this.

As an intermittent accompaniment to the grunts of the negroes I could hear the chatter of their teeth. Suddenly they gave a shout and looking upward I saw the edge of the rim a body length away. Another effort and I was lying beside them, the three of us panting like dogs, our heads hanging over the sulfurous pit. What was below was unknown to us —we could scarcely see ten feet down the inside of the crater, while around us swirled a chilly mist freezing the very strength out of us. A few minutes were enough and we slid down the side of the crater again to sunlight and food.

Looking up at Pelée from the streets of St. Pierre, one felt that surely no destruction from a crater so far off could reach the city before safety might be sought ; but as I sat upon the very slope of the crater I could easily imagine a burst of flaming gas that could roll down that mountainside and engulf the city below it in a minute or two of time.

It was half way down the mountain that the boy proved a blessing for we lost our way and suddenly found ourselves at the end of a butte whose precipitous sides fell a sheer five hundred feet in all directions around us, except that by which we had come. For an

129

hour we retraced our steps and cruised back and forth till at last the boy discovered a crevasse into which we lowered ourselves by means of the strong lianes which hung down the sides till we reached the bottom where we found a cool stream trickling through giant ferns. We lapped the delicious water like thirsty dogs. Again we were in the dry river bottom of the Blanche and we took to the beach for St. Pierre in the heat of the middle afternoon.

The climb had been a disappointment for I had particularly wished to find if there were any trace left of the immense monolith which had been forced above the edge of the crater at the time of the eruption and had subsided again. I also wanted a photograph of the crater which is less than a fourth the size of the Souffrière of Saint Vincent. But, as you may know, this is distinctly a part of the game and there is no need of casting glooms here and there over a cruise for the want of a picture or two.

So I forgot the photograph which I did not get of Pelée's crater and thought of the refreshing glass or two of that most excellent febrifuge "Quinquina des" which I might find at the little inn that had been erected over the ashes of its former self. This inn had been one of the meaner hotels of St. Pierre, close to the water front and facing the Rue Victor Hugo. When Pelée began to rumble, the proprietor had sent his wife and son to a place of safety, but he himself had remained, not that he did not fear the volcano but to guard his little all from the marauding that was sure to follow a more or less complete evacuation of the city. It had cost him his life and now the widow and her son were eking out an existence by supplying the wants of the few who chance to pass that way.

It was three o'clock in the afternoon when we reached the inn and it was still very hot. I stood for a few minutes, quite still, in the sun in order to cool off slowly and to dry my skin before I entered the grateful shade of the roof that partly overhung the road. In doing this I won great respect from my saccatra guide and the boy, both of whom did likewise, for they feared the effect of the exertions of the climb and the subsequent walk along the hot beach quite as much as I did.

It was here that I received my most forlorn impression of St. Pierre. The widow's son, a likable young fellow of about eighteen, had stepped out into the road to talk to me when a pathetic form in a colorless wrapper slunk from out the shadows of the walls and spoke to him. It was evidently me about whom she was curious, and he answered her questions in the patois which he knew I could not understand.

ALONE IN THE CARIBBEAN

She was a woman of perhaps forty, partly demented by the loss of her entire family and all her friends in the terrible calamity of nine years before. Her wandering eye bore the most hopeless expression I have ever seen and her grey, almost white hair, hung, uncombed for many a day, over her shoulders. Her feet were bare, she wore no hat and for all that I could see the faded wrapper was her only covering. Her questions answered, she stood regarding me silently for a moment and then passing one hand over the other palms upward so that the fingers slipped over each other, she said, "Il est fou —fou."

That night I read myself to sleep in the cockpit of the Yakaboo with my candle lamp hung over my head from the stumpy mizzen mast. But between the pages of the wanderings of Ulysses, which Whitfield Smith had given me at Carriacou, slunk the figure of the woman who had called me "crazy" —utterly forlorn. Remove the whole of Mount Pelée and you take away the northern end of Martinique whose shores from St. Pierre to the Lorain River describe an arc of 225° with the crater of the volcano for its center. When I left St. Pierre the next morning, then, I was in reality encircling the base of Pelée along 135° of that arc to Grande Rivière. There lived Monsieur Waddy of the Union Sportive who had made me promise that I would spend at least one night with him before I sailed for the next island.

"You can make the depart for Dominique from Grande Rivière," he told me. "I will keep a lookout for you." This would be entirely unnecessary, I told him. Could I get the canoe ashore all right? "Oh, yes! I shall watch for you." There was some reservation in that "Oh, yes !" For his own good reasons he did not tell me of the terrific surf that boomed continually on the beach where he lived —but it did not matter after all.

The trade in the guise of a land breeze lifted us out of the roadstead of St. Pierre and we soon doubled Point La Mare. A mile or so up the coast the white walls of Precheur gleamed in the morning sunlight. One cannot read far concerning these islands without making the friendship of Père Labat through the pages of his five little rusty old volumes. They are written in the French of his day —not at all difficult to understand —and the reading of them compelled me to form a personal regard for this Jesuit priest from his straightforward manner of writing.

We were now in the country of Père Labat and Precheur, before us, was where in 1693 he had spent the first few months of his twelve years in the West Indies. Du Parquet, who owned Martinique at that time, gave this parish to the Jesuit order of "Le Precheur" in

ALONE IN THE CARIBBEAN

1654 and it was only natural that here Labat should become acquainted with the manners and customs of the people before he took up his duties in the parish of Macouba near Grande Rivière. But here the wind failed me, it was Père Labat having his little joke, doubtless, and the lack of it nearly got me into trouble. I had been rowing along the shore for some time, following with my eyes the beach road that the priest had known so well, and had come to Pearl Rock. There is a channel between the rock and the shore and as I looked at my chart, folded with that particular part of the island faced upwards, it seemed to me that the name was somehow familiar.

Then I began to recollect some tale about an American privateer that had dodged an English frigate by slipping through this very place at night. I was trying to recall the details when a premonition made me look around. There, silently waiting for me not four strokes away, was a boatload of those accursed douanes! They had been watching for me since, two days before, they had received a message from their confrères down the coast that I had either been lost in the squall off St. Pierre or was hiding somewhere along the north coast. With an instinct that needed no telegram from my brain, my right arm dug its oar deep into the water while my left swung the canoe around like a skater who turns on one foot while the other indolently floats over its mate. The left oar seemed to complete the simile.

While the douanes were recovering from their surprise at this unexpected movement of the canoe which had been on the point of boarding them, I pulled with the desperation of a fly trying to crawl off the sticky field of a piece of tanglefoot —but with considerably more success as to speed. With a few yanks —one could not call them strokes —I was clear of the douanes and I knew they could not catch me. But they tried hard while I innocently asked if they wished to communicate with me. "Diable!' they wanted to see my papers and passport. I did not feel inclined to stop just then, I told them —they were easing up now —and if they wished to see my papers they could do so when I landed at Grande Rivière. And so the second batch of douanes was left in the lurch.

Along the four miles of coast from Pearl Rock to Grande Rivière there is no road, and the slopes of Pelée, which break down at the sea, forming some of the most wonderful cliffs and gorges I have ever seen, are as wild as the day when Columbus first saw the island. But if you would care to see these cliffs you must go by water as I did, for were you to penetrate the thickets of the mountain slopes you would not go far —for this is the haunt of the fer–de–lance. In starting the cultivation of a small patch of vanilla, which grows in a nearly wild state, Waddy killed a hundred of these vipers in the space of three months. But I gave no thought to the snakes —it was the cliffs that held me.

Imagine a perpendicular wall ranging from two to four hundred feet in height and covered with a hanging of vegetation seemingly suspended from the very top. No bare face of rock or soil, just the deep green that seemed to pour from the mountain slope down the face of the cliff and to the bright yellow sandy beaches stretching between the promontories. A surf, that made my hands tingle, pounded inshore and I watched with fascinated gaze the wicked curl of the blue cylinder as it stood for an instant and then tumbled and crashed up the beach. I was wondering how Waddy would get me through this when the measured shots from a single–loading carbine made themselves heard above the noise of the surf.

I turned the Yakaboo around that I might view the shore more easily and found that we were lying off a long beach terminating in Grande Rivière Point a few hundred yards beyond. A group of huts flocked together under the headland as if seeking shelter from the trades that were wont to blow over the high bluff above them. Where the beach rounded the point, the usual fringe of coco palms in dispirited angles stood out in bold relief. A line of dugouts drawn far up the beach vouched for Waddy's statement that here the natives caught the "thon."

Off the point a series of reefs broke the heavy swell into a fringe of white smother —inside was my salvation of deep blue quiet water. The blue of the sea and sky, the white of the clouds and broken water, the yellow of the deeper shoals and the beaches, the dark green background of vegetation lightened by the touches of red roofs and painted canoes, the sketchy outline of the point and the palms made a picture, ideally typical, of this north coast village.

A crowd of natives were dragging down a huge dugout which proved to be fully thirty feet long and made of a single log while a detached unit, which I recognized as the figure of Waddy, stood firing his carbine into the air. It was a signal, he explained later, to attract my attention and to call the people together to launch the dugout. When Waddy saw that I had turned the canoe he waved his large black felt hat frantically at the dugout and I waved back in understanding and waited.

But even under the protection of the barrier reef, there was a goodly surf running on the beach —too much for the Yakaboo —and I saw them wait, like all good surf men, till there was a proper lull, and then rush the dugout into the sea. For a moment she hung, then, as the centipede paddles caught the water, she shot ahead, her bow cutting into the menacing top of a comber mounting up to break. Up she went, half her length out of the water, her bow pointing skyward, and then down again as the sea broke under her, her bow men swung through a dizzy arc. If that were close work in a lull what were the large seas like?

In a few minutes they were alongside. Clearing away the thwarts half the natives —she was full of them —jumped overboard and swam ashore. I then unstepped my rig and passed over my outfit bags with which we made a soft bed in the dugout for the Yakaboo. I followed the outfit and we slid the empty canoe hull athwartships over the gunwale and then with a man under her belly like an Atlas, we swung her fore and aft, lifted her up while the man crawled out and then set her down gently in her nest. She looked like some strange sea–fowl making a ludicrous effort to hatch out an assortment of yellow eggs of various sizes and shapes.

In this way Waddy had solved the surf problem for me. If the Carib Indians were good boatmen, the Martinique tuna fishermen were better. First we paddled up shore to regain our driftage, and then in around the edge of the reef to a deep channel that ran close to the beach. We followed the channel for a hundred yards where we turned, hung for an instant —the seas were breaking just ahead and astern of us —and at a signal from the people on shore, paddled like mad. With the roar of the surf under us we passed from the salt sea into the sea of village people who dragged the dugout and all high and dry on the beach. It had been another strange ride for the Yakaboo and she looked self–satisfied, as if she enjoyed it.

As I jumped to the sands, Waddy received me, glowing and triumphant. It seemed that I was a hero! and great was his honor to be my host.

The Yakaboo and her yellow bags were carried to a sort of public shed where the crowd assembled with an air of expectancy which explained itself when I was ceremoniously presented to His Honor the Mayor. This dignitary then made a speech in which the liberty of the town was given me, to which I replied as best I could. Thus was I received into the bosom of the little village of Grande Rivière. Then up the hot dusty road to Waddy's large rambling house on the headland where a second reception was held, only the elect being present.

It was at this point, however, that the liberty of the town which had been presented me "paragorically speaking," as "Judge" Warner used to say, was about to be taken away from me. The street door was suddenly burst open and a band of hot dusty douanes came in to arrest the man who had defied their compatriots near Pearl Rock. But the Mayor, the priest, the prefect of police, and my fiery little host —an Achilles as to body if we may believe that the ancient Greeks were not large men —stayed the anger of the douanes while Waddy's servant —oh, the guile of these Frenchmen! —poured out a fresh bottle of wine which effectually extinguished the flame of their ire. My papers were duly examined and all was well again. When the douanes were at last on their way I told my protectors how I had dodged them at St. Pierre and Pearl Rock. This called for another bottle.

But I cannot keep you standing here in Waddy's house, for the little man was as eager to show me the sights of Grande Rivière as any schoolboy who races ahead of his chum, of a Saturday morning, two steps at a time, to the attic where some new invention is about to be born. He waved the select committee of the bottle very politely out of the front door and then grabbing his big hat he raced me up the steep road to the top of the cliff above the town. Time was precious. One could walk fast and talk at the same time.

In the first hundred yards I learned that he was born in Martinique, educated in Paris, and had specialized in botany and medicine. Cut off from the world as he had been for the better part of his life (I had all this as we cleared the houses of the village) he had developed the resourcefulness of a Robinson Crusoe. He would have made an excellent Yankee. He could make shoes, was a carpenter, something of a chemist, a philosopher, an expert on tuna fishing, and a student of literature. It seemed that his divertissement was the growing of vanilla and the raising of a large family.

He did not give out all this in a boastful way but merely tore through the facts as if he were working against time, so that we might understand each other the sooner and interchange as much of our personality as possible in the few hours I was to stay at Grande Rivière. By the time we reached the top of the cliff I had the man pat while he had me out of breath. He was the third I had met who would make life worth while in these parts.

ALONE IN THE CARIBBEAN

And here, looking up the valley of the Grande Rivière, I saw one of the most beautiful bits of scenery in all the islands. The river came down from Pelée through a cañon of green vegetation. On the opposite wall from where we stood, a road zigzagged upwards from the valley to disappear through a hole near the top of the cliff. Some day I shall travel that road and go through the hole in the wall to visit Macouba beyond where Père Labat spent his first years in the parish and where he practised those sly little economies of which he was so proud. He tells of how he brought home some little chicks, poules d'Inde he calls them, and gave them out among his parishioners to be brought up, in material payment for the spiritual comfort and the blessings which he, Père Labat, afforded them. And how his children came back to him, grown up and ready for his table. His sexton lived close to the sea by the river (probably just such a stream as this with a ford and the houses of the town close to its banks) and this gave him the idea of buying ducks and drakes and going in with the sexton on a half and half basis. When the ducks matured, Père Labat, who was steadily increasing his worldly assets, bought out the sexton at a low price. The sexton probably shared in the eating of the ducks for he was a singer and a good fellow, a Parisian, the son of an attorney named Rollet, made famous by Boileau in a shady passage of his "Satires." The son had changed his name to Rallet, fled the scenes of his father's disgrace and came to Martinique where he found peace and happiness in the parish of Père Labat. Although the priest and poor Rallet have been a–moldering these two hundred years I could not help hoping that it was a good cook who prepared their ducks and chickens.

The shadow of evening had already crossed the valley bottom and it followed a lone figure that was slowly toiling up the road toward the hole in the wall. We scrambled down again through the village, where the odor of French cooking was on the evening air, past a little wayside shrine to the beach where I had landed. We had left the evening behind us for a time and were back in the last hour of afternoon. It was hot even now, although the dangerous heat of the day was over. I had caught my breath on our coming down and my long legs made good progress over the soft sands —there is a knack in beach walking, the leg swings forward with a slight spring–halt motion, the knee is never straightened and the foot is used flat so that it will sink as little as possible in the sand. I had my little Achilles in the toils and I talked while he fought for breath.

For a quarter of a mile we trudged the sands till the green wall closed in on us and met the sea. A little spring trickled down through an opening in the rocks and we drank its cool water from cups which Waddy made of leaves. It was here that my friend was wont to come when he wished to be alone and he led me up through a crevasse to the top of a gigantic rock that overhung the surf some thirty feet. He could have paid me no greater compliment than to take me to this place, sacred to his own moody thoughts, where, like a sick animal or an Indian with a "bad heart" he could fight his troubles alone. Below us the surf curled over in a mighty roll that burst on the beach with a deafening roar, sending up a fine mist of salty vapor like the smoke of an explosion. This was Père Labat's country and as I watched the regular onslaught of several large seas I thought of a paragraph he wrote some two hundred years ago. "The sea always forms seven large billows, waves or surges, whichever you would call them, that break on the shore with an astonishing violence and which can be heard along the windward side where the coast is usually very high and where the wind blows continually on the sea. The three last of these seven waves are the largest. When they have subsided after breaking on shore there is a little calm which is called Emblie and which lasts about the time it takes to say an Ave Maria, after which the waves begin again, their size and force augmenting always till the seventh has broken on the shore."

We watched the sun go down and then silently crawled down to the beach. It was Waddy's wish that we should walk back in the darkness. The advance of night seemed to drive the last fitful twilight before it —one can see the light fade away from a printed page —and the stars came out. The moon would not rise yet awhile. "Look!" said Waddy, and he turned me toward the dark cliffs above us. Hanging over us was a deep velvet darkness that I could almost reach out and feel, and against this like the jewels of a scarf, was the glimmer of thousands of fire–flies —moving, blinking spots of light as large and luminous as Jupiter on the clearest night. They lived in the foliage of the cliff and it was Waddy's delight to come here of a night and watch them. "Chaque bête a feu clairé' pou nâme yo!" he said. (Each firefly lights for his soul.)

Dinner was waiting for us and with it the proud maman and two of the children. Some were away at school and some were too young to come to the table (at least when there were visitors) and we did justice to that of which she was proud, the food. That night we discussed till late the various means by which the "Touring Club" could see more of the Antilles as I was seeing them, but Nature finally had her way and I fell asleep talking —so Waddy said.

CHAPTER X. A LAND CRUISE —THE CALM OF GUADELOUPE.

I AWOKE in the morning to find that I had carelessly slipped into the second day of a windy quarter. There was no doubt about it ; the trade was blowing strong at six o'clock. I was impatient to be off shore before the surf would be running too high even for the thirty–foot dugout. After gulping down a hasty breakfast and bidding profuse adieux to Madame Waddy, I reached the beach with my friend just in time to see one of the fishing boats capsize and to watch the natives chase down the shore to pick up her floating gear.

It took nearly the whole male population of the village to turn the dugout and get her bow down to the surf. With a shout and a laugh the people carried the Yakaboo and placed her lightly in her nest. Ten of the strongest paddlers were selected and they took their places in the dugout forward and aft of the canoe while I, like the Queen of the Carnival, sat perched high above the rest, in the cockpit. For nearly half an hour —by my watch —we sat and waited. There were thirty men, on the sands, along each gunwale, ready for the word from Waddy. There was little talking ; we all watched the seas that seemed to come in, one after another, with vindictive force.

I was beginning to swear that I was too late when a "soft one" rolled in and we shot from the heave of a hundred and twenty arms plunging our bow into the first sea. Her heel was still on the sand and I feared she wouldn't come up for we shipped two barrels of brine as easily as the Yakaboo takes a teacupful. But with the first stroke she was free and with the second she cleared the next sea which broke under her stern. We were in the roar of the reef and if Waddy yelled good–bye it had been carried down the beach like the gear of the fishing boat. But he waved his hat like a madman and followed us along shore as we ran down the channel and turned out to sea.

Once clear of all dangers, eight of the men fell to bailing while the two bow men and the steersman kept her head to it. Then we swung the Yakaboo athwartships while I loaded and rigged her. We slid her overboard and I jumped in. The men held her alongside where she tugged like an impatient puppy while I lowered the centerboard. "Let 'er go!" I yelled —an expression that seems to be understood in all languages —and I ran up the mizzen, sheeting it not quite home. Then the jib. I shall never forget the sensation as I hauled in on that jib —it seems out of proportion to use the word "haul" for a line scarcely an eighth of an inch in diameter fastened to a sail hardly a yard in area. The wind was strong and the seas were lively.

When that sheeted jib swung the canoe around she did not have time to gather speed, she simply jumped to it. I made fast the jib sheet and prepared to steer by the mizzen when I discovered that the canoe was sailing herself. I looked back toward shore and waved both arms. Waddy was a crazy figure on the beach. The day was delirious. A tuna dugout that had been lying into the wind fell away as I started and raced ahead of me, reefed down, her lee rail in the boil and her wild crew to windward. My mainsail was already reefed and I let the canoe have it. By the high–tuned hum of her board I knew that the Yakaboo was traveling and the crew of the tuna canoe knew it, too, for we passed them and were off on our wild ride to Dominica.

My channel runs were improving. The sea, the sky, and the clouds were all the same as on the other runs, but the wind was half a gale. What occupied my mind above all, however, was the discovery that the canoe would sail herself under jib and mizzen. I had thought that no boat with so much curve to her bottom could possibly do such a thing —it is not done on paper. The fact remained, however, that the two small sails low down and far apart kept the canoe on her course as well as I could when handling the mainsheet.

I checked this observation by watching my compass which has a two–inch card floating in liquid and is extremely steady. I also learned that I did not have to waste time heading up for the breaking seas, except the very large ones, of course. Sometimes I could roll them under —at other times I let them come right aboard and then I was up to my shoulders in foam. The canoe was tighter than she had ever been and it was only the cockpit that gave trouble. When she began to stagger from weight of water, I would let go the main halyard and she would continue on her course while I bailed. In all the two thousand miles of cruising I had hitherto done, I learned more in this twenty–five mile channel than all the rest put together. Some day —I promised myself —I would build a hull absolutely tight and so strong and of such a form that I could force her through what seas she could not easily ride under. Also, what a foolish notion I had clung to in setting my sails only a few inches above deck ; they should be high up so that a foot of water could pass over the deck and not get into the cloth. In this run, if the Yakaboo had been absolutely tight and her sails raised and if I had carried a small deck seat to windward, I could have carried full sail and she would have ridden to Dominica on a cloud of brine—smelling steam. As it was, she was traveling much faster than at any time before and I did not know that the most glorious channel run was yet to come.

I laid my course for Cape Cachacrou (Scott's Head), a peculiar hook that runs out to westward of the south end of Dominica. For the first two hours I could not see the Head, then it popped up like an island and began slowly to connect itself with the larger land. The going was excellent and in short time the head was right over our bow, with Dominica rising up four thousand feet to weather. We were not more than half a mile off shore when I took out my watch. I figured out later that our rate had been six miles an hour including slowing up to bail and occasionally coming to a dead stop when riding out a big sea bow on. I could ask no better of a small light craft sailing six points off the wind, logy a part of the time and working in seas that were almost continually breaking.

Fate was indulgent, for she waited till I had stowed my watch in its berth to starboard. Then she sent a sea of extra size —it seemed to come right up from below and mouth the Yakaboo like a terrier —and before we got over our surprise she gave us the tail end of a squall, like a whiplash, that broke the mizzen gooseneck and sent the sail a—skying like a crazy kite. I let go all my halyards and pounced after my sails like a frantic washerwoman whose clothes have gone adrift in a backyard gale. The mainsail came first and then the jib. The truant mizzen which had dropped into the sea when I slipped its halyard came out torn and wet and I rolled it up and spanked it and stowed it in the cockpit.

The sea had come up from the sudden shoaling where in a third of a mile the bottom jumps from a hundred and twenty fathoms to twelve, and as for the squall, that was just a frisky bit of trade that was not content with gathering speed around the end of the island but must slide down the side of a mountain to see how much of a rumpus it could raise on the water. I had run unawares —it was my own stupid carelessness that did it —on the shoals that extend to the southeast of Cachacrou Head where the seas jumped with nasty breaking heads that threatened to turn the Yakaboo end for end any minute.

With the mizzen out of commission I might as well have stood in pink tights on the back of a balky farm horse and told him to cross his fingers as sail that canoe. I might have hoisted my jib and slowly run off the shoals to the westward, but that would have meant a hard tedious beat back to shore again for a good part of the night. I chose to work directly across the shoals with the oars. But it was no joking matter. My course lay in the trough of the sea and it was a question of keeping her stern to the seas so that I could watch them and making as much as I could between crests.

Most of my difficulty lay in checking her speed when a comber would try to force her along in a mad toboggan ride and from this the palms of my hands became sore and developed a huge blister in each that finally broke and let in the salt water which was about it' plenty. For an hour I worked at it, edging in crabwise across the shoals till the seas began to ease up and I pulled around the Head to the quiet waters under its hook. Have you walked about all day in a stiff pair of new shoes and then come home to the exquisite ease of an old pair of bedroom slippers? Then you know how I felt when I could take a straight pull with my fingers crooked on the oars and my raw palms eased from their contact with the handles.

Cachacrou Head is a rock which stands some two hundred and thirty–four feet up from the sea and is connected with the coast of Dominica by a narrow curved peninsula fifty yards across and half a mile in length. There is a small fort on the top of the Head and here on the night of September the seventh, in 1778, the French from Martinique, with a forty–nine gun ship, three frigates and about thirty small sloops filled with all kinds of piratical rabble, captured the fort which was in those days supposed to be impregnable. It was the same old story ; there is always a weak point in the armor of one's enemy —thirst being the vulnerable point in this case. The night before the capture some French soldiers who had insinuated themselves into the fort, muddled the heads of the English garrison with wine from Martinique, and spiked the guns. The capture then was easy. By this thin wedge, the French gained control of Dominica and held the island for five years.

Rowing close around the Head, I found a sandy bit of beach just where the peninsula starts for the mainland and with a feeling that here ended a good day's work, hauled the Yakaboo up on the smooth hard beach. The sun —it seems that I am continually talking about the sun which is either rising or setting or passing through that ninety degree arc of deadly heat the middle of which is noon (it was now four o'clock) —was far enough on its down path so that the Head above me cast a grateful shade over the beach while the cool wind from the mountains insured the absence of mosquitoes.

The lee coast of Dominica stretching away to the north was in brilliant light. You have probably gathered by this time that the Lesser Antilles are decidedly unsuited for camping and cruising as we like to do it in the North Woods. In a few isolated places on the windward coasts one might live in a tent and be healthy and happy, such as my camp with the Caribs ; but to cruise and camp, that is travel and then rest for a day on the beach —this is impossible. In this respect my cruise was a distinct failure.

When I did find a spot such as this, where I could still enjoy a part of the afternoon in comparative comfort, I enjoyed it to the utmost. I did not unload the Yakaboo immediately —I merely took those things out of her that I wanted for my present use. Tabac de Diable, for instance, and my pipe, and then a change of clothes ; but before I put on that change I shed my stiff briny sea outfit and sat down in a little sandy–floored pool in the rocks. There I smoked with my back against a rock while the reflex from the Caribbean rose and fell with delightful intimacy from my haunches to my shoulders.

For some time I rested there, with my hands behind my head to keep the blood out of my throbbing hands and the salt out of my burning palms. Across the bay was the town of Souffrière, not unlike the Souffrière of Saint Lucia, from a distance, while a few miles beyond was Point Michelle and another few miles along was Roseau, the capital town of the island. Away to the north Diablotin rose nearly five thousand feet, within a hundred feet of the Souffrière of Guadeloupe, the highest mountain of the Lesser Antilles.

After a while I got up, like a lazy faun (let us not examine the simile too closely for who would picture a sea faun smoking a Three–B and with a four days' stubble on his chin?). On a flat–topped rock near the canoe I spread out my food bags. Near this I started a fire of hardwood twigs that soon burned down to a hot little bed of coals over which my pot of erbswurst was soon boiling. This peameal soup, besides bacon and potatoes, is one of the few foods of which one may eat without tiring, three times a day, day in and day out, when living in the open. It is an excellent campaign food and can be made into a thin or thick soup according to one's fancy. I have eaten it raw and found it to be very sustaining. At home one would quickly tire of the eternal peameal and the salty bacon taste —but I never eat it when I am at home nor do I use in general the foods I take with me when cruising. The two diets are quite distinct.

While the pot was boiling, I betook myself to a cozy angle in the rocks which I softened with my blanket bag, and fell to repairing my mizzen. My eye chanced to wander down the beach —is it chance or instinct? and finally came to rest on a group of natives who stood watching me. Modesty demanded something in the way of clothes so I put on a clean shirt and trousers and beckoned to them. They were a timid lot and only two of them advanced to within fifty feet of the canoe and then stopped. I talked to them, but it was soon evident that they did not understand a word I said, even the little patois I knew got no word from them. Finally they summoned enough courage to depart and I was left to my mending.

I had finished my sail and was enjoying my pea–soup and biscuits when my eye detected a movement down the beach and I saw a lone figure which advanced without hesitation and walked right into my camp where it smiled down at me from an altitude of three inches over six feet. "My name ess Pistole Titre, wat you name and frum war you cum?"

I told him that my name was of little importance and that I had just come from Martinique. "Frum war before dat?"

"Saint Lucia."

"Frum war before dat?"

"Saint Vincent.

"Frum war before dat?"

"Grenada."

"An' you not afraid?"

"Why should I be afraid? The canoe sails well."

"I no mean de sea, I mean jumbie. How you don't know w'en you come to strange ilan de jumbie no take you?"

There might be some truth in this but I answered, "I don't believe in jumbies." This he interpreted into, "I don't believe there are jumbies HERE." The fact that I did not believe in jumbies, the evil spirits of the Africans, was utterly beyond his conception —of course I believed in them, everybody did, but by some occult power I must know their haunts and could avoid them though I had never visited the place before. "I know jumbies no come here, but how you know? You wonderful man," he concluded.

ALONE IN THE CARIBBEAN

While this conversation was going on, I was secretly admiring his huge lithe body —such of it as could be seen through an open shirt and by suggestive line of limb ; he might have been some bronze Apollo come to animation, except for his face. His face was an expression of good—will, intelligence, and energy that came to me as a refreshing relief from the shiny fulsome visage of the common native.

The jumbies disposed of for the time being, Pistole sat down on a rock and made rapid inroads on a few soda biscuits and some pea—soup which I poured into a calabash. The native can always eat, and the eating of this salty soup with its bacon flavor seemed the very quintessence of gastronomic delight. When he had finished he pointed to a steep upland valley and told me he must go there to milk his cows. He would bring me a bottle of fresh milk, he said, when he came back again, for he was going to fish that night from the rocks under the Head. As he walked away along the beach, the breeze brought back, "An' he no 'fraid jumbies. O Lard!"

My supper over, I turned the canoe bow toward the water and made up my bed in the cockpit. It would be too fine a night for a tent and I tied my candle light part way up the mizzen mast so that I could lie in my bed and read. At sunset I lit my lamp for the beach under the Head was in darkness. While the short twilight moved up from the sea and hovered for a moment on the highest mountain tops my candle grew from a pale flame to a veritable beacon that cast a sphere of light about the canoe, shutting out night from the tiny rock—hedged beach on which we lay. But Ulysses did not make me drowsy and I blew out my light and lay under that wonderful blue ceiling in which the stars blinked like live diamonds. The Dipper was submerged with its handle sticking out of the sea before me and Polaris hung low, a much easier guide than in the North. Just overhead Orion's belt floated like three lights dropped from a sky rocket. Through the low brush over the peninsula the Southern Cross tilted to westward.

As I lay there stargazing, the rattle of a displaced stone told me of the coming of Pistole who laid down a long bamboo pole and seated himself on his haunches by the canoe. I relit my lamp that I might observe him better. Suspended from a tump line passing over the top of his head was a curious basket—like woven matting. From its depths he drew forth a bottle, known the world over, a four shouldered, high—sided termini that proclaimed gin as its original contents, but which was now filled with milk and corked with a wisp of upland grass.

ALONE IN THE CARIBBEAN

I stuck the bottle in the sand beside the canoe where the morning sun would not strike it and then dug around in my cozy little burrow and brought forth a bag of tobacco. Pistole did not smoke. He was supporting his mother and an aunt ; it was hard work and he could not afford luxuries. Here certainly was a paradox, a native who forbore the use of tobacco!

Pistole came here often, he said, when there was not much moon, to fish at night from the rocks, using the white squid that shines in the water for bait. Sometimes he filled his basket to the top with little rock fish and at other times he got nothing at all. He lighted his flambeau from my candle lamp and departed, leaving the pleasant odor of the burning gommier like an incense. I watched his progress as the light bobbed up and down and was finally extinguished far out on the rocks.

Tired as I was, my throbbing hands kept me awake till Pistole returned some time later —the fish did not seem to be biting —and he lay down in the sand by the canoe. Had he seen a jumbie or was there a sign of lajoblesse? The huge creature edged in as close to the planking of the Yakaboo as he could get, like a remora fastened to the belly of a shark. The monotone of his snores brought on sleep and when I awoke the sun was well up above the mountains of Dominica. A lengthy impression in the sand was all that remained of the native who had long since gone to tend his cattle.

There is one morning when I feel that I have a right to spread myself and that is on Sunday. It is from long force of habit that began with my earliest school days. There was no need for an early start and as for my breakfast, I spared neither time nor trouble.

First I very slowly and very carefully reversed Pistole's bottle so as not to disturb the cream and then I let out the milk from under it. This was for the chocolate. The cream which would hardly pour and which I had to shake out of the bottle I set aside for my oatmeal. This I had started the night before and it only needed heating and stirring. I made the chocolate with the native "stick" and sweetened it with the Muscovado sugar and I even swizzled it and sprinkled nutmeg on the heavy foam on top after the old Spanish manner. That "head" would have put to shame the "Largest Schooner in Town." I also made a dish of scrambled eggs and smoked flying fish that Waddy had given me. It was a breakfast fit for a king and I felt proud of myself and congratulated my stomach on its neat capacity as I stretched out by a rock like a gorged reptile and lit my pipe. There was nothing, just then, that could increase the sum of my happiness. I should have been glad to have spent the day there but I knew that the sun would soon make a hell's furnace of this delightful spot so when my pipe was finished I washed my dishes and loaded the canoe. I was having my "last look around" when I saw a crowd of natives coming up the beach with Pistole at their head. They were probably coming to see the canoe and to say good–bye so I sat down on a rock and waited for them. Pistole, who had apparently been appointed spokesman, said that they all lived in a village, not far off, but hidden from view by the bush. They were very anxious to show me their village —would I come with them?.

Pistole led the way along the peninsula to a crescent of beach that might have been on the lagoon of an atoll in the South Sea islands. Under the coco palms that hung out over the beach almost to the water's edge were the canoes of the village. Behind the scrubby growth that fringed the beach was a double row of huts with a wide path between them parallel to the shore. Down this path or avenue I was led in review while the homes of the persons of distinction were pointed out to me. These differed from the ordinary huts in that they were sided with unpainted boards. One or two were built of American lumber, painted and with shingled roofs. Half the village followed us while the other half sat in its respective doorways. Oh! the luxury of those door steps ; to those who sat there it was like beholding a Memorial Day procession from the carpeted steps of a city house. This world is merely one huge farce of comparison. At the end of the avenue —let us give it as much distinction as possible —we retraced our steps and the march came to an end at the house of Pistole's mother. This, I might say, was one of the finest and contained two rooms. The big native was very proud of his mother and aunt who received me with the graciousness of women of royalty and brought out little cakes and glasses of cocomilk and rum. The heat was growing outside and I must get off the beach, so I said "Good–bye" and went back to the canoe followed by a small caravan bearing offerings of the village, waternuts and pineapples.

The wind was roaring down the mountainsides, for this quarter continued fresh, and I left the beach with the reefed mainsail only. The sea was like a floor and with a small gale for a beam wind the reefed sail lifted the Yakaboo along like a toboggan. I held in for the town of Souffrière in order to keep the smooth water and when I was part way across the bay the lightish water under me suddenly turned to a deep blue —the color of sea water off shore. There was a sharp well–defined line which I crossed again and was once more in lighter water. It was L'Abime, Dominica's submarine crater.

ALONE IN THE CARIBBEAN

In less than an hour I lowered sail off the main jetty of Roseau.

It was not quite twelve. The whole town had begun breakfast at eleven and was still eating. I may not be absolutely correct in saying that the whole town was eating for there was one individual who was on duty and enjoying a nap in the shade of the custom–house at the shore end of the jetty. There was another also —but he did not belong to the town —the captain of the coasting steamer Yare, a jolly little Irishman whom I came to know better in St. Thomas. He was not at breakfast and he yelled a welcome from the bridge of his steamer at her Sunday rest by the big mooring buoy in the roadstead. I ran up my ensign on the mizzen halyard and yelled at the man inshore. He rubbed his eyes but did not seem to know why he should be disturbed. "Where is the harbor–master?"

"At him breakfus' —w'at you want?"

"I want to land. Don't you see my ensign?"

"O Lard! I t'at it wuz de Umium Jack."

At this Wilson, of the Yare, sent out a great roar across the water. "You don't think that ebony ass knows the difference between one flag and another, do you?" he inquired much to the offense of the e. a. With some sheepishness, the revenue man came down to the landing place where I prepared to tie up the Yakaboo while awaiting the answer from the harbormaster. But no, I could not even fasten my painter to one of the iron piles, —I must lie off in the roads till word came that my papers had been passed upon. There might be the chance that I had yellow fever aboard. In an hour the boatman returned with word that I might come ashore. In view of what followed I should add that when I handed my papers to the boatman I told him that I had already landed at Scott's Head under stress of weather and that he should report this to the harbor–master. Some days later while I was fitting a new goose–neck to the mizzen of the Yakaboo in the courtyard of the Colonial Bank, word was brought that I was "wanted" by the Acting Colonial Treasurer. I knew from the tone of the demand that something was in the air. When I was ushered into the presence of that august little personage, I was asked with considerable circumlocution why I landed at Scott's Head before making official entry at Roseau. "Who told you?" I whispered, as if he were about to disclose an interesting bit of gossip.

ALONE IN THE CARIBBEAN

"The police officer of Souffrière telephoned this morning that he saw your camp at Scott's Head on Sunday morning." (It was now Friday, five days later.) I said that I hoped the lazy officer at Souffrière had been duly reprimanded for not having reported me sooner.

"What!" the little man shouted. "You are the one to be reprimanded for having landed and not having mentioned the fact when you gave up your papers at Roseau. Do you know that you are liable to two weeks' quarantine?"

By this time my ire should have been goaded to the loud–talking point. I leaned forward in a confidential way and whispered (he seemed to dislike this whispering), "Let's have in the boatman who took my papers on Sunday morning." They might have been the dying words of some unfortunate victim of a street accident asking for his wife or his mother.

The boatman came in due time accompanied by loud tones of authority which issued from his thick–soled boots. The weight of the Empire was in every step. Then I stood up and looked hard into a pair of hazel eyes while I asked the owner if I had not mentioned, when I handed him my papers, the fact that I had spent the night at Scott's Head under stress of weather. I owned those eyes while he spoke the truth and said, "Yes."

"Don't you know, Mr. S —," I asked, "that under stress of weather —my mizzen having blown away —I may land at any convenient beach and then proceed to the nearest port as soon as repairs are effected?" One would think that we were talking about some great steamer instead of a sailing canoe. I did not, however, mention my visit to the village on the peninsula.

When the Yakaboo was ready for sea again, I chucked her into the basement of the Colonial Bank and started on a land cruise through the hills of the island. I would hire a small horse and circumnavigate the island on its back, carrying with me a couple of blankets, a pail and a frypan. But the idyll stops there.?

? Sunset—St. Pierre. ?

?

? Ruins of the cathedral. ?

ALONE IN THE CARIBBEAN

Soon after I arrived at Roseau, word came to me that a Mr. B of Chicago was visiting his uncle on a plantation near the town. It turned out that I knew this man and in the course of time we met. When he heard of my plan to ride around the island, he embraced the idea with great warmth —as some would put it —in fact he not only embraced it ; he adopted it and when it came back to me it was entirely changed. It no longer belonged to me, it was a sad little stranger whom I knew not. Instead of camping near the roadside with a bully fire at night and the horses tethered close by, this was all done away with by means of letters of introduction. Our blankets and our pots and pans were whisked away by folded pieces of paper inside of other pieces of paper. Our food we need no longer trouble about. I felt like asking, "Please, ma'am, may I take a little eating chocolate and my pipe and tobacco?"

It was on Friday then, oh, unlucky day for the skipper of the Yakaboo! that I obtained a pony from the harbor–master. I did not see the horse till the next morning —a few minutes before the start which was scheduled for eight o'clock. I have inferred that there is but little humor or the sense of it in the English islands, at least, but this animal was a pun —the lowest form of humor. To have called him a joke would have put a burden on him that would eventually have swayed his back till a fifth wheel would have been necessary to keep his poor paunch off the ground. And as for that poor paunch —there was the seat of all the trouble. It had not been filled often enough nor full enough and as in nature we come to liken the things we eat, this poor beast was becoming of necessity an ethereal being. I asked the man who brought it if they taxed horses in the island by the head or by the pound. The colored groom very politely informed me —for was I not traveling in the West Indies in search of information ? —that there was, of course, a tax on every horse in the island, and as for the pound, there was a small fee levied on every animal that got astray and was brought there. If you were sitting with me in my cozy little cabin and we were discussing that horse I should say, "Poor brute, I felt damn sorry for him," in that earnest tone which you would understand.

I am not heavy in build, however, neither did I have any luggage to add weight, for a porter had been engaged to carry our extra duffle on his head. With a small cargo of chocolate to port and a supply of tobacco and matches to starboard, I adjusted the stirrups and mounted my poor animal. Even then I felt him go down below his Plimsoll marks. I wore my ordinary sea outfit which I had carefully washed. I had one suit of "store clothes" but I was not going to befoul them on any uncurried West Indian skate for any man, no matter how exalted his position might be. B—, rather chunky of build, arrived well mounted at the stroke of the hour and at a brisk canter. If he were not what one might call au fait, he bore some aspects of the gentleman–rider even if he wore his trousers stuffed into leggings instead of "breeks." He had apparently noticed that there was a figure mounted on a horse by the roadside but until he was close upon me he did not realize that this was to accompany him on his ride around the island. When he recognized me his face fell like a topsail taken aback and he instinctively looked around to see if any one saw him with me. "Good God!" he muttered, "you're not going to ride in that rig, are you?"

"You don't expect me to wear a hunting coat on this caricature, do you? Let's be off."

"Yes, let's be off," he said, as he put spurs to his horse and raced along the road toward Laudat.

"Let's be off," I whispered into the ear of my Rosinante —for he was a she —and with a thwack I started her clattering after my friend.

By careful husbanding the strength of my animal we reached Laudat at ten o'clock. That is, I did. My friend had arrived there several times and had gone back occasionally to note my progress.

Laudat is a little settlement nearly half way across the island where one takes the trail for a rather arduous climb to the Boiling Lake in the Souffrière mountains. Through the courtesy of a priest in Roseau a rest house was put at our disposal. Here we feasted on raspberries, coffee and bread, after which we started for the Boiling Lake. I shall not weary you with a laborious description of a laborious climb along a narrow trail, muddy and slippery and root–crossed, nor of the everlasting din of the anvil bird that somehow makes a noise like the ringing of steel against iron, nor of the Boiling Lake. The next day we finished our crossing and followed the road along the windward side to the estate of Castle Bruce where we stopped for the night.

The following day we rode to Melville Hall where we were received by the Everingtons. It was along this coast, somewhere between Crumpton and Pagoua Points that Columbus tried to land on the morning of November 3rd, when he gave Dominica its name and then proceeded to the northward and set foot the same day on the shores of Maria Galante which he named after his ship. From Melville Hall we rode to Hampstead and then across the northeast corner of the island to Portsmouth.

Lying in the smooth waters of Prince Rupert Bay were three American whalers, a remnant of a fleet of sixteen that had gathered there to transship oil. As you may remember from your early American history, the English government has always been extremely fond of gaining revenue through petty taxation. They even tax rowboats in some of the islands and in Saint Vincent the crude little catamaran on which the Black Carib boy is seated (?photo) is taxed thrupence per foot. Imbued with this idea, a petty official of Dominica once suggested to the skipper of an American whaler that he should be made to pay a tax for the use of the shelter of the island. To this the Yankee skipper replied, "Go ahead and make your law and your tax, we'll tow one of our own damn islands down here and use that."

I have said little about my Rosinante, who seemed, somehow, to improve on the good food she was getting. She bore up well ; I rode her with a loose girth and took the best possible care of her. If I could only nurse her for a month or so I might make a presentable beast of her. As it was, I felt that I was riding a rather tough skin in which an old piece of machinery was moving with considerable lost motion. I remember speculating as to what price the harbor–master would charge me if the mare died while in my care and wondering what return I might gain from her carcass. There was this comfort, her skin was tough and should she drop on some precipitous path her bones and eternal economy would not burst out and go clattering down into the valley below. I was sure of what might be left of her and in a pinch I could skin her and sell the flesh to the natives, break up the bones for fertilizer and use her hoofs for gelatin. It was an absorbing bit of speculation but did not interest B—, whose mind was usually occupied with problems of much higher finance. But there was no real cause for worry. On the last day we covered fully twenty–five miles of road that was mostly up and down hill. I gained as much respect for her as most any West Indian I had met.

It was the loose girth which caused me to lose my last shred of dignity. We were descending a steep path down the side of a valley in the bed of which flowed a small fordable stream. There was no mishap until we reached the river bank which dropped away steeply to the water's edge. For some unaccountable reason I and Rosinante were ahead. Slowly Rosinante felt her way down the bank and then stood, bow down, like the Yakaboo scending a sea. In a detailed description I should have said that she was built for'ard somewhat like a cow —lacking shoulders. The saddle of its own accord had begun

151

to slide forward. I reached for her tail and missed it. Her forefeet were in ten inches of water while her after props were still on dry land. Even then I might have saved myself by taking to the after deck. Slowly she lowered her muzzle to the stream. There was nothing for it, the saddle slid down the sharp ridge of her neck and I landed with my hands in the water as if I too would drink. As I rolled off into the stream I thought I caught Rosinante in the act of winking her eye —or was it only a fly that bothered?.

Our land cruise ended that evening and I bade goodbye to my friend. Rosinante was returned to the harbor—master and I went back to the Yakaboo.

Traveling up the Dominica shore I had my first taste of calm. It was not the blazing calm that I was to experience a few days later but it was a good foretaste. In light weather there is usually a calm spot along the northern half of the coast line up to Prince Rupert Bay. Just around the bluff the trade strikes the sea again and here I set sail and ran into Toucan Bay where there is a little coast village. Here was the last bit of beach whence I could make my departure for Guadeloupe and I hauled the canoe out on the sand at the far end from the village.

The people came down to the beach and insisted upon carrying my canoe well up from the water. They asked me where I was going to sleep and I pointed to the cockpit of the Yakaboo. At this one of the head men said that I must sleep in the village. He would see to it that a room in one of the houses was cleaned out for me and that his wife would cook my evening meal. I conceded this last point and taking up my food bags walked with him to the village.

While my supper was cooking, a woman came to me and asked if I would see her son. He was dying, she thought (the native is always dying with each complaint, however slight), and the coast doctor would not reach the village for several days. I told her that I was no medicine man, but she would not believe that I could travel alone as I did without some mystic power to cure all diseases. I found the boy, about eighteen years old, in great distress, suffering possibly from acute gastritis —a not uncommon ailment of the West Indian negro. I muttered some Latin à la Bill Nye and gave him a pill that could do no harm and might do some good. I dare say my diagnosis and prescription were not much wider of the mark than those of many practitioners of high repute. I was playing safe, for if the boy died subsequently I knew it not. I returned to my supper of chocolate and jack fish and then made up my bed in the canoe.

ALONE IN THE CARIBBEAN

Long before the sun began to throw his light over the mountains of Dominica I had folded my blankets and was eating a scanty breakfast, for the day promised well and I was anxious to be sailing. My channel runs, so far, had been boisterous and exhilarating, like a race from tree to tree in a game of blindman's buff, the trees being distant conical patches of grey–blue land ; but this run of the Saints was a pleasant jaunt. Seventeen miles to the northwest lay Les Saintes, a group of picturesque islands that stood out fresh and green even as I cleared Dominica. Ten miles farther on my course was Guadeloupe. Nineteen miles to the northeast lay the larger island of Marie Galante and when I opened the Atlantic to the north of her I could make out the hump of distant Desirade.

It was in these waters that Rodney caught up with the French fleet under De Grasse on the morning of April 12th, 1782. It is difficult for us to realize that in these islands that now appear to us to be of such little importance, a battle such as this —the Battle of the Saints —should be one of the turning points which led directly to the supremacy of Great Britain on the sea. England stood alone against the world. The American colonies had declared their independence and Cornwallis had surrendered at Yorktown. France and Spain were eager to end, once for all, the power of England's navy. The Dutch had been defeated off the Dogger Bank and the year before, Rodney had captured their island of St. Eustatius and unroofed Oranjetown, as you shall see when I take you there in the Yakaboo.

The French fleet was considered a perfect fighting machine and while De Grasse had thirty–three ships to Rodney's thirty–five they were considered to have the advantage on their side, due to greater tonnage and a larger number of guns per ship. But the French were weak in one point and that was sailing to windward —this was offset in a measure by their superior ability to run off the wind and escape from their foes, should the battle go against them. On the morning of April 12th, Hood led the British fleet, which was apparently to windward, while Rodney in the Formidable was in the center. The French fleet was in a line parallel to the English and a safe distance to leeward. The wind was evidently light. Then, we are told, "a sudden gale of wind gave the British admiral his chance —abruptly turning his flagship to larboard he broke through the French line." This "gale of wind" was probably the usual freshening of the trade at about eight o'clock, which Rodney's ships received first because he was to windward of the French. By breaking into the line as he did, the whole of Rodney's fleet was concentrated on two–thirds of the French and the English could use both broadsides at one time while the French could only use one. In the cannonading which followed, a rooster which had escaped from the coops on board the Formidable stood on the bowsprit and crowed defiantly. "It was a good omen to the sailors, who worked their guns with redoubled vigor." Six of the French ships were captured and the rest fled to leeward, mostly in a crippled condition.

Rodney at this time was sixty–three years old, a roué ; a gambler, and crippled with gout. But he was considered the best admiral whom the British had. Some years before, he had fled to France to escape debt and it was a Frenchman, Marshall Biron, who paid his debts and made him return to England because he did not want to have his country deprived of the glory of beating the British with their best admiral at their head. It had been too rash a gamble. Although Rodney's tactics, in the Battle of the Saints, were conceived on the spur of the moment, unknown to him, they were first evolved by a Scottish minister, John Clark of Eldin, and were a lesson to Nelson who embodied them in the "Nelson touch" at Trafalgar.

I passed close to the Saints and looked with great longing on a pretty little fishing village on the lee coast of Terre d'en Bas. There were some white people on the beach where several smart looking fishing boats were drawn up on the sand. I would have given much to have been allowed to land there, but I knew there was no port of entry in the Saints and remembering my Martinique experiences I held my course for Basse Terre on Guadeloupe. Soon after, the wind left us and I rowed into the roadstead of Basse Terre at the very peak of the heat of a calm day, that is, three o'clock in the afternoon.

It was the eighth of May and getting on toward June when the light winds and calm weather of the hurricane season begin. There is no doubt as to the degeneracy of the white man in the tropics due to the heat. First comes the loss of temper. I noticed this in my own case. I had become short tempered and swore at the slightest provocation.

When I rowed in close to the seawall of the town and located a small building where a douane boat was hung in davits under a roof to protect it from the sun and over which a customs flag hung limp from a staff, I felt that I was reasonably correct in guessing that this was the office of the harbor–master. There were a few loafers on a jetty that stood half–heartedly just far enough out from shore to clear the surf. I addressed these as best I could and asked for the harbor–master. They did not seem to understand, neither did they care. I asked again and louder, then I flung my wretched French to the oily sea and used the most concise and forcible English I could command —not that I thought it would do any good but just to let off the steam of my ire. A miracle occurred! A head and shoulders became visible in one of the windows of the customs' office, for such it was, and yelled :.

"Keep your shirt on, old man, we're not fussy here. Come right ashore and I'll take your papers after we've said, 'How do you do.' " This was the greatest shock I had yet received in the Caribbean. When I recovered myself —I had been standing in order to swear the better —I sat down to row ashore. Basse Terre is built along an open roadstead somewhat like St. Pierre but with a retaining wall built up from a steep shelving beach to the level of the streets fifteen feet above. I beached the Yakaboo under the sea wall where a number of boatmen lifted her up and carried her to a place of safety. The English–speaking harbor–master, who really was an American, came out, grabbed my hand, and led me into his office.

"It's a darn small ensign you carry, but it does my heart good to see it," he said, and then he began to introduce me to some of his cronies who had been helping him to pass away a hot calm afternoon with a gossip and a smoke. There were Henri Jean–Louia (Homme de Lettres, Chargé de mission agricole par la Chambre d'agriculture de Point–à–Pitre et le Conseil général de la Guadeloupe), and Hubert Ancelin (Négociant–Commissionaire, Secrétaire–Trésorier des Chambres de Commerce et d'Agriculture, Agent de la Compagnie "Quebec Line") —I am reading the titles of these dignitaries from the cards they gave me —and there was a small French–looking man with a great deal of dignity who seemed very much interested in everything we said.

Jean–Louia, the newspaper man, asked me if I would care for a little refreshment. I replied that since I was no longer in a whisky–and–soda country any liquid refreshment he might choose would be very acceptable. In a short time some cakes and a bottle of champagne were brought in. My health was proposed (there were certainly no outward signs of my immediate decline) and we drank the delicious wine in delicate champagne glasses. Bum that I was, —you shall have an accurate description later, —if I had been suddenly dropped into the middle of a ball room I would not have felt more incongruous than drinking champagne and eating bits of French pastry less than a quarter of an hour from the time I had left the Caribbean and the Yakaboo.

But I must bring forward the little man who has shown great interest in our conversation. He was dressed in white duck, trousers loose and baggy, coat with military cut, and he wore mustachios, —a typical Frenchman. I had been doing my uttermost with the meager vocabulary that I could claim my own when I bethought myself of the little man who had listened but had not said a word. Neither had he been introduced to me as yet. I turned to Magras and said in English, "And who is this little Frenchman?" at which the "little Frenchman" piped up, "I'm no Frenchman, I'm a Yankee but I suppose I've been down here so darn long I look like one. My name is Flower," he continued, "and I came to ask if you would care to spend the night with me at my house."

This certainly was a day of misjudgments and for a second time I could have been floored by a mere breath. I thanked Mr. Flower and told him that I should be delighted to spend the night with him.

There were still two hours of daylight when I left the harbormaster's office with Mr. Flower, who with the energy characteristic of the small man in the tropics, led me through unshaded deserted streets to the outskirts of the town to the half–ruined Fort Richepance on the banks of the Galion River. Basse Terre cannot be said to be picturesque ; there is an arid barren aspect about the town that would not appeal to the tourist. That it has been a place of some importance one can see from the military plan of the wide streets, squares and substantial stone, brick and concrete houses. It was evidently not laid out by a civil governor. One might easily reconstruct a past full of romance and stirring incidents, for Basse Terre was the West Indian hotbed of revolution bred from the ferment in Paris. It was here that Victor Hugues began his notorious career. Born of mean parents in some part of old France he was early placed out as an apprentice. Whatever his character may have been, he was a man of spirit for he soon became master of a small trading vessel and was eventually made a lieutenant in the French navy. Through the influence of Robespierre he was deputed to the National Assembly. In 1794 he was appointed Commissioner at Guadeloupe. Should his life history be written it would be a fascinating tale of cupidity, intrigue, murder and riot —a reflection of the reign of terror in the mother country. Had he been less of a rogue France instead of England might today have been the dominant power in the Lesser Antilles.

The next day I experienced my first real calm in the tropics. My log reads : —"Tuesday, May 9th, 1911. Off at 8 :30 (could not disturb my host's domestic schedule in order to make an early start) and a long weary row along the lee shore of Guadeloupe. Blistering calm with shifting puffs at times. Deshaies at 6 P.M. Distance 27 miles. Beautiful harbor but unhealthy —turned in at local jail."

ALONE IN THE CARIBBEAN

I tried to sail in those shifting puffs but it was a waste of time. The lee coast of Guadeloupe is noted for its calms and on this May day when the trade to windward must have been very light, there was at times not a breath of air. I settled down for a long row. The heat did not become intense till eleven when what breeze there had been ceased and on all the visible Caribbean I could detect no darkened ruffle of its surface. The sun was well advanced into his danger arc. I had on a thick pair of trousers, a red sleeveless rowing shirt and a light flannel over–shirt open at the collar to let in as much air as possible. I made a nest of a bandana handkerchief and put it on my head. On top of that I lightly rested my hat. To protect the back of my neck I wore a red bandana loosely tied with the knot under my chin —just opposite to the fashion of the stage cowboy who wears his handkerchief like a napkin.

Then, with the least possible effort, I rowed the canoe along shore, rarely turning my head but keeping the corner of my eye along the shore which is nearly straight in its general trend —a little west of north. From time to time I would stop and hold both oars in one hand while with the other I gently lifted the cloth of my trousers clear of the burning skin beneath. For a time I rowed with my sleeves down but the burn of the salt sweat and the friction of the cloth more than counteracted the benefit I might gain by shading my forearms and I rolled up my sleeves again.

My forearms, one would suppose, had, after these three months of continual exposure, all the tan possible, but I found that after a while the skin was blushing a deep red and somewhat swollen and painful. The glare from the water was intense and to protect my eyes I screwed my face into the grin of a Cheshire cat, to elevate my cheeks and bring down my eyebrows. Try it and half close your eyes and you will know just what I mean. The sea heaved in long shallow groundswells as though laboring heavily for breath.

The dazzling beaches quivered in the heat waves while the mountains stood up sharp and strong in the fierce sunlight. There was not the slightest sign of fish and it seemed as though the sun had driven them to the coolest depths below. At twelve o'clock I stopped for a few minutes to eat a "pine" the natives had given me at Toucan Bay. This pineapple which, I believe, was originally brought from Antigua where the best pines of the West Indies are found, has a golden flesh, sweeter than the white fibrous fruit which we of the North know and yet with all of the tang. The core is soft and partly edible and one can eat the whole of one of these fruits with a pleasing absence of that acrid taste which leaves the after effect of putting one's teeth on edge. There are many fruits to which we refer as "delicious" and "refreshing" in our paucity of descriptive adjectives but these two words cannot be applied in a better sense than in describing the pineapple of the Lesser Antilles.

Two o'clock came and then, thank the Lord, the sun began to go appreciably to the westward so that by slightly raising the mainsail I could get some protection. My long pull at last came to an end when at six o'clock I rowed into a beautiful little bay and beached the canoe at the very doorsteps of the village of Deshaies. The bay was a deep pocket walled by green hills on three sides and open to seaward where the sun with a guilty red face was hurrying to get below the horizon so that he could sneak around again as fast as possible in order to have some more fun scorching inoffensive canoe people.

The bay, a snug enough harbor for small coasters, struck into the land like a tongue of the ocean mottled with shoals and coral reefs while the green of the hills was barred from the blue water by a narrow strip of white sand. The charm of the place was strong and I forgot the hot toil of the day while I stood on the beach by the Yakaboo and looked about me. Scarcely two canoe lengths from the water's edge stood the outposts of the village, those meaner houses of the fishermen, the beachcombers, and the keepers of small rum shops.

The people, of the lighter shades of the mulatto, were loafing as to the male portion on this common back porch of beach, while the women were busy over ovens and coalpots, preparing the evening meal. With the apathy of the island native they had watched me row into their quiet harbor and had waited till I was actually on the beach at their very door steps before they got up from their haunches to flock around the canoe. But now there was great excitement. They looked at me and at the canoe and there was nothing they saw about either of us that was at all familiar. To give them a thrill I pulled on the mizzen halyard and let it go again —the sail fanned out, crawled up the mast, slid down again, and folded up.

Surprise and curiosity showed in all their features but they made no move to touch my things, they merely looked. Some one with an air of importance dispatched a boy for some one else who had official authority and soon after the acting mayor came down to the beach. The mayor, it seemed, was laid up with an attack of fever. The acting mayor was a dapper little person, very civil, and not at all officious. Could he do anything for me? I told him that from the evening set I believed there was promise of a strong wind on the morrow and that I was now preparing my canoe for an early start in order to jump the thirty−eight miles of open water to Montserrat before the trade might grow into a gale. Therefore I did not want to make a camp. I also said that I feared I had come to a fever hole —at which he grinned assent —and if he could find some place where I could sleep without the company of mosquitoes I would be deeply indebted to him.

He told me that he would place the town "hotel" at my disposal and said that while he was attending to my papers he would get the key. As for the Yakaboo, she would be perfectly safe where she lay on the beach. In the meantime I would stretch my legs and see a bit of the town during the few remaining minutes of twilight. Deshaies was of a régime which had lasted until recent years and the substantial houses of its main street reminded me of those of our "before the war" cities in the Southern states. Dilapidation was everywhere ; there were no actual ruins. The old prosperity was gone and the town was waiting dormant till the coming of that more stable inheritance which is the natural right of a soil wonderfully fertile.

There were iron grills and balconies and bits of paved roadway and courtyard and there were faces among those easy−going people that took my mind back to Mayero and the descendants of the Saint−Hilaire family. But the banded Anopheles were coming from the Deshaies River bed in millions and I returned to the beach where I found the acting mayor waiting for me. He had borrowed a sheet of my note paper which he now returned, a neatly written document to the effect that I had landed that evening at Deshaies sans rien d'anormal —on my way to Montserrat. Then he showed me a great iron key and led me across the street to that "hotel" which is less sought after than needed.

It was the town lock−up ! —consisting of a detached building of one story and having two rooms, perhaps more properly cells, which were heavily barred and shuttered. In the first room a deal table stood in the middle of the floor. On this I put my food bags and my candle lamp which I lit, for it was now dark outside. There was but one thought in my mind, to get as much rest as possible, for the next day might prove a hard one.

I borrowed a coalpot and while I cooked my supper I chatted with the acting mayor. He was to be married, he said, and that night there was to be a dance in honor of his betrothal. He would deem it a great honor if I would come to the dance, but I declined, saying that unless I was very much mistaken the morrow would be the last day for two weeks in which I might safely cross the channel and that I feared to remain in this fever hole any longer than I could possibly help. To avoid the possibility of being annoyed by rats, I carried my food back to the canoe where I stowed it safely under the hatches.

The acting mayor bade me good night and left me to smoke my evening pipe on the doorstep of the jail. After a while the preliminary scale of a flute and the open fifths of a violin announced that the ball was about to begin and I closed the ponderous door of the jail on the strains of the first dance. I had long since put out my light lest it attract mosquitoes and as I made up my bed on the floor I heard the scampering of rats in the darkness. I must confess to a childish horror of rats that is even greater than that of snakes and I finally put a new candle in my lamp so that it might burn all night. I was awakened at five o'clock in the morning by the acting mayor who was returning from the dance. The town did not awaken at five, it seemed, and there was no glowing coalpot to be had. To my disgust there was not a stick in the canoe and on the beach there were nothing but soggy coco–tree fronds. At last a door creaked and from the woman who opened it I bought some charcoal. In spite of my precautions of the night before, it was an hour and twenty minutes before I finally shoved off in the Yakaboo.

CHAPTER XI. WE MAKE OUR BEST RUN.

WE LEFT the beach in a dead calm. The sun was nearly an hour above an horizon of trade clouds and even as I rowed I could see the wind that was coming begin to darken the water in patches to the eastward. In half an hour the wind caught up to us and soon after I set sail. We were scarcely free of Guadeloupe when the canoe began to move with the first light breaths, over a long easy swell. Montserrat was a hazy blur on the horizon, and I should have to look sharp lest I miss it.

For a while I held directly for the blur, but as the wind freshened it began to work into the south'ard and I shifted my course till I was running wing and wing with the island two points to weather. I did this so that later in the day I would not have a hard wind and a heavy sea directly abaft —the most ticklish and nerve–tiring condition for canoe sailing. The wind was increasing steadily and I knew I was in for half a gale —and a good run. I also knew that while it was necessary to make as much speed as possible, I should have to keep a sharp eye on my gear, for if anything crippled my rig for windward work I was in for an adventure on the Caribbean. This wind held for a week and were I blown clear of Montserrat there would be no choice but to keep on with some sort of rig up till I struck Saint Croix, one hundred and seventy–five miles away.

If ever at any time on this cruise, I was now sailing along the thin edge of things. Although it was a second quarter that had come in soft, it seemed that a fifth day had slipped in somehow for the weather was on a rampage. We were nearing the end of the regular trade season and might expect our almost infallible weather signs to break down. I found that my barometer showed but little variation during the time I was in the Lesser Antilles and only kept tabs on it in order to note the decided drop which might indicate the approach of any weather more severe than the ordinary blow.

As far as I could see to windward, north and south, squalls were now chasing down as though there were two conditions of wind ; one a stiff breeze and the other a series of squalls moving independent of and through the first. The canoe was traveling so fast —we were making a good six knots —that I could easily dodge most of the squalls by tacking down the wind like a square rigger. Once I was actually running off on the port tack WSW while the course from Deshaies was NW1/4W. There was no harm in being thrown off my course to the south and west for it ultimately served to place Montserrat all the more to windward.

When the wind which was blowing from east–southeast finally declared itself a young gale, I found to my great relief that I had worked my way so far to the westward that my course for the island was now a little better than NWbN. Instead of having to run within one point of being dead before the wind our course was now two points farther to windward. Nearly every sea was breaking and we were making a continual succession of toboggan rides, the breaking seas at times carrying us up the back of the sea ahead so that we were actually traveling a little faster than the waves themselves. This surf–riding soon became a regular habit and I was forced to reef the mainsail and mizzen lest the Yakaboo turn end for end. We now slowed down to a more reasonable speed.

One might imagine that at a time like this I would have little chance for observation and yet with my senses alert to their highest efficiency there was very little that escaped me. My eyes wandered on a continual circuit from the compass in my cockpit into the belly of my mainsail, up the mast and down again to the seas about me. Then we swung on a

161

quick circuit through a hundred and eighty degrees from the seas under our bows to the squalls astern, taking in the skies on our return.

It was on this mind panorama that I saw more distinctly than at any other time the manner in which these islands gather moisture from the trade clouds. For a time after we had left Deshaies, Montserrat moped mist–wrapped on the horizon. Then slowly the heat of the morning sun prevailed and the island became more and more definite in outline till it at last showed clear and distinct —a volcano on the horizon. The island is made up of two peaks but from my position they were almost directly in line so that I saw only the outline of the southernmost and larger, the Souffrière.

The wind was then blowing lightly and the sky was clear of clouds except in the east where they were advancing in droves with the wind before the sun. The trade overtook us first and then came the clouds, fleecy and bulging, like ships before the wind, each with a squall under it. I watched a small cloud, one of the first of the van, approach the peak with unslackened speed till it lodged against the mountainside two thousand feet above the sea, where it came to a full stop. It seemed almost to recoil a bit. Then it slowly embraced the peak and more slowly began to draw away again to the westward. When it was finally clear of the island I saw that it had lost half its bulk. Montserrat had taken her toll in mountain showers.

For a space the peak was again clear in outline, two volcanic curves that came out of the sea to meet three thousand feet above. Next a large stately cloud, a ship of the line among the others, enveloped the peak and came to a stop. There it hung and diminished in size till it was reinforced by another cloud and for the rest of my run the upper third of the island was hidden in a cloud cap, which diminished and increased in volume like slow breathing.

The wind seemed to be continually freshening and I found that although I had reduced my sail area by nearly one–half, I was again catching up to the seas ahead and tobogganing. I had moved the duffle in my cockpit as far aft as I could and sat on the deck with my back against the mizzen mast. Just above my head I lashed my camera —the most precious part of my outfit. At the first indication of broaching–to I would take hold of the mast and force her over on her weather bilge till she was almost before the wind. Then I would let her come up to her course and hold her there till she took the bit in her teeth again when I would have to pry her back as before.

ALONE IN THE CARIBBEAN

My blood was up and I told her that she could turn end for end if she wanted and tear the rig out before I would take in any more sail. A bit of anger is a great help at times. Another time, when I go canoe cruising on the sea, I shall carry a small squaresail and a sea anchor that I can readily trip. In spite of all my efforts it seemed that we should be forced to weather of Montserrat and that I should have to run off for a while to the southeast. But we were sailing faster than I suspected and at last fetched up abreast of the southern end of the island and about a quarter of a mile off shore. Then I brought her into the wind and hove–to with the reefed mizzen and let the wind carry us into the calm water under the lee of the island.

I looked at my watch and found that it was just eleven–thirty. We had made our last long jump, the most exciting of all our channel runs in the Caribbean. We had covered thirty–five miles in five hours and ten minutes. We had sailed thirty–three miles in four hours and forty minutes —our average speed had been a little more than seven miles an hour. For some time, however, after I had made sail our speed was not much more than five miles, and I believe that the last nine miles had been covered in an hour, with fifty square feet of sail up! Except in a racing canoe I had never sailed faster in a small craft than on this run.

The wind, eddying around the end of the island, was carrying us directly along shore and I lowered my mizzen while I ate my luncheon. It was pleasant to drift along without thought of course and to watch the shore go by at a three–mile gait. I had just settled myself comfortably in the cockpit when I noticed a native who had come down to the beach waving his arms frantically. That we drifted as fast as he could walk along shore was good evidence that the wind was blowing strongly. I learned afterwards that he thought me to be the sole survivor of a fishing boat that had been lost a week before from Nevis. She was never heard from. After I landed at Plymouth I was told that a sloop had been dismasted that morning in the roadstead.

At the time it was a genuine source of satisfaction, not that I was happy in the ill luck of the sloop, but I regarded this as proof of the sturdy qualities of the Yakaboo. One must, however, always be fair in such matters and it is only right for me to say that after further acquaintance with the sloops of the Lesser Antilles it is a marvel to me that they stand up as well as they do. The credit does not rest with the Yakaboo but rather with the freak luck of the West Indian skipper. God, it seems, has greater patience with these fellows than with any other people who have to do with the sea —I have purposely avoided

163

calling the natives of the Lesser Antilles sailormen.

There was not much in Montserrat for me. Thirty miles to the northwest lay Nevis and St. Kitts —stepping stones to St. Eustatius and Saba. A nearer invitation than these was Redonda, a rounded rock like Diamond off Martinique which rose almost sheer to a height of a thousand feet out of deep water with no contiguous shoals, a detached peak like those of the Grenadines —a lone blot with Montserrat the nearest land, eight miles away. On the 10th of November in 1493 Columbus coasted along Guadeloupe and discovered Monserratte, which he named after the mountain in Spain where Ignatius Loyola conceived the project of founding the Society of Jesus. "Next," says Barbot, "he found a very round island, every way perpendicular so that there seemed to be no getting up into it without ladders, and therefore he called it Santa Maria la Redonda." The Indian name was Ocamaniro.

It was on the morning, when I was loading the Yakaboo for the run to Redonda, that I came as near as at any time to having a passenger. As I was stowing my duffle, there was the usual circumcurious audience, beach loafers mostly, with a transient friend or two who had come down early to see me off. The forehatch was still open when the parting of the crowd proclaimed the coming of a person of superior will, not unaccompanied by a height of figure, six feet two, strong and raw–boned, the masculine negress of the English islands. She carried a large bottle of honey and a jar of preserved fruits. "My name is Rebecca Cooper," she said by way of introduction, "an' I cum to ask if you take a passenger to Nevis wid you."

I looked at the cockpit of the Yakaboo and at her tall figure. "Oh, me seafarin' woman, me no 'fraid. Oh, yas, I been Trinidad —been aal 'roun'!"

"I'm sorry," I said, "if you're to be the passenger the skipper will have to stay ashore."

"Das too bad. Annyway I bring you a bottle of honey an' some Jamaica plums an' cashews."

I stowed the bottle and the jar in exchange for which she very reluctantly took a shilling. She lived somewhere up in the hills and having heard fantastic tales of the Yakaboo she had come down to see the canoe and its skipper with her offering of mountain honey and preserves. It was unselfish kindness on her part and she only took the shilling that she might buy "some little thing" by which to remember me. There are many like these in the islands, but they are scarcely known to the tourist —sad to relate.

While Rebecca Cooper was silently examining the canoe, I took out the clearance paper which the Collector of Customs had given me the day before. It read as follows : *****

MONTSERRAT
Port of PLYMOUTH.

THESE are to certify all whom it doth concern, that F. A. Fenger master or commander of the Yakaboo, burthen 1/4 tons, mounted with __ guns, navigated with __ men Am. built and bound for Nevis having on board Ballast &Captain hath here entered and cleared his vessel according to law. Given under my hand at the Treasury, at the Port of Plymouth, in the Presidency of Montserrat, this 18th day of May, one thousand nine hundred and eleven. EDWARD F. DYETT
1st Treasury Officer

*****

It was the "Ballast and Captain" that made me think. My outfit —not perfect as yet, but still the apple of my eye —was put down as "Ballast" and to add ignominy to slight I was put down under that as "Captain." I dislike very much this honorary frill —Captain —it is worse than "Colonel."

The wind was light from the southeast and we —the Yakaboo and I, for we left Rebecca on the beach with the crowd —slipped off with eased sheets at a gentle gait of three miles an hour.

The early settlers of Montserrat and Nevis were largely Irish. Strange to say, among the first Europeans to see the West Indies were and Englishman, Arthur Laws or Larkins, and an Irishman,m William Harris of Galway, who sailed with Columbus. We are inclined to think that the crews of the Admiral's fleet were made up wholly of swarthy Portuguese, Spaniards, and Italians. Churchill, in speaking of Redonda, says that most of the inhabitants were Irish —but what they could find for existence on this almost barren rock with its difficult ascent is hard to understand. It is true that Redonda proved to have a considerable commercial value, but not until 1865 when it was found that the rock bore a rich covering of phosphate of alumina. The rock is not nearly exhausted of its rich deposit, but I was told in Montserrat that I should find a crew of negroes in charge of the company's buildings.

One must always take the words of early explorers —as well as modern ones —with a grain of salt in regard to the wonders of nature, but when Barbot called Redonda a "very round island, every way perpendicular so that there seemed to be no getting up into it without ladders," he did not exaggerate. When I lowered the sails of the Yakaboo under the lee of Redonda, I saw that the sides of the rock rose sheer out of the water like the Pitons of Saint Lucia, except for one place where a submerged ledge supported a few tons of broken rock which had tumbled down from the heights above. This could hardly be called a beach and it was no landing place for a boat.

Built up from this ledge of debris was a concrete pier which stood some ten feet above the water and was surmounted by a wooden cargo boom. Anchored in the rock near the pier was a steel cable that ran up like the thread of a gigantic spider to a point some four hundred feet above, where I made out a sort of staging. I rowed close to shore and shouted, but there was no answer. Then, thinking that I was too far under the cliff, I rowed off a bit and began to fire my thirty–eight–forty. A voice from somewhere up there shouted down to me but what it said I could not understand. I located two figures busy on the staging and presently a miner's bucket began to slowly slide down the cable. There was something novel in this; sailing up to an immense rock in the sea, firing off a revolver as a signal to natives I had never seen before, and having a bucket lowered for me from a height of four hundred feet.

While I was watching the descending bucket a boat with four men in it came from around the end of the rock. The sea being smooth they were fishing on the weather side of Redonda and when they saw me they came post haste for they had been expecting me. They rowed alongside and I put aboard the duffle I should require for the night. Then we fastened the painter of the Yakaboo to a large mooring buoy used by steamers when taking on their cargo from lighters towed up from Montserrat when the occasion requires. I very carefully examined the buoy with its seven–eighths chain and asked the men if it would hold the canoe in case of a blow. "Shur! an' it's th' same moorin' we use fer th oiland whin a hurricane is blowin'," said one with a brogue as broad as any just over from the Isle.

ALONE IN THE CARIBBEAN

The speaker was Frederick Payne, as pleasant a native as I have found in the islands, who if you put him in another room and heard him talk you would wager the soul of your maternal grandmother against a thrupenny bit was no other than a red–whiskered Irishman.? ? Hauling in the boat. ?

?

? The capstan. ?

?

? The bucket. ?

The canoe made fast, we rowed ashore and clambered up the iron ladder on the face of the pier. The boom was swung out, tackle lowered and the boat hoisted inboard like a piece of cargo. The bucket which had come down with a load of phosphate, we emptied and climbed aboard for our aerial ride The winch was started and we were slowly hauled up the cable which follows a ravine–like cleft in the rock. On either side was a scanty growth of scrub brush and cactus which seemed to grow for the sole purpose of giving perches to the noddies and gulls that eyed us from a fathom's length or two with the all–seeing idle curiosity of a cash girl of a dull afternoon.

Little by little the Yakaboo diminished in size till she looked like the weak dash of an exclamation point with the buoy for an overgrown period. The sea was sinking away from us. I took out my barometer and we watched the needle while it swung from "Fair" to "Change." Finally the needle stopped and we were hauled on the staging by the two sweating natives who had wound us up. By an easy path, we climbed three hundred feet more to the company's buildings.

What an eagle's nest from which to look down upon a world of sea! Montserrat was a near neighbor, high Nevis not much farther off brought out of the place queer thoughts of school days when Hamilton was a mere bewigged effigy on the glossy page of a history book. What right had he to be born down here in the Caribbean? There was Antigua to windward of the arc of our cruise; what right had she and Nevis to know Nelson whom our young minds inferred spent his entire life at Trafalgar and the battle of the Nile? Edging out from the weather shoulder of Montserrat lay Guadeloupe in a shroud of mist as though keeping to herself some ferment of a modern Victor Hugues. But the redundant thought was always of the riches that have been in these islands and the extraordinary selfishness and sordidness that have been the motives of nearly every act since the discovery of the West Indies by Columbus.

We were too high for the glare of the sea and I wandered about through the whole delightful afternoon on the top of the rock to descend at sunset to the enclosed verandah of the manager's house where I satisfied a righteous appetite with a roasted chicken of Ethiopian–Irish upbringing.

In the morning I was lowered from this giant's stepping stone and was once more cockpit sailing, in a light breeze, for Nevis. Except for the distant sight of a goodly "gyaff topsail" on the first day when I skirted the Grenada shores, I had seen no indications of large sharks. What had at first been a haunting bugaboo had now become a forgotten possibility. We were approaching the banks which lie to the southward of Nevis and I sat on my blanket bag, bent up behind me like a cushioned easy chair with a lazy–back.

There was just enough breeze to allow me to lean with my elbow on the weather deck. Sharks were as far removed from my thoughts as the discussion of the Immaculate Conception —I believe I was actually deciding that my first venture upon escaping the clutches of the chosen few who guard our national customs would be a large dish of ice cream which I would eat so rapidly that it would chill the top of my head and drive from it forever the memory of the calms of Dominica and Guadeloupe. My mind was fondling this chilly thought when suddenly the flash of a yard of rainbow under my bows announced the arrival of a Dauphin, or, as they called them in the days of Labat, a Cock Dorade. By the shape of its square–nosed head I could see that it was the male of the species. I have often wondered whether this was not the dolphin of the dying colors —it surpasses even the bonito in the marvellous changes in its hues when expiring. These fish are common near the northern coast of Martinique. Père Labat says that in order to catch the dorade without bait one must troll with a fly made of two pigeon feathers on each side of a hook and smeared with dog grease. I watched him leisurely cruise for a while back and forth under the bow when suddenly there was a mighty swirl under the nose of the canoe and I saw the greyish white torpedo form of a huge shark heave after him. The dauphin was not to be caught unawares —the Lord knows how long Mr. Shark had been watching him from under the shadow of the Yakaboo —and the pair tore away through the sea, the shark a lagging second. After a hopeless dash the shark gave up the chase.

ALONE IN THE CARIBBEAN

I watched the dorsal fin make a wide circle to windward and then coming up from astern he settled down for a comfortable loaf under the canoe where he could again lie in wait for a careless dauphin that might happen along. I leaned over and watched him as he hung, indolently, just to leeward of the tip of my centerboard. He seemed almost as long as the Yakaboo —once when he drifted a little off-side, I got his measure, his length reaching from the forward point of the canoe's shadow to the upright line of the mizzen; by this he must have been a little over twelve feet in length. If he were not as "big 'roun' as a barril" he certainly would have been a good armful had I jumped overboard to embrace him, —but I had no such intention. He must have been too slow and ponderous to feed on such swift fish as the dauphin unless he caught one by surprise as he had tried to get this one from the shadow of the canoe.

No wonder these fellows become desperate at times and go in packs like hungry wolves to some whale pasturage where they can drag down their cattle by sheer force of numbers after the manner of their land relations. I had no reason to believe he would trouble me unless I was foolish enough to throw something overboard or otherwise attract his attention by leaning too far out to look at him. A sly peek over the edge of the gunwale was enough and I made that with my arsenal ready. What he thought this could be sailing so slowly above him with a belly like a fish and a fin that did not scull and two white wings sticking up into the air from its back, I don't know, for I am as yet unfamiliar with the working of a shark's mind. Had he known there was a tasty scrap (pardon this subtle bit of self-flattery) only three feet away should he choose to butt that stiff fin, his actions might have been different.

I watched his wicked pig eyes but he did not seem to look up or take notice of the canoe. He merely hung there in its shadow, an almost imperceptible flexation of his body and a sculling of his tail being sufficient to move him along at three knots an hour. We were scarcely two miles from Redonda when he had come back from his dash after the dauphin and from that time for over ten miles, till we were well within the Nevis bank, he hardly varied his position a foot. I have somehow or other always associated the presence of sharks with calm weather and oily seas. The story books always have it so. In the West Indies the shark is more in evidence during the calms of the hurricane months than at any other time. On this account the French call him requien which is a corruption of requiem. Rocheford says, "Les François & les Portugais luy donnent ordinairement ce nom de Requiem, c'est à dire Repose, peutetre par ce qu'il à accoutumé de paroître lors que le tems est serain & tranquille . . ." (The French and the Portuguese usually call it Requiem,

169

that is to say Repose, perhaps because it usually appears when the weather is serene and tranquil.) At last he slipped away, a gruesome shape, to cruise about ghostlike on the shoals. I almost felt lonely after his departure —his absence was like that of a sore tooth which has been pulled out.

The shark took with him what little wind there was and I rowed around the corner of Nevis to its port of entry, Charlestown. Nevis runs up into a single peak, the lower slopes sweeping down to the sea like a train checkered with sugarcane plantations. The island seems more wind-swept than Montserrat; it has a fresh atmosphere quite different from all the rest of the Lesser Antilles —still it is one of the oldest and was settled in 1608 by Englishmen from St. Kitts. To me there is a singular fascination in going ashore in a place like this and coming upon some old connection with the history of our own republic. I had purposely loafed on my way from Redonda so that I could land in the cooler part of the afternoon.

As soon as I had shown my papers to the harbormaster, he said, "Can I do anything for you?" "Yes. Show me the birthplace of Alexander Hamilton."

It was like asking for the village post office in some New England seacoast town. A walk of two minutes along the main road brought us to the place where I took a photograph of a few ruined walls. Here I could gape and wonder like any passing tourist and reap what I could from my own imagination. They tell me that a famous writer of historical romance once spent a day here to absorb a "touch of local color." An admirable book and written in a style which will bring a bit of history to many who would otherwise be more ignorant of the heroes of our young Republic. It is history with a sugar coating but the "touch," I am afraid, is like that artificial coloring which the tobacconist gives to a meerschaum that is to become a pet. In all these islands there is no end of "atmosphere" to be easily gotten, but what of the innermost history of these places?

Nevis has always been a land of sugar, open country and fertile and in its time wondrously rich —the ruins of old estates like that of the Hamiltons show that —and in secluded places such as the little village of Newcastle on the windward side with its top bay, extremely picturesque. But in these places one must of necessity scratch around a bit and get under the top soil of things. What about the camels that were brought here from the East to carry cane to the mills? Who brought them here and when? Did the young Alexander know the sleepy-eyed, soft-footed beasts? There were one or two on the island as late as 1875 and I talked with a lady who as a small child used to be frightened at their groanings as they rose, togglejointed, from the roadway beneath her window. To learn the intimate history of these islands one must first visit them for acquaintance sake and then go to Europe and dig up stray bits from letters and manuscripts sent from the islands to the old country. Of papers and correspondence there is very little to be found here and it is at the other end of the old trade routes that one must search.

I left Nevis on a hot calm Sunday morning for Basse Terre, the port of St. Kitts. The row was twelve miles and the calm hotter than that of Guadeloupe. There was no perceptible breeze, just a slow movement of air from the northeast —not enough to be felt —a sluggish current that stranded a ponderous cloud on the peak of Monkey Hill, its head leaning far out over the Caribbean where I rowed into its shadow. When I was still half a mile from the town I stood up in the cockpit and took off my clothes. After I was thoroughly cooled I enjoyed a shower bath by the simple expedient of holding one of my water cans over my head and letting the water pour down over my body. Then I put on my "extra" clothes. They were extra in that they were clean. The shirt was still a shirt, for there is no alternate name for that which had degenerated into a mere covering for one's upper half, but the trousers were pants. They were clean; I had done it myself on the deck of the Yakaboo. Some day when I build another canoe I shall corrugate a part of the forward deck so that I can cling the better to it when I am trying to get into the hatch in a seaway and also so that I can use it as a rubbing board when there is washing to be done.

The shade of this cloud was something extraordinary. At first I thought there would be a heavy downpour of rain but the air was too inert and the cloud hung undecided. like most other things West Indian. For the first time in four months I could take off my hat in the daytime! I enjoyed this shade while I could and I ate my luncheon, the canoe drifting slowly northward on the tide. It was just the time and the place for another shark and I thought of my friend of the Nevis bank. I saw no fish and threw out no invitations and when I had had my fill I rowed into Basse Terre where I was received by the fourth unofficious harbormaster I had yet encountered.

But we shall not be long in St. Kitts, or Sinkitts as the authoress puts it by way of a little impressionist dab of "color." I found some interesting old newspapers in the cool library of Basse Terre where I spent several days reading the English version of the war of 1812. "Now!" I promised myself, "I shall see something of the island to which the Admiral gave his own name." But promises on a cruise like this, however, are not worth the wasting of a thought upon.

CHAPTER XII. STATIA —THE STORY OF THE SALUTE.

DON'T WASTE your time hâre," he said in the swinging dialect of the northern islands, "you will be among your own at Statia and Saba." I had met this Saba man on the jetty, Captain "Ben" Hassel of a tidy little schooner, ex–Gloucester, and he told me of the Dutch islands and their people. He was my first breath of Saba and my nostrils smelt something new.

Saba had been a love at first sight for I had already seen her at a distance from the deck of the steamer as we had passed southwards in January. The Christmas gale which had chased us down from Hatteras passed us on to that more frolicsome imp of Boreas, the squally trade on a "chyange ob de moon" day. It was the same Captain Ben's schooner that I had watched running down for the island under foresail. Through the long ship's telescope I had made out the cluster of white houses of the Windward Village, plastered like cassava cakes on the wall of a house, but as I came to know later, nestled in a shallow bowl that tipped towards the Atlantic. Although we were within the tropics, it blew down cold and blustering with an overcast sky more like the Baltic than the Caribbean. I did not then know how I should come to long for just such an overcast sky to shut off for a few hours that blazing ball of fire known to us of the North as the smiling sun. His smile had turned into a Sardonic grin. As Saba began to grow indistinct, the sharper outlines of Statia had brought me to the opposite rail and with hungry eyes I swept the shores which were all but hidden by the obstinate rain squall that had come down from the hills and was hanging over the cliffs of the Upper Town as if to rest awhile before starting on its weepy way westward to vanish later in the blazing calm of the Caribbean.

And that is why you shall hear nothing of St. Kitts for the day after I spoke with Captain Ben, I was again in the Yakaboo. The offshore wind that helped us up the lee of St. Kitts carried with it the sweet rummy odor of sugarcane that kept my thoughts back in the old days. Then, as we were well up the coast, there came another odor, a mere elusive whiff of sulphur, that went again leaving a doubt as to whether it were real, and my thoughts were switched to the formidable Brimstone Hill, now towering above us inshore, shot some seven hundred feet out of the slope of Mount Misery by a volcanic action which had all but lacked the strength to blow the projectile clear of the land. It was the beginning of a new volcano, but the action had stopped with the forcing up of the mass of rock which now forms Brimstone Hill. On the top of the rock is Fort George, one of the most fascinating masses of semi–ruin I have ever seen. With the atmosphere of the place still clinging to me I had read Colonel Stuart's "Reminiscences of a Soldier." He had spoken of Bedlam Barracks through which I had just been wandering, in his first letter to England. "Bedlam Barracks, Brimstone Hill, Mount Misery," he said, "are not the most taking of cognomens, but what's in a name?"

Until recent years there stood on Brimstone Hill the famous bronze cannon which bore the inscription : "Ram me well and load me tight, I'll send a ball to Statia's Height."

The wind freshened and St. Kitts with its Mount Misery and Brimstone Hill was rapidly slipping by as I passed into the shoal channel where "Old Statia" stood up seven miles away. The channel was "easy" on this day and I could give myself up to that altogether delightful contemplation of the approaching island. Characteristic from the east and west in her similarity to the two–peaked back of a camel, Statia is more striking when approached from the south where the Atlantic on its way to the Caribbean has cut into the slope of the "Quille," exposing the chalky cliff known as the White Wall. Blue, snow–shadowed, the White Wall gives an impression of freshness that seemed to belie the weathered battery which I could begin to make out at its western end. Here, during the calms of the hurricane season, the sperm whale comes to rub his belly and flukes against the foot of the cliff where it descends into the blue waters of the channel, to scour away a year's growth of barnacles.

Farther to the westward, de Windt's battery took form, while a thatched negro hut or two on the lower slopes of the "Quille" were the only evidence of human habitation. Behind it all, the perfect crater of the "Quille" rose, covered with an almost impenetrable tropic verdure which had flowed up the sides and poured into the bowl as the rain, from the time of the last eruption, had changed the volcanic dust into a moist earth of almost pre–glacial fecundity.

ALONE IN THE CARIBBEAN

We had hardly passed mid–channel, it seemed, when the wind, eddying around the south end of the island, swept the canoe with lifted sheets past the corner of Gallows Bay, and I found myself bobbing up and down in the swell off the Lower Town of Oranje. As I lowered my rig and made snug, I could see below me, through the clear waters, what had once been a busy quay. The long ground swell dropping away from under threatened to wreck the centerboard of the Yakaboo on the ruined wall of a warehouse that had once helped to determine the success of the American colonies. On shore, an excited group of negro fishermen had gathered from the shadows of the broken walls to join the harbormaster who had lumbered from his hot kantoor (office) to the still hotter sands, in shirt and trousers —and not without an oath. "Watch de sea!" he yelled as half a dozen negroes waded in up to their waists.

"Look shyarp ! —NOW!" and I ran the surf, dropping overboard into the soapy foam while the canoe continued on her course riding the shoulders of the natives to a safe harbor in the custom house.

"Oi see you floy de Yonkee flag," he said in greeting as I came dripping ashore, more like a shipwrecked sailor than a traveler in out–of–way places.

"Yes. My papers are in the canoe. "No hurry," he returned, "the first thing we do here, is to have a glass of rum —it is good in the tropics.

And so I was welcomed to Statia, in the same open manner that the Dutch had welcomed and traded for centuries, and by the last of a long line of them —one of the old de Geneste family.

While we were drinking our rum, the harbormaster seemed to suddenly remember something. Pulling me to the window, he pointed up to the ramparts of Fort Oranje hanging over us. "You know de story of de salute ? —No ? —Well, I'll carry you to de Gesaghebber (governor) an' to de Fort an' we'll find de Doctor–HE can tell you better than I —but you can't go this way."

Nor could I, for I had no coat but the heavy dogskin sea jacket, chewed and salt begrimed and altogether too hot for the oven–heat on shore. My shirt of thin flannel, once a light cream color, was now greased from whale oil and smoke stained from many a fire of rain–soaked wood. A hole in the back exposed a dark patch of skin, burned and reburned by the sun. My trousers were worn thin throughout their most vital area, the legs hanging like sections of stove pipe, stiff and shrunken well above my ankles with lines of rime showing where the last seas had swept and left their high water mark. My feet were bare, tanned to a deep coffee from continual exposure to the sun in the cockpit.

The third article of my attire and the most respectable was my felt hat, stiff as to brim from the pelting of salt spray and misshapen as to crown from the constant presence of wet leaves and handkerchiefs inside. The world may ridicule one's clothing and figure, but one's hat and dog had best be left alone. Still I cannot say that I was ill at ease or embarrassed for I was entirely in keeping with my surroundings. Marse James' office was neat and clean to be sure, but outside, up and down the beach there was nothing but ruin and heart—sinking neglect.

A razor, honed on the light pith of the cabbage palm, and a tin basin of fresh water contributed largely to the transformation which followed. Shoes and stockings from the hold of the canoe added their touch of respectability. It is remarkable what an elevating effect is produced by a mere quarter of an inch of sole leather. A neat blue coat and trousers borrowed from the harbormaster changed this cannibal attire to that of civilization. True, there was some discrepancy between our respective waist measures, but this was taken care of by a judicious reef in the rear and since it is hardly polite to turn one's back on a governor there would be nothing to offend this august official. With the coat buttoned close under my chin so as to show the edge of a standing military collar there would be nothing to betray the absence of white linen beneath.

They say that once upon a time the dignity of the Gesaghebber, whose authority extends over an area of scarcely eight square miles, was sorely tried by one of his own countrymen. An eminent scientist who came to investigate the geologic formation of the island, landed with much pomp and circumstance, wearing a frock coat and a silk hat. His degeneracy, however, was as the downward course of a toboggan, for only a few weeks later, upon his departure, he dropped in to bid the governor good—bye, attired in pajamas, slippers and a straw hat and smoking a long pipe that rested on the comfortable rotundity which was all the more accentuated by his thin attire.

I combed my hair and with my papers stuffed in my pockets set out to climb the famous Bay Path with the puffing de Geneste.

ALONE IN THE CARIBBEAN

Built against the cliff which it mounts to the plateau above in a zigzag of two flights, the Bay Path belies its name. It is in fact a substantial cobbled roadway with massive retaining walls run up to a bulwark breast high to keep the skidding gun carriages of the early days from falling upon the houses below. That it had been built to stand for all time was evident, but even as I climbed it for the first time I could see that its years were numbered. The insidious trickling of water from tropical rains had been eating the soft earth away from its foundations and making the work easy for the roaring cloud bursts which take their toll from the Upper Town. The bulwarks that had comforted the unsteady steps of the belated burgher were now broken out in places and as we passed under the Dominican Mission the harbormaster drew my attention to the work of the last cloudburst which had bared the cliff to its very base. There was no busy stream of life up and down the wide roadway. As we stumbled up the uneven cobblestones we passed a lone negress shuffling silently in the shade of a huge bundle of clothes balanced on her head, down to the brackish pool where the washing of the town is done. Her passing only emphasized the forlorn loneliness of the hot middle day. We gained the streets of the Upper Town where the change from the simmering heat of the beach to the cool breezes of the plateau was like plunging into the cool catacombs from the July heat of Rome.

The Gesaghebber was still enjoying his siesta, we were informed by the negress who came to the door. In the crook of her arm she carried a sweating watermonkey from St. Martin's. She had addressed the harbormaster, but when she noticed that it was a stranger who stood by his side she dropped the monkey which broke on the flagging, trickling its cool water around our feet. "O Lard —who de mon?" she gasped.

"Him de mon in de boat," de Geneste mimicked —for as such I had come to be known in the islands.

Leaving the servant to stare after us, we retraced our steps to the fort which we had passed at the head of the Bay Path. Saluting the shrunken Dutch sentry who stepped out from the shadow of the Port, we crossed over the little bridge which spans the shallow ditch and passed through to the "place d'armes" of Fort Oranje.?

? The old guns at Fort Oranje, St. Eustatius. The date 1780 may be seen on the trunnion of the nearest gun. ?

ALONE IN THE CARIBBEAN

Forming the two seaward sides of an irregular quadrangle was the rampart, its guns with their hooded breeches pointing valiantly out over the roadstead and sweeping the approaches of the Bay Path. In the angle where the rampart turns back toward the town, stood the flagstaff, with topmast and cross trees, and stayed like a sloop, from which the red, white, and blue flag of Holland flapped in the trade wind. From just such a staff, held in that stepping before me, the Flag of Holland had been the first of a foreign power to dip in honor of the ensign of the infant navy of our Continental Congress. From this very rampart the first foreign salute had been delivered to our naval flag one hundred and thirty-five years before. Whether you will or not you must have a small bit of the history of Statia.

From her earliest days Statia belonged to the Dutch, who, before the British, were masters of the sea and for long years were supreme in maritime commerce. They have always been sailors as you shall see. The policy of the Dutch has always been for free trade and by this they became rich in the West Indies. Oranjetown, on the lee side of the island, half on the cliff, half on the beach, Upper and Lower Town as it was called, with its open roadstead where at times two hundred trading vessels have lain at anchor, possessed no advantages except those of free trade. Statia became a port of call. When our thirteen colonies broke away from the mother country the old Dutch Republic sympathized with the young one and the Dutch made money in the commerce that followed. When the struggle for independence broke out Statia was one channel through which the colonies procured munitions of war. Every nation has its blackguards and it seems that English traders at Statia actually supplied to the American colonists powder and cannon balls which were made in England and sent to them in Statia. This Rodney knew and he had for a long time kept a hungry eye on the rich stores of Oranjetown. If he ever took Statia his fortunes would be recouped and —perhaps Marshall Biron knew this when he paid the debts of the old fighting roué and sent him back to London. It was on account of these English merchants —"vipers" Rodney calls them —that upon returning to the West Indies one of his first acts was to loot Statia. His most plausible excuse, however, was because here at Port Oranje, on the cliff above the bay, the first foreign recognition was made of our naval flag. You shall have the story "just now, as they say in the islands.

It was on the 16th of November, 1776, that the brig Andrea Doria, fourteen guns, third of our infant navy of five vessels, under the command of Josiah Robins sailed into the open roadstead of St. Eustatius and dropped anchor almost under the guns of Fort Oranje. She could have borne no more fitting name than that of the famous townsman of Columbus, who, after driving the French out of his own country in 1528, founded the republic of Genoa and with the true spirit of democracy, refused the highest office of the grateful government which he had established. The Andrea Doria may have attracted but little attention as she appeared in the offing, for in those days the two miles of roadstead from Gallows Bay to Interloper's Point were often filled with ships. But with the quick eyes of seafarers the guests of Howard's Tavern had probably, even as she was picking out her berth, left their rum for the moment to have their first glimpse of a strange flag which they all knew must be that of the new republic.

Abraham Ravené, commandant of the fort, lowered the red, white, and blue flag of Holland in recognition of the American ship. In return, the Andrea Doria fired a salute. This put the commandant in a quandary. Anchored not far from the Andrea Doria, was a British ship. The enmity of the British for Holland and especially against Statia was no secret. In order to shift the responsibility, Ravené went to consult Johannes de Graeff, the governor, who was at that time living in the hills at Concordia, his country seat. De Graeff had already seen the Andrea Doria, for Ravené met him in the streets of the Upper Town. A clever lawyer and a keen business man, the governor had already made up his mind when Ravené spoke. "Two guns less than the national salute," was the order. And so we were for the first time recognized as a nation by this salute of eleven guns. For this act, de Graeff was subsequently recalled to Holland, but he was reinstated as Governor of Statia and held that position when the island was taken by Rodney in 1781. The Dutch made no apology to England. Two years after this salute of '76, John Paul Jones was not served so well at Quiberon, for the French gave him only nine guns, the number at that time accorded to republics. This, of Statia, may well stand as our first naval salute.

Near the flag stepping was a bronze sundial mounted on a base of carved stone, its creeping shadow marking off the long listless days of the stagnant island as it had measured the too short hours of the busy port. It was like the tick of a colonial clock in the abode of the spinster remnant of a once powerful family. As I stood on the edge of the rampart and looked down on what was left of the Lower Town, it was hard to realize that the ruined walls below us had once held fortunes in merchandise and that in the empty Road before me had ridden ships captained by the same hard shrewd Yankee skippers that we still know on our own coast —skippers as familiar with the bay and the rum shops of Oranjetown as their own neat little gardens at home.

ALONE IN THE CARIBBEAN

Forming the two inshore sides of the quadrangle was a row of one–storied buildings, pierced near one end by the vaulted Port through which we had entered. The largest of these, a few steps above the southern end of the rampart, was built of stone. Here in the very room that Ravené had used as Commandant of the island, I gave my papers to the present officer. He was a new arrival from the Old Country and as yet knew no other language than the crackling speech of Holland. As he took the papers, he stepped to the window and his superior smile vanished when he saw that there was no boat lying in the Road. Mars James came to my rescue in the unintelligible fusillade that followed. While the harbormaster unsnarled the tangle of red tape, I improved the opportunity to look about me. In his report of the military defenses of the island in 1778, Ravené describes the building as a stone structure having two rooms ; the first a sort of council chamber and the second a gun room. The latter still contained the old gun racks which held the modern descendants of the old snaphaanen. He also mentions the barred cellar beneath, which was used as the criminal and civil prison. Some days afterward, while poking about in its musty depths, I found some of the old flintlocks and a pile of grape shot, rusted to a depth of a quarter of an inch, like those which Statia furnished to the needy army of Washington. There was still use for a jail, I found, for in one of the wooden shanties of that tumbledown row a negress was confined awaiting transportation to the penitentiary at Curaçao. She had an incurable mania for theft.

My papers duly viséd for Saba, we again made our way to the Gesaghebber. We found him, very much awake this time, in an animated discussion over a horse trade with the Medical Officer. "Frigid little lump of ice!" I muttered to myself at the curt nod he gave me. The Doctor was another sort. A Welshman by birth, an American by education, and a sailor by nature, I found that he had traveled widely and we were soon so deep in conversation that the pompous little governor, who knew no English, was forgotten for the moment. The harbormaster and the horse trade slipped away unnoticed. Another horse galloped in, the hobby of the Doctor. "Did you know that the original cannon used in the first salute to your flag are still lying in the sand where they have been thrown down from the ramparts of the fort?"

I feigned ignorance, thus removing a dam which might have held back some of those interesting bits which so often drift out on the stream of a story, unimportant perhaps in itself. Next to the art of sitting on a log, the ability to listen well is one of the crafts of life in the open. And then, as a diamond, in the vast sheet of blue mud which flows over the sorting tables of the Kimberley mines, is caught on the oily surface, a new name was spoken, that of a hero. Although I have since spent many hours in search of it, I have not found it in print. Krull —a name which goes well with kruit (powder) and cannon, —Krull–Krut–Kah–non —the gallant Dutch Admiral who fell in one of the most heroic sea fights of his time.

Rodney, upon the capture of Statia, learned that a convoy of vessels had left the island shortly before his arrival. They were under the protection of a lone Dutch man–of–war in command of Admiral Krull. In a letter of February 4th, 1781, to Phillip Stephens, Esq., Secretary to the Admiralty, he says: "A Dutch Convoy, consisting of 30 sail of Merchant Ships richly loaded, having sailed from St. Eustatius, under the protection of a 60 gun ship, about Thirty–six Hours before my arrival, I detached Captains Reynolds [later Lord Ducie] of His Majestie's ship Monarch, with the Panther and the Sybil, to pursue them as far as the Latitude of Bermudas, should they not intercept them before he got that length."

The slow–sailing convoy was caught and Krull commanded the ships to hold their course while he waited to stand off the three English men–of–war. He was killed in the unequal fight that followed. Lord Rodney says: Since my letter of the 4th instant, by the Diligence and Activity of Capt. Reynolds, I have the Pleasure to inform you that the Dutch Convoy which sailed from St. Eustatius before my arrival have been intercepted. I am sorry to acquaint their Lordships that the Dutch Admiral was killed in the action. Inclosed, I have the honour to send Captain Reynold's letter; and am, etc."

In a letter of February 10th, he says: "The Admiral, who was killed in the action with the Monarch, has been buried with every Honour of War."

In spite of this anger against St. Eustatius and the Dutch, Rodney had only admiration for the brave Krull.

We made our excuses to the governor and were soon scrambling among the ruins of the Upper Town. A fascinating mixture of old–world houses, surrounded by high walls which gave the streets the appearance of diked canals, of ruins and of negro shanties palsied by the depredations of millions of ants, Upper Oranjetown bore a character quite distinct from any of the West Indian towns of the lower islands. Here was no trace of a preceding French régime to give the houses uncomfortable familiarity with the streets and breed suspicion by their single entrances, nor did the everlasting palm thrust its inquiring trunk over the garden walls like the neck of a giraffe to inform the humbler plants within what was going on in the street. It lacked the moss—stained and yellow—washed picturesqueness of Fort de France and St. George's and for that very reason the novelty of it was restful. Above all was the feeling that here at one time had existed the neat thrift of the Dutch. With thrift comes money and with money comes the Jew. One wonders how the Jew with his feline dread of the sea, first came to Statia, knowing the long boisterous passage of those days. The reason may very properly have been the excellent seamanship of the Dutch traders. In the early history of Cayenne we are led to believe that the "fifteen or twenty families of Jews" were brought over by the Dutch. The Jew brings with him his religion and so we find the ruins of a one time rich little synagogue in one of the modest side streets. Whereas the Jew brings his religion with him as part of his life, the Christian brings it after him as part of his conscience. Thus we find, not far off, the tower of the Reformed Church with its unroofed walls. The Dutch "Deformed" Church as they have called it ever since a hurricane swept the Upper Town. In the shadows of the walls the Doctor showed me a long line of vaults where lie the old families, de Windts, Heyligers, Van Mussendens and last, the almost forgotten tomb of Krull, with no mark to proclaim his bravery to the world, and what need, for the world does not pass here —the dead sleep in their own company in a miasm that seems to come up out of the ground and permeate the very atmosphere of the island.

As in Fort de France, I became a part of the life of Statia ; here was a place where I could live for a time. In six hours I had boon companions. There was the Doctor —he would always come first and there was that inimitable Dutchman, Van Musschenbroek of Hendrick Swaardecroonstrasse, the Hague, who had an income and was living in a large house in the town which rented at $8.00 the month and was doing —God knows what. His English was infinitely worse than my German and it was through this common medium that we conversed —Dutch was utterly beyond my ken.

He used to come of a morning in his pajamas, hatted and with a towel on his arm and wake me for our daily bath. In that delicious fresh morning which follows the cool nights of the outer Antilles we three would scramble down to the Bay, the Doctor pumping the lore of the island into my right ear, the Dutchman rattling of outdoor expedients into my left. He, the Dutchman, was a well—built man, barrel—chested and with a layer of swimmer's fat, for he had once been the champion backstroke of Holland and a skater, and had geologized all over the world.

ALONE IN THE CARIBBEAN

But we'll listen to the Doctor. Our favorite walk was to Gallows Bay, where there was a clean sand beach. We walked in a past that one could almost touch. As we took up the Bay Path, that first morning, just below the fort where a sweet smelling grove of manchioneel trees, tempting as the mangosteen of the Malays and caustic as molten lead, made dusk of the morning light, the Doctor touched my arm. There in a shallow pit, two yards from our path, lay seven rusty cannon, half buried in the sand. He did not have to tell me that these were the last of the old battery of eleven which had belched forth their welcome to the Andrea Doria. Some time after the salute, the guns were condemned and piled up near the present Government Post–Office in the fort where they remained till the late seventies. At that time an American schooner, cruising about for scrap iron, came to Statia to buy old cannon. The trunnions were knocked off so that they would roll the easier and they were thrown over the edge of the cliff.?

? The tomb of Admiral Krull. ?

Iron cannon, as a rule, bore the date of their casting on the ends of their trunnions whereas the bronze guns were dated near the breech. These bore no date, but they must have been old at the time of the salute. The schooner took four of them, but did not return for the rest. So these seven have remained as unmarked and unnoticed as the silent grave of Krull on the plateau above.

Farther along, on our way to the beach, was an immense indigo tank with its story. In the ken of the last generation, a ship had been driven ashore in a southwester, the tail of a hurricane. Most of the crew perished in the sea, but three came safely through the surf when Fate decided that after all they must join their comrades on the other shore. They clambered up the broken walls only to fall into the disused tank, now filled with brackish water, where they drowned like rats in a cistern.

Passing the walls of the last sugar refinery in operation on the island, we came to the beach. A blue spot in the sand caught my eye and I picked up a slave trading bead of the old days. It had been part of a cargo of a ship bound for Africa; her hulk lay somewhere out there in the darker waters of Crook's reef where it had lain for the last century or more, sending its mute messages ashore with each southwest gale, ground dull on their slow journey over the bottom of the Caribbean

ALONE IN THE CARIBBEAN

The Bay was only habitable during the early morning hours, before the sun got well over the cliff above. The rest of the day I spent on the plateau where the sun's heat was tempered by the trade which blew half a gale through the valley between the humps, a fresh sea wind. The active men of Statia go to sea; there is little agriculture besides the few acres of cotton and sisal that cry for the labor of picking and cutting for here the negro is unutterably lazy.

I used to see from time to time a ragged old native; whose entire day was spent sitting in a shady corner, blinking in the sunlight like a mud-plastered turtle, dried-caked. Some one must have fed him, but I can assure you that this was not done from sunrise to sundown and he must have gone somewhere to sleep but during the light of day I never saw him stir. I passed him for the sixth time one day —I wondered what was going on in the pulp of that brain pan; not conscious thought I was certain —when a man hailed me from the doorstep of what was once a prosperous burgher's house —a last white descendant of that very burgher. The excuse was a bottle of Danish beer but I read through that —he wanted a breath of the outside world and I gave him what I had. He was not a poor white —just another like de Geneste, left by an honorable old family to finish their book —their last page. He lived with a negress whom he extolled and not altogether in self-defense. They were married and I took his word for it. She was cooking and washing in the kitchen when I came in and at the call of her master brought the beer and glasses on a tray with a peculiar grace mixed with an air of wifely right —there was no defiance in her bearing but there was that which I might best describe as an African comme il faut. There was no attempt at an introduction and she left us immediately to resume her labors. We sat on a broken sofa —they wear out and break down in Statia exactly as they do in some of the houses we know where first cost is the only cost —but here they never go to the woodshed. I happened to glance through an open doorway into what was once a drawing room and there, reared up like a rocking horse about to charge forward from its hind legs, was a barber's chair. "What in the name of Sin have you got that in there for?"

"Oh, oy cuts hair," he answered with that soft weatherworn tone that belongs to Statia alone. Whether this hair cutting was a partial means of livelihood or merely a pastime for the accommodation of his friends I did not ask. I was not even inquisitive enough to ask how the thing came to the island. My host asked me if I would like to have my hair trimmed and I said that I should be delighted. It was like accepting another bottle of beer. I adjusted my bones to the cadaverous red upholstery that showed its stuffing while my friend tied the apron around my neck. He did no worse than many a country barber I have met and with less danger from showerings of tonics and laying on of salves. Instead of fetid breathings of Religion, Politics and League Baseball, I listened to tales of old Statia. Some time when I am dining out and find an old Statia name beside me —there are many in our eastern cities —I may be tempted to say, "Gracious! are you a de ——? I have had the pleasure of a haircut in your great grandfather's drawing room."

It was while I was in the barber's chair that I was a witness to a scene that many times since has made me stop whatever I have been doing —and think a bit. A sloop was lying in the roadstead bound that evening for Porto Rico. One of her passengers–to–be was the colored son of this man, who would seek his fortune in the more prosperous American island. The boy had been about town for a last palaver with his friends and now, in the late afternoon, had come to his home to say good–bye. He had already seen his mother and now came in where his father was cutting my hair. Oh, the irony of that parting! The boy showed little concern —he was perhaps eighteen and dressed in store clothes of Yankee cut. It was the poor miserable father who was hurt —a white man breaking down over the parting with his rather indifferent colored offspring. My friend excused himself to me and then putting his arms around the boy's neck sobbed his farewell on the boy's shoulder. His was a figure equal to the mad woman of St. Pierre, to his last shred paternal. I could say more but this is enough; may I be forgiven this intimate picture.

One morning the town awoke to find that a Dutch man–of–war was lying in the Roads and then Statia came to life for two days. The ship was the Utrecht, an armored cruiser stationed in the West Indies. In the late afternoon the ship's band climbed the Bay Path to the fort where I listened to the concert and struck up an acquaintance with a Russian captain of marines who cared not a whit for the beauties of the dying day and cursed the sun for his everlasting smile and prayed for a day of the grey weather of the Baltic. To tell the truth I was coming to it myself. The next morning I saw him at play with his clumsy Dutch marines —they were having landing drill and a more cloddish lot I have never seen. They landed in three feet of water, mostly on all fours, from the gunwales of the ship's boats and one fellow —I stood and watched him do it —actually managed to sprawl under the boat and break his arm.?

? "Here was a town walled in by Nature." ?

ALONE IN THE CARIBBEAN

The grand event of the Utrecht's visit, however, was on the night of the second day when a dance was given in the governor's house in honor of Her Majesty's officers. Before the dance a select few of us were invited to tea at the house of Mynheer Grube, the former governor. I accepted the invitation, borrowed some clean "whites" from the Doctor, combed and brushed my hair, and went.

There was something very placid and restful about this home of the old Dutch gentleman and his wife —the quiet dignity of a useful life frugally lived and of duties conscientiously performed. There were old clocks and cupboards in it and a Delft plate or two just as we find them in our Dutch colonial houses of the north. If you examine the outer walls carefully you will find a round place, plastered up as though at some time a cannon ball must have gone through. One did and it was not many generations ago when just such a quiet Hollander as Grube was living there as Governor.

It was some time after the looting of Oranjetown, when Statia had been sucked dry by the English and flung back to the Dutch like a gleaned bone, that a French frigate in passing fired upon the Upper Town just to see the mortar fly. It was in the trade season and she bowled along, close under the lee of the island with her weather side exposed as if to say, "Hit me if you can."

One of her shots passed through the very room in which the governor sat reading. His wife, —I wonder if she had been in the kitchen overlooking the making of some favorite dish ? —rushed into the room and found her husband calmly reading with the debris of stone and plaster littered about him, as though nothing had happened. She begged her husband in the name of all that was sane to move from his dangerous position. "Be calm," said the governor, "don't you know that cannon balls never strike again in the same place?"

But he was not altogether right. Down on the beach, just beyond Interloper's Point, lay the little old battery of Tommelendyk —Tumbledown–Dick they call it. There had been but little use for the guns of late and there was no militaire now stationed on the island. There was, however, one man on Statia, a one–armed gunner whose blood was roused when he saw the wanton firing of the Frenchman. He was working in his field, not far from Tommelendyk and he remembered that there was still some powder and shot left in the magazine and that one of the guns at least was in good order for signaling purposes. He rushed down to the battery followed by his friends.

ALONE IN THE CARIBBEAN

In a twinkling the breech–hood was off and the gunner blew through the touch–hole to make sure that the passage was clear. Measuring the powder by the handful, he showed his friends how to ram home the charge and the ball. By this time the Frenchman was almost abreast the battery. The gunner's first shot was a good "liner," but fell short. He had not lost his cunning in guessing the speed of a ship. The impromptu crew reloaded in quick time and as they jumped clear of the smoke they gave a yell of delight. The shot had struck the Frenchman in the hull close to the waterline. Two more shots were planted almost in the same place before the frigate could clear the island.

When she ran into the choppy seas her crew found that their ship was rapidly making water. They dared not beat to windward to St. Martin's and were forced to make for St. Thomas, the nearest port to leeward. With her guns and stores shifted to port she must have been a weird spectacle as she bore down on the Danish island, with a free wind and heeled as though she were beating into a gale.

Grube had been Governor in the same way that his predecessors had held office —burghers performing their duty to the state without political influence and by right of a worthy life. We had our tea and cakes and drank our Curaçao in the short evening that brought with it the last music of the band at the fort. Then we arose and went to the house of the present Governor where most of the white people of Statia were already gathered as one huge family. The room was on the upper floor —there are never more than two in these islands —to which we gained access by an outside stairway, from the courtyard, a most convenient arrangement by which a large crowd of guests could not invade the privacy of the rest of the house. Most of the officers of the Utrecht were there and the midshipmen —young boys such as you might meet at almost any dance in Edgewater or Brookline.

It had been a long time since I had danced and I reveled in this party of the Governor of Statia. I danced with Heyligers and de Windts and Van Mussendens and no end of names that had been in the island long before the coming of Rodney. I danced with names and my spirit was in the past. The tunes they played were old ones, some of them English and some handed down from the time when the Marquis de Bouillé made the island French for a year. There were quaint French themes, some of which I recognized. To these same tunes, in this same room, the ancestors of these people had danced many a time. Then the orchestra switched to more modern things —"Money Musk" and the old sailor's delight "Champagne Charlie" which you will only hear in our parts in some wharfside saloon, befuddled through the lips of some old rum laden shellback. But withal this ancient atmosphere and the dire poverty of these descendants of once prosperous burgher families there was no sadness at the Governor's that night. If these people were always talking of the glorious Past their introspection had not made them morbid. They were seafarers and their philosophy was a hopeful one. Here was the gathering of a congenial happy family. I have never dropped into a community where I felt so immediately and completely at home as here and at Saba. There is one word which applies to these people more than any other and that is —Good-hearted. They are not super-educated surely but they have a far wider knowledge of the world in general than our average farmer community. They retain a refinement of family which generations of poverty have not been able to down and they have survived the fires of want with a spirit that is one of the paradoxes of the world.

The orchestra finally reached the limit of its strength and stopped playing through sheer exhaustion —they were not professionals, just friends who were glad to do this service. From time to time one of the players would lay aside his instrument and join the dancers for a while till by rote each had had his share. The ending of the music seemed to be the accepted signal for refreshments and those who did not take up trays of coffee and small cakes lined up along the walls as before the dance. The coffee had an awakening effect but the dance did not continue. Presently a whisper found its way from mouth to ear till it reached Van Musschenbroek in a far corner. His perspiring face smiled assent and he stepped into the middle of the cleared room. In laughable broken English he announced that he would now delight the audience with an imitation of a fiddler crab. It was a clever stunt and from the way in which he skittered about the floor in arcs of wandering centers weaving his claws in the air, I knew that he knew beach life. And so the second part of the evening was started. There was no assumed modesty that needed coaxing —whoever was asked deemed it a pleasure to do his part of the entertaining ; was this not a way in which he might honor the Governor and his wife? The midshipmen of the Utrecht entered into the spirit of the thing and one of them sang a Dutch song. Most of these chaps had been on the Utrecht when she attended the Hudson-Fulton celebration in New York and for a time we had a bit of Keith's circuit on the boards. George M. Cohan did not sound a whit better than when we hear him imitated at home. There is a limit to all good things and these people live in moderation and never reach the limit —the party broke up when we were all happily tired.

I became attached to Statia as I had become attached to Point Espagñol and Fort de France, but I found that little by little my eyes sought the sea more and more. The channel was calling again and peaked Saba became a aggravating invitation. With all the fascination of the old fort and the batteries, the stories of the privateers and the brisk companionship of the Doctor, the call was stronger than the present love, and so one morning I took to the shimmering channel and left the island of England's wrath for her sister where the Dutch rule the English.

CHAPTER XIII. SABA.

TO LAND at Saba in a small boat you must choose the right kind of weather. If there is no wind you cannot sail, if there is too much wind you cannot land, for the seas swinging around the island will raise a surf on the rocky beaches that will make a quick end of your boat. For a week there had been too much wind. One day the trade eased up a bit and de Geneste said, "You better make a troy in de mornin'." I made ready.

The next morning seemed to promise the same kind of day as that on which I rushed from Guadeloupe to Montserrat and I feared trouble when I should reach Saba. The wind was already blowing a good sailing breeze and we took to the water at seven o'clock and with Saba a little north of WNW and the wind nearly east I sailed west for an hour wing–and–wing. Then I laid my course for the island. Half an hour later I was obliged to reef because we were making too much speed in the breaking seas. "A fine layout this!" I thought, for if I did not reach the island before the surf ran heavy, I had visions of joining my long painter to all my halyards, sheets, and spare line and swimming ashore with it to let the canoe tail off in the wind, moored to some out–jutting rock or perhaps lying off under the lee of the island for a day or two till the seas calmed. It was all unnecessary worry. The direct distance from island to island was only sixteen miles and was across before the seas had grown too large.

Saba one might call the Pico of the West Indies ; not as high by half, but the comparison may stand for all that. From a diameter of two miles she rises to a height of nearly three thousand feet, her summit lost in the low–lying trade clouds which tend to accentuate the loftiness of this old ocean volcano. The West Indies pilot book gives three landing places and of these I was told by de Geneste to try the south side or Fort Landing, four cables eastward of Ladder Point.

I knew the place when I sailed in toward the island for there was a little shack perched about fifty feet above the beach where the revenue officers, they are called brigadiers, sought shelter from the sun's heat. Above the surf a fishing boat lay on rollers across the rocks, for here is no sand. To the westward, like a terrace, under Ladder Point was a levelled cobble beach some twelve feet above the water where they used to build sloops and schooners before they found that they could get them better and cheaper from Gloucester. Winding upward in a ravine–like cleft were flights of steps hewn out of the solid rock and connected by stretches of steep pathways.

The shack and the pathway up the ravine were the only signs of human habitation and from the barren aspect of the island with its low scrubby vegetation one would not suspect that the steps and paths led to the homes of some three thousand people. When I had made my rig snug and hoisted my centerboard I rowed as close to shore as I dared. As at Statia, a number of black watermen waded out into the sea to lift the canoe clear of the rocks. I rowed a bit to windward to counteract a strong current and then as we swept down toward the men, I jumped overboard and swimming with my hands on the stern of the Yakaboo I waited till we were opposite the men and then shoved the canoe into their arms.

One of the brutes might have taken her weight on his head for my food bags were flat and my outfit thinned out, and for the crowd of them she was a mere toy which they lifted clear of the surf and carried ashore to a couple of rollers without even grazing a stone. The skipper, having a proper regard for his bones, washed himself ashore like a limp octopus.?

? At the head of the Fort Ladder. ?

?

? "Here Freddie Simmons teaches embryo sailor–men, still in their knee trousers, the use of the sextant and chronometer." ?

ALONE IN THE CARIBBEAN

Now there was one person whom I came to know in Statia but whom I have not mentioned as yet because our friendship really belonged to Saba and it was here she was buried only a few weeks after I left the island. She was a kindly elderly woman and a good friend to me. She had been head nurse at the Government Hospital at Antigua and had been under the care of the Doctor at Statia for some time. He suspected cancer, he told me (she told me that she knew it was cancer), and since he could do nothing for her, he advised her to go to Saba to live up in the air where no breeze hung about long enough to lose its freshness and where the chill of night brought with it sound sleep. She had gone on to Saba a few days after my arrival at Oranjetown. One afternoon when I had been complaining of dizziness and nausea the Doctor gave me a kindly shaking and said, "Now see here! you yellow–headed Scandihoovian, you've had just a little too much of old Sol and we've made a little plan for you, Mrs. Robertson and I. When you get to Saba, you'll forget your 'little green tent' for a time and you'll stay with Mrs. Robertson till you're straightened out. Do you mind!" The Doctor could be a bit fierce upon occasion and he was a strong man who would knock you down as soon as not if he thought he could right matters by force.

So when I picked myself up from the wet rocks and followed the Yakaboo up the beach I was accosted by a white man, one Freddie Simmons —they are for the most part Simmons or Hassels here and you can't go far wrong in calling them by one or the other name.

He was a young man, seafaring evidently, not from any traditional roughness, but from an indefinable ease of gait, scarcely a roll, and from a way of taking in everything as he looked about him as though he were used to scanning the deck of a vessel. He had an open pleasant face that spoke kindly before he opened his mouth and mild blue eyes that could not lie. "My name is Simmons —they call me Freddie Simmons." He pronounced it almost like "Fraddie."

"I'm a Freddie too," I answered as we shook hands.

"So Mrs. Robertson said. She's breakfast waiting for you up at Bottom —I'll carry you there just now."

"How the devil did she know I was coming to–day?" I asked. Then he told me how a man up in St. John's had almost looked his eyes out for a week watching for me and was at last rewarded by the sight of a queer rig that could be no other than that of "de mon in de boat."

"But I'll have to stow my canoe somewhere before we start," I told him.

"Oh, we'll take the canoe along," at which he nodded to four black giants who lifted the Yakaboo and started for the path —two with grass pads on their heads where she rested bow and stern while the others walked at each side like honorary pall–bearers to steady the load. And so we proceeded on our way, eight hundred feet up, to the bed of an old crater where the town of Bottom lies, out of sight of all who pass unless they travel in aeroplanes.

Now I am going to take advantage of the fact that you are soft and short–winded and not used to climbing flights of stairs and steep paths. While you can do little but puff and perspire I shall tell you a little of this strange island. What ancient documents Saba may have possessed were whisked up and blown out across the wide seas over a century ago when a hurricane swept the island in 1787 and took with it almost every vestige of human habitation except the low–set concrete covered rain tanks and the tombs of the ancestors of the present inhabitants. For nearly a century after the island was sighted by Columbus probably no European picked his way up the cleft to the upper bowls of the island. There may have been Caribs living here but I have seen no mention of them. When the Dutch began active trading operations in the West Indies in the early part of the 17th century we find them (the Dutch) already settled in Statia and Saba. For nearly three–quarters of a century the island lived in peace.

In 1665, seventy English buccaneers from the company of Lieutenant–Colonel Morgan who had captured Statia, sailed over to Saba and captured the island with little or no resistance. The main expedition returned to Jamaica but a small garrison was left on each of the islands. Most of the Dutch inhabitants were sent to St. Martin's whither they returned later to Statia. It is from this small handful of English buccaneers that were left in Saba in 1665 by Morgan, that the present white population has descended and while Saba has almost continuously belonged to the Dutch except for a short break in 1665 and in 1781 and also about 1801 it has been truly said that here the Dutch rule the English. There has been little marriage outside of the island by these English people and no mixing with the negroes. Saba is the only island in the West Indies where the whites predominate and the proportion to the blacks is two to one. But the greatest paradox of all is to see here in the heights of this island, six degrees within the tropics, the fair skins and rosy cheeks whose bloom originated in old England in the reign of Charles the Second and has kept itself pure and untarnished there two and a half centuries.

By this time you have clutched my arm and stopped in the pathway long enough to catch your breath and ask, "Yes, but what do these two thousand whites and one thousand negroes live on?" There is little gardening and for the most part the men of the island go to sea where they earn money to support their families and keep their tidy little homes shipshape and neatly painted. As I sit and write this, now that I know the island, I can think of no truer description than that given by the Abbé Raynal in 1798. "This is a steep rock, on the summit of which is a little ground, very proper for gardening. Frequent rains which do not lie any time on the soil, give growth to plants of an exquisite flavor, and cabbages of an extraordinary size. Fifty European families, with about one hundred and fifty slaves, here raise cotton, spin it, make stockings of it, and sell them to other colonies for as much as ten crowns (six dollars) a pair. Throughout America there is no blood so pure as that of Saba ; the women there preserve a freshness of complexion, which is not to be found in any other of the Caribbee islands."

The porters, before us, halted and the Yakaboo came to an aerial anchorage at the crest of the path where the mountainside seemed broken down. It was in reality a "V" blown out of the side of an old crater. No wonder the Yakaboo had come to a stop. She may have seen things unusual for a canoe but she had by no means lost her youthful interest —she was not blasé. There, before her, spread out on the floor of an ancient crater, was the prettiest village imaginable. Cozy little homes, a New England village minus chimneys, all seemingly freshly painted white with green shutters and red roofs. To guard against the "frequent rains which do not lie any time on the soil" the streets were lined with walls, shoulder high, which were in reality dikes to direct the torrents which are suddenly poured into Bottom Town from the slopes which surround it. A remarkable coincidence that here, high up in the air, the colony should use the dikes of its mother country but for an entirely different reason. What struck me most forcibly was that while there was no hint of monotony the houses gave the outward appearance of a uniform degree of prosperity ; here must be a true democracy ; If any man had more money than his neighbor he did not show it, yet there was no hint of greasy socialism, all of which I found true as I came to know the island.?

? The "dikes" of Bottom Town. ?

ALONE IN THE CARIBBEAN

The Bottom, as the crater floor is called, is a circular plain about half a mile in diameter and surrounded on all sides by a steep wall, continuous except where we stood at the top of the path from the South Landing which we had just climbed and at another point on the west side where the rim is broken and the path called the Ladder descends to the West Landing. Up the rim on the eastern side a path zigzagged and disappeared through a notch in the outline to the Windward Side, the village I had seen from the steamer four months before. Lost in the mist, the summit of the island towered over Bottom to the northward.

Here was a town walled in by Nature. The cleft into which the path was built ended in a small ravine that broke into the level plain of the Bottom and it was across this ravine that Freddie Simmons pointed out the ultimate anchorage of the Yakaboo and the asylum of her skipper. Our procession started again —we stopped once or twice to meet a Simmons or a Hassel —to make a starboard tack along the western side of the ravine, a short tack to port, and we put the canoe down on the after deck —I should say the back porch —of a cool airy house where we were to keep in the shade for a matter of ten days.?

? A cozy Saba home. ?

Here then was the end of my cruise in the Lesser Antilles. I had swung through the arc from Grenada to Saba and in the doing of it had sailed some six hundred miles. My destination was the Virgins and their nearest island lay a hundred and ten miles away. "Oh!" I thought, as I looked down at the canoe, "if I could only be sure that I could make you stay absolutely tight and be reasonably sure of the wind, I would not hesitate to make the run in you." Even if I did get her tight and encountered a calm I knew that I would have little chance of withstanding the heat. Mrs. Robertson had come out to welcome me and I heard her step behind me. She had guessed my thoughts for as I turned she said, "You had better not think of it." At that Freddie put in his oar. "Be content, my boy ; the boat could do it, but one day of no wind at this time of the year would finish you and you don't want to be found a babbling idiot with the gulls waiting to pick out your eyes."

Sense was fighting desperately with the spirit of adventure but at last sense won out —perhaps through some secret understanding with cowardice. "Yes, I believe you're right —I'll let some other damn fool try it if he likes," and that ended the matter.

ALONE IN THE CARIBBEAN

It is in the evenings that one comes to know the people of Saba. They go quietly about their business during the hours of daylight and then, after supper, for hey always eat in their own homes, they meet some place —it was at Mrs. Robertson's that first night —to thresh out the small happenings of the day. News from the outside world may have come by sloop or schooner from St. Kitts or Curaçao. Then when the gossip begins to lag, a fiddle will mysteriously appear and an accordion will be dragged from under a chair while the room is cleared for the "Marengo" or a paseo from Trinidad.

I could have no better chance to observe the "rosy cheeks of Saba," and to me the delight of the evening was to be once more among people who lacked that apathetic drift of the West Indies which seems to hold them in perpetual stagnation. The women danced together for the most part to make up for the lack of other men. From the very first, these people have been seafaring and the few men on the island are those crippled by rheumatism or too old to go to sea. You will find Saba men all over the West Indies, captains and mates and crews of small trading schooners in which they are part owners or shareholders. They have learned the trick of spending less than they earn.

Once in a conversation with the port officer of Mayaguez, at the mention of Saba men, he told me that their shore spree consisted in walking to the playa where hey would indulge in ice cream and Porto Rican cigars. On one occasion a Saba foremast hand sought his advice in regard to investing money in a certain coconut plantation in Porto Rico. That they are good sailormen does not rest on mere fanciful sentimentalism for they have been brought up to it from their very boyhood.

In a little house, on the north side of the ravine which the Yakaboo had doubled in the forenoon, was a nautical school provided by a wise government. Here Freddie Simmons teaches embryo sailor–men, while still in their knee trousers, the use of the sextant and chronometer and the mathematics that go therewith. To me, Saba is a memory of living in a bowl over which the sun swung in a shortened arc. Here in Bottom Town the day was clipped by a lengthy dawn and a twilight. As the sun neared the rim to the westward, I used to stroll to the "gap" at the Ladder Landing to enjoy the cool of the late afternoon and watch the "evening set" from the shadows of the rocks. Behind me was twilight ; on the rocks below and on the Caribbean before me was yet late afternoon.

Here was a place for a dream and a pipe of tobacco. I used to wonder how near Columbus had passed on his way to Hispaniola. Why did he give her the name of Saba? Was it from

194

the Queen of Sheba or St. Sabar? And then when the sun had finally gone down behind his cloud fringe and the short twilight had been swept out by night, I would turn back into the dark bowl with its spots of square yellow lights from the windows of the Saba people. The stars seemed close here as though we had been pushed up to them from the earth. Later the moon would appear ghost–like over the southern rim and float through the night to the other side.

One morning Captain Ben's schooner was reported under the lee of the island and that afternoon we carried the Yakaboo down the Ladder and put her aboard. She had gone across Saba. I made my last round of good–byes in Bottom Town and then scrambled down the Ladder in the hot afternoon sun. In half an hour a lazy breeze pushed us out into the Caribbean. Saba stood up bold and green in the strong light, her outline distinct with no cloud cap. Little by little the shadows in the rocks at her feet began to assert themselves, blue–black, while her green foliage became a cloth and lost its brilliancy, blue–green it was —there was distance between us and the snug island. When the sun went down she was a grey–blue hump between sea and sky.

CHAPTER XIV. SIR FRANCIS DRAKE'S CHANNEL AND "YAKABOO"

WE AWOKE with the Virgins dead ahead. We were approaching them as Columbus had —from the eastward. His course must have been more westerly than ours, but had he seen them first in the morning light as I did the effect must have been very nearly the same —a line of innumerable islets that seemed to bar our way. Herrera says, "Holding on their course, they saw many islands close together, that they seemed not to be numbered, the largest of which he called St. Ursula (Tortola) and the rest the Eleven Thousand Virgins, and then came up with another great one called Borriquen (the name the Indians gave it), but he gave it the name of St. John the Baptist, it is now called St. Juan de Puerto Rico." The largest island to windward he named Virgin Gorda —the Great Virgin.

ALONE IN THE CARIBBEAN

I spread my chart of the Virgins on the top of the cabin and tried to pick out the southern chain of islands that with Tortola and St. John's form Sir Francis Drake's Channel. On the chart were various notes in pencil which I had gathered on my way up the Lesser Antilles. On the lower end of Virgin Gorda, or Peniston as it is called, a corruption of Spanish Town, I should find the ruins of an old Spanish copper mine and here was that remarkable strewing of monoliths that, as I brought them close up with my glasses, looked for all the world like a ruined city, more so even than St. Pierre —and was called Fallen Jerusalem.

Next in line came Ginger with a small dead sea on it, Cooper and Salt Islands where the wreck of the Rhone might be seen through the clear waters if there were not too much breeze. Directly on our course through the Salt Island passage was a little cay marked Dead Chest and called Duchess by the natives. Completing the chain were Peter, and Norman, which might have been the Treasure Island of Stevenson. It was these names, Ginger, Cooper, Dead Chest, Peter, and Norman's that awoke the enthusiasm of Kingsley and from the suggestion of this Dead Chest, Stevenson wrote his famous, "Fifteen men on the Dead Man's chest, Yo–ho–ho, and a bottle of rum!"

It was Thursday, June 22nd, the Coronation Day of George Fifth and Queen Mary when we dropped anchor in the pretty harbor of Road Town in Tortola. How ancient will it all sound should some one read this line a hundred years from now! I put on respectable dress, for I had with me my trunk which had followed by intermittent voyages in sloops, schooners and coasting steamers, and from its hold I pulled out my shore clothes like a robin pulling worms of a dewy morning. Shaved and arrayed, I was taken to meet the Commissioner, Leslie Jarvis, who, like Whitfield Smith, deserves better than he has received.?

? Christian the Ninth, St. Thomas. ?

That night as I smoked a parting cigarette with the Commissioner on the verandah of Government House and feasted my eyes on Salt and Cooper and Ginger across the channel in the clear starlight, I told him that I should see a little of Sir Francis Drake's Channel before I finished my cruise at St. Thomas. "We are starting to–morrow in the Lady Constance for a round of the islands and you had better leave your canoe and come with us."

ALONE IN THE CARIBBEAN

"I'll go with you as far as Virgin Gorda if I may and leave you there." And so was my last bit of cruising in the West Indies planned.

The Lady Constance is a tidy little native built sloop, the best I had seen in all the islands, about eighteen tons, used as a "Government Cruiser" to keep smuggling within reasonable limits and as a means of conveyance for the use of the Commissioner on his tours of inspection. She is also used for carrying mail to St. Thomas, a run of about twenty-seven miles. "Oh, by the way," said the commissioner, as I was half way down the steps, "we take the two ministers with us —you won't mind that?"

"How can I?" I answered. "It's the Government's party and I suppose they are quite harmless."

"Quite," came from the dark shadows of the verandah.

In the morning, at a reasonable time, when everybody had enjoyed his breakfast and settled it with a pipe, we got aboard. The Commissioner was accompanied by all the accouterments of an expedition, guns, rods, a leather case with the official helmet within, and most important of all, innumerable gallons of pineapple syrup, baskets of buns and boxes of aluminum coronation medals for each deserving school child in all the British Virgins. The Yakaboo we put aboard forward of the cabin trunk —the ministers brought with them their nightgowns and a pleasant air of sanctity.

Somewhere there lurks in my mind a notion to the effect that professional men of religion are among sailors personae non gratae at sea. A thing may in itself be quite harmless and yet may bring down disaster to those about it. Perhaps it is just a whim of the Lord to test his self-proclaimed lieutenants when they venture into the open. There seems always to be trouble at sea when a minister is aboard. The harm we received was trifling but it was a warning. The breeze was fresh when we started and the Lady Constance had already bowed once or twice to the seas when we close-hauled her for the beat up the channel. Suddenly a wave boarded us and with an impish fit gathered the little deck galley in its embrace and with a hiss and a cloud of briny steam carried the box with its coal-pot and cooking dinner and swept the whole of it into the sea. I looked at the Commissioner and we both looked at the parsons. There was a warning in this. Titley, the big colored skipper, felt it too and from that time our sailing was done with great care. So much for superstition, it seems to grow on me the more I have to do with the sea.

197

ALONE IN THE CARIBBEAN

The channel was full of fish, Jarvis had told me, and with our towbait we would take at least one fish on each tack. We made a good many tacks and got one small barracuda. Of course we knew where the trouble lay. We spent the night under East End where in the morning the Commissioner landed and put an official touch to the depositing of syrup and buns in sundry little dark interiors and gave out medals for outward adornment. Thus in the outermost capillaries of the United Kingdom was the fact of the coronation brought home, and, most truly is the stomach of the native the beginning and end, the home and the seat of all being. Then we slipped across to Virgin Gorda and a day later were in Gorda Sound, a perfect harbor, large enough, some say, to hold the entire British Navy.

It was from Gorda Sound that I began my little jaunt about the Virgins. I had been looking forward to sailing about in the Drake Channel, for in many ways it is ideal canoe water. Here is an inland sea with a protected beach at every hand, blow high or low. Columbus may have been far off when he named them the "Eleven Thousand," but as I sit here and glance at the chart I can count fifty islands with no difficulty, all in range of forty miles.

The Virgins are mountainous but much lower than the Lesser Antilles and while they are volcanic in origin they do not show it in outline and must be of a much older formation than the lower islands. They are the tail end of the range which forms Cuba, San Domingo, and Porto Rico.

I bade good–bye to the Lady Constance one morning, and sailed out before her through the narrow pass by Mosquito Island, while they took the larger opening for low Anegada, which we could not see, twelve miles to the northeast. I hauled up along the shores of Virgin Gorda and made for West Bay. What a contrast was this sailing to our traveling in the lower islands. Instead of the large capping seas of the trades here was an even floor merely ruffled by a tidy breeze. For a change it was delightful, but too much of it might prove tiresome and in the end we would probably be seeking open water again. I was soon in the bay and running ashore at the western end I dragged the Yakaboo across the hot sands and left her under the shade of the thick sea grapes that form a green backing to the yellow beach. There is no town on Virgin Gorda, merely clusters of native huts that might be called settlements, the two larger having small school houses which are also used as churches.

ALONE IN THE CARIBBEAN

The life in these small outer cays is of a very simple nature. There are no plantations and the negro lives in a sort of Utopian way by raising a few ground provisions near his hut and when he wishes to change his diet he goes fishing. To obtain cash he sends his fish and ground provisions to the market in Tortola or St. Thomas and strange to say his most urgent need of cash is for the buying of tobacco.

Once, during the hurricane season, it chanced that all the sloops were at St. Thomas when Virgin Gorda found that it had run out of tobacco. The sloops had been gone for a week and were due to return when suspicious weather set in and no one dared leave port even for the shortest run. What with the hand to mouth existence these people lead and the small stock in the shops, there is never more than a week's supply of tobacco on Virgin Gorda and that notwithstanding the fact that the negroes here are inordinate smokers. The first day after the tobacco had given out was lived through with no great difficulty. On the second, however, the absence of the weed began to make itself felt.

The dried leaves of various bushes were tried but with little success. Dried grass and small pieces of bone were burned in pipes and finally those most hard pressed took to pulling the oakum out of the seams of an old boat that lay on the beach of West Bay. When day after day followed and the sloops from St. Thomas did not return, the whole population finally gave itself over to the smoking of oakum and watching for the return of their sloops. Even the oakum in an old beached fishing boat will not furnish smoking material for a couple of hundred natives for any great length of time and finally the island was quite smokeless, a state which to these people borders close onto starvation.

At last the sullen threat of a hurricane passed off and the next day the lookout reported white sail–patches beating up the channel. When the sloops beat into West Bay late that afternoon, the whole population of Virgin Gorda was waiting for them. As soon as the boats were beached the first business of the island was to enjoy a good smoke. To have been there with a camera and to have caught the two hundred columns of bluish smoke drifting aslant in the light easterly breeze!.

In the morning I was again on the summer sea of the channel. We had cleared Virgin Gorda and were lazing along toward Ginger when I saw the mottled fin of a huge devil fish directly on our course. I was in no mind to dispute his way —not being familiar with the disposition of these large rays —so I hauled up a bit and let him pass a hundred feet or so to leeward. I stood up and watched him as he went by and swore that some day I would harpoon just such a fellow as that from a whaleboat and take photographs of the doing. Just now I was leaving him alone. His fin, mottled brown and black like the rest of his upper surface, stood nearly three feet high and I judged his size to be about eighteen feet across from tip to tip.

For my nooning, I went ashore on a little beach on Cooper where I built a fire in the shade of beach growths. The sun, it seemed, did not have the deadly spite in its rays as in the lower islands but this may have been wholly surmise on my part. It was a great joy to be able to do a bit of beach work —that is to live more on the beaches than I had been doing in the Windward and Leeward islands. I sat for a while under the small trees where the cool wind seeped through the shade and set myself to a real sailor's job of a bit of needlework on the mainsail where a batten had worn through its pocket.

There is a peculiar freshness about these small cays that seems to do its utmost to belie any suspicion of a past. The beaches are shining, the sand and pebbles look new and in a sense perhaps they are, for one does not find here the thin slime on the rocks that is an accompaniment of long years of near–by civilization. Man befouls. The vegetation is for the most part new, for excepting an aged silk cotton tree, there are no growths of great age. The palms grow for a generation or two and pass away. The small woody growths of coarse grain and spongy fiber quickly bleach out and rot away upon death. They almost seem to evaporate into the air. Here are places of quickly passing generations that suggest eternal youth. Were our impressions of these places not biased by brilliantly colored pictures which we have seen in our youth of pirates and adventurers of a former age portrayed on brilliant white beaches with a line of azure sea and a touch of fresh green, we would swear that they were no older than a generation. But all these beaches of perpetual youth knew the rough–booted pirates of centuries ago and the Indians before them. Here in the channel between these outer cays and Tortola, three centuries ago, convoys of deeply laden merchant ships under clouds of bellying squaresails used to collect like strange seafowl to sail in the common strength of their own guns and a frigate or two for the European continent. Drake and Morgan and Martin Frobisher, whom we think only as of the Arctic, and the Admiral William Penn knew these places as we know the environs of our own homes.

When I had finished my sewing and had washed my dishes I shoved off again and in a few minutes —what a toy cruise ! —I was ashore on the beach of Salt island where a few huts flocked together under the coco–palms. Here I found a native by the name of

ALONE IN THE CARIBBEAN

William Penn. I asked him if he had ever heard of the old Admiral. Penn, he told me, was an old name in these islands, there having been many Williams. In all probability the name was first assumed by the slaves in the old days and then handed down from generation to generation.

It was here, in 1867, that the Royal Mail Steamer Rhone was wrecked in a hurricane. William Penn showed me in one of the huts a gilded mirror which had been "dove up" and he told me that the natives were still diving–up various articles from the wreckage. We put off in our canoes and rowed around to the western shore where the steamer lies in some forty feet of water. She must have been broken up on the rocks during the first onslaught of the hurricane and then blown out to where she now lies about two hundred yards from shore. The conditions were not particularly good, yet we could see what was left of her in large masses of wreckage literally strewn about on the ocean floor.

Then I hoisted sail again and was off across the channel to Dead Man's Chest where I would camp for the night. The surf was too high, however, and I had to content myself with a photograph and to sail on to Peter where I came ashore in the cool of the evening on a sandy turtle beach. A native came out of the bush and without any word on my part immediately turned to and built my evening fire. There was a good deal of the simple coast African in him —he freely admitted that it was curiosity that brought him to see me and the canoe and in return for a civil word he was only too glad to do what service he could. He showed the same pride of his village (these negroes all have a strong appreciation of the picturesque) that I found all along the lee coasts and he begged that I visit the snug little bay where he lived, when I set sail in the morning.

The night promised clear with a small new moon crescent —perfect for sleeping without cover. I had no sooner settled myself down in my tiny habitation than the wind began to drop and thousands of mosquitoes came out of the bush on a rampage. Instead of pitching my tent on the ground I ran the peak up on the mainmast which I stepped in the mizzen tube. The middle after–guy I ran to the foot of the mizzen mast which was now in the mainmast tube. The sides I pegged in the sand under the bilges of the canoe and in this way I had a roomy canoe tent which gave access to the forward compartment in case of rain.

After I had rigged the tent I beat the air inside with a towel so that when I fastened down the mosquito bar there was no one inside but myself. I found, however, that I was plenty of company. While the night air outside was cool enough I soon found that the heat from my body accumulated in the tent till I lay on my blankets in a bath of perspiration. A loose flap in the top of the tent would have taken off this warm air as in a tepee. Had there been one mosquito to bother me sleep would have been impossible. At last a gentle night breeze sprang up, I wiped my body dry, and dropped off to sleep.

The next day was July first, the last of the cruise of the Yakaboo, and almost of the skipper. I was up with the sun —many evil days begin just that way —and off the beach after a hasty breakfast. My destination was Norman Island —I would come back to Peter again, where there were caves in which treasure had actually been found and where there was a tree with certain cabalistic marks which were supposed to indicate the presence of buried treasure. I cleared the end of the island and hauled up for Norman, passing close to Pelican Cay. Norman is a long narrow island with an arm that runs westward from its northern shore, forming a deep harbor which gives excellent protection from all quarters but northeast.

In a rocky wall on the extreme western end of the island where the harbor opens out to the channel are two caves which can be easily seen when sailing through the Flanagan passage into Sir Francis Drake's Channel. These caves are the ordinary deep hollows one commonly finds in volcanic rock formation close to the sea and were for years unsuspected of holding hidden treasure. They say that a certain black merchant of St. Thomas, who had literally become rich over night, found his money in the shape of Spanish doubloons from an iron chest which he dug up in the far end of one of the caves. The man had bought Norman, had spent some time there and for no apparent reason had suddenly become rich. One day a curious fisherman found the empty chest by the freshly dug hole in the cave and there were even a few telltale coins that had rolled out of range of the lantern of the man who dug out the treasure. And there must have been another place for one day a small schooner came down from the north and entered at the port of Road Town. She picked up a native from Salt island and one night she ran down to Norman's. The next morning she put the native ashore on his own island and sailed for parts unknown —as to what happened on Norman the native, it seems, was strangely silent. There's the whole of the tale except what's known by the crew of the schooner.?

? The jetty at Norman's Island. ?

ALONE IN THE CARIBBEAN

As I sailed into the harbor, I saw a sandy beach at the far end where a small wooden jetty stood out in the calm water. Fringing the beach was a row of small coco palms, behind which the island bowled up into a sort of amphitheater of scrubby hillside. What a place for a pirate's nest! There is scant printed history of Norman and what is written is for the most part in some such records as led the schooner to the island. I rowed in to the beach, the hill to the eastward cutting off all moving air so that a calm of deathly stillness held the head of the bay in a state of quivering heat waves. The low burr of wind in the upper air outvoiced whatever sound might have come from the surf on the windward side of the island.

There was something peculiarly uncanny about the place which was all the more accentuated by the lonely jetty and a pair of pelicans that launched forth in turn from their perch on the gallows–like frame at its end, to float in large circles over the clear sandy–floored harbor, remounting again in lazy soft–pinioned flaps. They flew off as I tied up to the jetty but completed their circle as I stepped ashore and sat eyeing the Yakaboo as if detailed there on sentry duty. The heat was intolerable and if I were to camp on Norman I should have to find a cooler spot than this.

First, however, I would hunt the pirate tree, but I had not gone far into the bush before I began to feel faint and sick. The bush was close but shaded and as I retraced my steps to the jetty and came out again into the full glare of the beach the heat came upon me like a blow. I needed water and I knew where I could get it, lukewarm, in my can in the after compartment of the canoe. I tried to stoop down from the jetty but nearly fell off so I followed the safer plan of lying down on the burning boards and reaching into the compartment with my arms and head hanging over.

The hatch came off easily enough and with it rose the hot damp odor of the heated compartment mixed with the smell of varnish. I took out a bag or two and found them covered with a sticky fluid. Then I discovered my varnish can lying on its side with its cork blown out, spewing its contents over all my bags. When I lifted my water–can it came up with heartsinking lightness. I took it up on the jetty and sat up to examine it. There in the bottom was a tiny rust hole where the water had run out. Then I lay down again and dabbled my fingers in half an inch of water and varnish in the bottom of the compartment. I had sense enough to know that I was pretty well gone by this time and I went ashore where I lay for some time under the shade of the young coco palms.

ALONE IN THE CARIBBEAN

If I could only get one of those water–nuts I should feel much better and although the trees were young and the nuts hung low they were still nearly three feet above my reach. Perhaps I could shoot them down, so I went back to the canoe and got the rifle which so far had been of little use to me. The will of the good Lord was with me for I found that I could almost touch the nuts with the muzzle of my rifle. By resting the barrel upward along the trunk of the tree I could poke the muzzle within a few inches of the stems. Any one could have made the shot, but I missed because I forgot that the sight was raised a good half inch from the center of the bore. It took me some time to reason this out and I had to sit down for a while to recover from the shock of the recoil. Then the idea came to me. I aimed the rifle this time with its axis in line with the stem and pulled the trigger. Down came the nut and I blew off its head and drank its cool liquid. In like manner I shot another coconut. Stalking the fruit of a coco palm may sound like the keenest of sport, but no hunting ever gave me keener satisfaction than shooting these two nuts in the neck.

The milk was cool and refreshing and I believe it pulled me out of as tight a corner as I have ever been in alone. There was no one living on the island. The coming on of nausea and the feeling that I did not exactly care what happened was hideous to my better sense and I felt that at all costs I must make an effort to refresh myself and then leave the island as soon as possible. By sheer luck of super caution I got into the canoe and untied the painter (I found it trailing in the water when I got out in the channel later) and then in one last effort of fostered strength I rowed out of the cove into the breeze where I quietly pulled in my oars and lay down.

A little time later the quick roll of the canoe roused me and I found that I was clear of Norman and close upon Flanagan Island. The wind was cool and I made sail for Tortola. I was still very faint but I had held that mainsheet for so many miles that even half insensible I could sail the Yakaboo into Road Harbor —perhaps she did a little more than her half of the sailing. For three days I was taken care of at Government House and then feeling perfectly well I prepared to sail for St. Thomas. The anxious Commissioner would not hear of this and the doctor forbade me to go into the sun again, warning me to take the next steamer for New York.

On the afternoon of July Fourth I was bundled aboard the Lady Constance, together with the Yakaboo, and in the evening we sailed into the Danish port of Charlotte Amalia.

ALONE IN THE CARIBBEAN

So here ends the cruise of the Yakaboo after nearly six months of wanderings in the out–of–the–way places of that arc which swings from Grenada to St. Thomas. Six months may seem a long time to you of the office who at the most can get a month of it in the woods or along shore, but to me these months had been so full of varied interest that they were a kaleidoscope of mental pictures and impressions, some of them surprisingly unreal, that I had gone through in weeks. Had it not been for the heat I should have kept on and cruised along Porto Rico, San Domingo, and Cuba, crossing the large channels by steamer if necessary.

But it is the sun which makes impossible the true outdoor life in these islands as we know it in the north. I was content with what I had seen. I did not think back with longing of Norman where I had failed to spend the days I had planned, nor of Diamond Rock off Martinique where I had wished to land, nor of the half–French, half–Dutch St. Martin's that was out of reach to windward, nor of Aves, the center, almost, from which the arc of the Caribbees is swung, for I decided, should the opportunity offer, I would come down here again in a boat large enough to sleep in off shore and in which I could escape the heat of the day at anchor in the cool spots where the down draft of the hills strikes the smooth waters of protected coves.

One morning the Parima nosed her way into the harbor and I put off to her in a bumboat with my trunk and outfit aboard and the Yakaboo towing astern. The trunk and outfit followed me up the companionway and after a talk with the First Officer I rowed the Yakaboo under one of the forward booms which had swung out and lowered its cargo hook like a spider at the end of its thread. I slipped the canvas slings under the canoe's belly and waved for the mate to "take her weight." She hung even and holding on to the hook I yelled to the head and shoulders that stuck out over the rail to "Take her up!"

"'Take her up,' he says," came down to me and we began to rise slowly into the air. We were leaving the Caribbean for the last time together and were swung gently up over the rail and lowered to the deck.

The steward led me to a Stateroom that I was to share with an American engineer returning from Porto Rico. Here was one who did not know of my cruise and I was glad to escape a torrent of questions. He, the engineer, looked askance at my rough clothes and I chuckled to myself while he hung about the open door in the altogether obvious attempt to forestall any sly thieving on my part. I don't blame him. I shaved and packed my suitcase with my shore clothes and then hied me to the shower bath whence I emerged an ordinary person of fairly respectable aspect.

Then some confounded maniac walked along the deck clanging a bell and I knew that it was the call to breakfast. I went below and took my seat opposite the engineer from Porto Rico who recognized me with a start. I embarked on a gastronomic cruise, making my departure from a steep—to grapefruit that had been iced and coming to a temporary anchorage off a small cay of shredded wheat in a sea of milk —foods of a remote past. I was tacking through an archipelago of bacon and eggs when I heard the exhaust of the steam winch and the grind of the anchor chain as it passed in over the lip of the hawse pipe, link by link. I had cleared the archipelago and was now in the open sea of my first cup of coffee and bound for a flat—topped island of flapjacks when I felt the throb of the propeller slowly turning over to gather the bulk under us into steerage way. Presently the throb settled down to a smooth vibration —we were under way.

Some one at my right had been murmuring, "Please pass the sugar ? —may I trouble you for the sugar? —I BEG your pardon but" —and I woke up and passed the sugar bowl. Someone else said, "I see by the papers" I was back in civilization again and as far from the Yakaboo and the Lesser Antilles as you, sitting on the back of your neck in a Morris chair.

Printed in the United States
50074LVS00003B/20